Raising Digital Families

FOR DUMMIES®
A Wiley Brand

by Amy Lupold Bair

Raising Digital Families For Dummies®

Published by
John Wiley & Sons, Inc.
111 River Street
Hoboken, NJ 07030-5774

www.wiley.com

Copyright © 2013 by John Wiley & Sons, Inc., Hoboken, New Jersey

Published simultaneously in Canada

For general information on our other products and services, please contact our Customer Care Department within the U.S. at 877-762-2974, outside the U.S. at 317-572-3993, or fax 317-572-4002.

For technical support, please visit www.wiley.com/techsupport.

Wiley publishes in a variety of print and electronic formats and by print-on-demand. Some material included with standard print versions of this book may not be included in e-books or in print-on-demand. If this book refers to media such as a CD or DVD that is not included in the version you purchased, you may download this material at http://booksupport.wiley.com. For more information about Wiley products, visit www.wiley.com.

Library of Congress Control Number: 2013934419

ISBN 978-1-118-48508-8 (pbk); ISBN 978-1-118-48509-5 (ebk); ISBN 978-1-118-48510-1 (ebk); ISBN 978-1-118-48511-8 (ebk)

Manufactured in the United States of America

10 9 8 7 6 5 4 3 2 1

About the Author

Named one of the most powerful women in social media by Working Mother magazine, **Amy Lupold Bair** is the owner of Resourceful Mommy Media, LLC (www.resourcefulmommymedia.com), a social media marketing company that includes the blogger network Global Influence as well as her own site, Resourceful Mommy (www.resourcefulmommy.com). She's loved the Internet since she first heard the whir whir click of a dial-up modem. Her first home online was a Geocities community, and she still maintains a Prodigy e-mail account for sentimental reasons. Amy's primary digital addiction is Twitter where she is always available as @ResourcefulMom.

Prior to her career as a social media consultant, writer, and speaker, Amy taught middle school English and drama. She and her social media–averse husband live in the Washington, D.C. suburbs where they are raising their own digital family.

Dedication

This book is dedicated to my husband, Jason, and our two amazing, tech-savvy kids. All three believe whole-heartedly that I can accomplish anything and support me without question as I pull them along on this crazy journey that is my life.

Author's Acknowledgments

Thank you first and foremost to John Wiley & Sons, Inc. for giving me this opportunity and welcoming me to the *For Dummies* family.

Special thanks to Ellen Gerstein who changed my life with the best Twitter direct message ever as well as Amy Fandrei who took a chance on this very grateful blogger. Your support and encouragement through this process has been incredible.

Brian Walls, my project editor, thank you for having patience, a sense of humor, and the courage to edit a blogger's writing. Thanks to the rest of the editing team who took the ideas on the page and turned them into something *For Dummies* worthy. Jennifer, Chantal, and the rest of the marketing team, thank you for your part in bringing this book to its readers.

I am grateful for the support and love of my family who gave up weekends and helped out in countless ways, all in the pursuit of deadlines.

Thank you to the blogging community for your friendship, encouragement, inspiration, and trailblazing. Shannan, there would be no me without you, and I am eternally grateful. Kelby, Melanie, Andrea and the rest of the KA room, thank you for your expertise and camaraderie. The Safe House Blobbers, I could not get through my days without you.

I would be remiss if I did not thank Mr. Herb who never allowed me to be satisfied with "good enough" writing, Mrs. Readinger who made writing fun, and Mrs. Bolich who insisted that I learn one new word a week. I still love ennui and undulate because of you.

Finally, I want to acknowledge Samantha Hall, the nom de plume I created as an eight year old girl, certain that Amy Lupold could never write for a living. I think, somehow, we've done this together.

Publisher's Acknowledgments

We're proud of this book; please send us your comments at http://dummies.custhelp.com. For other comments, please contact our Customer Care Department within the U.S. at 877-762-2974, outside the U.S. at 317-572-3993, or fax 317-572-4002.

Some of the people who helped bring this book to market include the following:

Acquisitions and Editorial

Project Editor: Brian Walls

Acquisitions Editor: Amy Fandrei

Copy Editor: Teresa Artman

Technical Editor: Joe Waters

Editorial Manager: Kevin Kirschner

Editorial Assistant: Annie Sullivan

Sr. Editorial Assistant: Cherie Case

Cover Photo: © Chris Bernard / iStockphoto

Composition Services

Project Coordinator: Sheree Montgomery

Layout and Graphics: Jennifer Creasey, Joyce Haughey

Proofreaders: Lindsay Amones, Shannon Ramsey

Indexer: Steve Rath

Publishing and Editorial for Technology Dummies

> **Richard Swadley,** Vice President and Executive Group Publisher

> **Andy Cummings,** Vice President and Publisher

> **Mary Bednarek,** Executive Acquisitions Director

> **Mary C. Corder,** Editorial Director

Publishing for Consumer Dummies

> **Kathleen Nebenhaus,** Vice President and Executive Publisher

Composition Services

> **Debbie Stailey,** Director of Composition Services

Contents at a Glance

Table of Contents

Introduction

. . . .

As the mom of two elementary school-age kids, I understand that parenting "digital natives" — that is, children born into this digital age in which we live — can be overwhelming at times. The technology that your children and their friends use daily may be unfamiliar to you. Even if you dive right into technology as quickly as your children do, you may not be aware of how your children experience the same platforms and devices. You also may not be familiar with the challenges and dangers associated with these technologies — dangers that are often unique to them.

Still, understanding current technology — from mobile apps to tablets — is about far more than safety. Raising a digital family also means monitoring access to seemingly unlimited resources online. Educational websites guide children in learning and practicing necessary skills, while family resource sites allow family members to stay connected. Apps help parents remember everything from when to buy milk to directions to play dates. If embraced and understood and monitored, today's technology offers fabulous tools to help you raise your digital family.

This book will equip you — as a digital parent — to become the head of your digital family, protecting your loved ones from online pitfalls and guiding them to make the most of this amazing and ever-growing world of technology.

Here are some of the things you can do with this book:

- ✔ Change browser settings to protect your family's privacy.
- ✔ Identify hidden online advertising aimed at your children.
- ✔ Manage Facebook privacy settings.
- ✔ Plan meals with the help of online tools.
- ✔ Help kids find fun yet safe entertainment sites online.

Foolish Assumptions

In writing this book, I assume that you have a home computer, at least one member of your family has a smartphone, and you know the basics of using today's technology devices (such as web browsers and Wi-Fi). I assume that you're interested in creating rules and guidelines for your family's use of digital devices, but you may not know where to start. I also assume that you have an e-mail address and are familiar with social media, even if you don't have a Facebook or Twitter account.

Conventions Used in This Book

When you see a term *italicized,* look for its definition in the context of raising a digital family. I sometimes give step-by-step instructions that direct you to enter specific text onscreen, and that text appears in **bold**. Website addresses (URLs) and e-mail addresses are in `monofont`. I sometimes refer to your children as "digital natives" because they've been born into a world of mobile devices, touchscreens, and Wi-Fi, while we as parents were born before the invention of many of the technologies we use today. I also refer often to the "digital family," which is composed of the members of your nuclear family.

How This Book Is Organized

Raising Digital Families For Dummies has six parts. You don't have to read the book sequentially, and you don't even have to read all the sections in any particular chapter. You can use the Table of Contents and the index to find the information you need and quickly get your answer. Here is what you'll find in each part.

Part 1: Living in the Digital Age

Part I introduces you to today's digital family, exploring some of the pros and cons of raising children in today's digital age. This part guides you through creating a *Digital Family Policy,* which is a tool to create and manage the digital rules for your family. For example, how much screen time are your kids allowed on a weekday? Are they allowed to have a Facebook account? It also dives into the safety concerns that many parents face, such as online predators and cyberbullying. This section also lays some ground rules for basic online etiquette, empowering you with the tools you need to talk to your children about what's appropriate online.

Part II: Navigating the Digital World Kids Live In

In this section, I introduce some of the digital gadgets that kids use daily, such as game consoles and social media games. This part tackles the issue of cyberbullying as well as online chat platforms and privacy settings. Not only does this part of the book guide you to change search engine filters to protect your family, but it also helps you identify online advertising targeting your children.

Part III: Grasping Social Media's Effect on Your Family

Part III dives head-first into social media, exploring not only the most popular social media platforms for teens and adults, but also taking a close look at social networking sites created specifically for children. This section also walks you through creating a YouTube account, giving you access to both privacy settings and filters. Finally, Part III delves into the world of online entrepreneurship as it relates to kids, including kids who blog.

Part IV: Left to Their Own Devices

This section focuses on handheld devices, such as video game systems and tablets. Part IV introduces tablets created with kids in mind while also taking a look at how your tablet can easily become the family tablet. Considering a mobile phone for your child? See how to decide whether the time is right — as well as how to keep your child safe.

Part V: Utilizing Online Family Resources

Navigating the world of digital parenting is not only about understanding terms of service and privacy settings. There are also amazing resources available online. Many cool apps are available to help parents balance family budgets, create weekly meal plans, and more. Part V looks at the educational resources available online for kids as well as the parenting tools available on the Internet for parents.

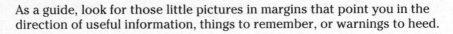

Part VI: The Part of Tens

Familiar to *For Dummies* readers, these Parts of Tens chapters include basic tips for digital parents, a closer look at online locations your teenagers may frequent, and also some of the most popular websites for kids.

Icons Used in This Book

As a guide, look for those little pictures in margins that point you in the direction of useful information, things to remember, or warnings to heed.

The Tip icon points out helpful information that may make something easier or point out something you may find useful.

This icon notes a piece of information that you may want to use later.

The Warning icon highlights lurking danger. When you see this icon, pay attention and proceed with caution.

When you see this icon, you know that there's techie material nearby. If you're not feeling very techie, you can skip this info.

Where to Go from Here

You don't have to read this book sequentially, and you don't even have to read all the sections in any particular chapter. You can skip over sidebars and just read the material that helps you complete the task at hand. Your first stop might be to read the Table of Contents and find the sections of this book that you need.

You may want to read just the chapters that apply to you now, or jump right into the Part of Tens for some quick tips. Chapters can be read in any order you choose. When you're ready to create your Digital Family Policy, see Chapter 2 — the policy, however, doesn't have to be completed before you read Chapter 3. I do recommend reading the chapters that apply to your family before finalizing your family's digital guidelines, though.

Each chapter stands on its own and can help you tackle specific tasks. For example, if your child has asked for his first mobile phone, you probably want to head to Chapter 17. If your child recently opened a Facebook account and you're concerned about privacy settings, check out Chapter 12.

This book is accompanied by a companion website that includes a Digital Family Policy template as well as other material to help you raise your digital family safely and smartly. To access this additional content, point your web browser to `http://www.dummies.com/go/raisingdigitalfamilies`.

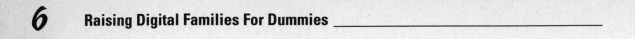

Part I
Living in the Digital Age

getting started
with
raising
digital
families

In this part . . .

- ✔ Meet today's digital family and explore what parents face as they raise digital natives, including some of the pros and cons of growing up in the digital age.

- ✔ Create a Digital Family Policy for your own family, addressing issues ranging from device usage rules by age to creating a smart phone contract for your children.

- ✔ Become familiar with some of the top safety concerns of parents raising children in the digital age including online predators and identity theft.

- ✔ Gain an understanding of basic online etiquette and how to talk to your children about appropriate online behavior.

- ✔ Get to know more about hidden screen time and the surprising places where kids are spending time plugged in.

Chapter 1

Meeting the Digital Family

In This Chapter
- ▶ Understanding "digital natives"
- ▶ Exploring areas that concern parents

According to the U.S. Census, the average American family has 2.6 children, 3 televisions, and at least 1 home computer. Most kids receive their first mobile phone by middle school, and with nearly one-quarter of American adults owning a tablet device according to Pew Research Center, many children are growing up with access to digital applications nearly from birth. We cannot deny that we live in a digital age with everything from our phones to our kitchen appliances connected to the Internet. Many parents have begun to feel like it's impossible to keep up with the ever-changing digital landscape and that their plugged in children speak a different language. There are also vast possibilities for learning, growth, and entertainment that we did not experience in our own childhoods.

As parents, even if we don't understand every nuance of the digital world that our children (and we) live in, it's important to set rules and parameters to help our kids navigate this brave new world. This book is chock-full of nuggets to help you become the digital parent you want to be for your digital native children, creating what I refer to as the "digital family." This book covers the places where kids of various ages spend the most time online or otherwise enjoy technology as well as the basics of the most commonly used devices. All throughout this book, I show you how to use online resources for education, entertainment, and even family management.

Whatever concerns you had before picking up this book worry you most, being the parent of a digital native can be overwhelming. The technology that your children are growing up with may be unfamiliar to you. Even if you dive right into technology as quickly as your children, you may not be aware of how your children are experiencing the same platforms and devices and the challenges and dangers that are unique to them.

This book will equip you, though, as a digital parent, to become the head of your digital family, protecting them the best you can from online pitfalls to guide them to make the most of this amazing and ever-growing world of technology. Feel empowered! This is a brave, new world you are living in, and there is so much that it has to offer today's parents and children.

Guiding Your Digital Natives

Children today are "digital natives," born into the world of smartphones, touchscreens, and connectivity like never before in history. You, the parent, must learn about this technology and the risks and rewards it holds for your children to help them maximize its benefits as well as mitigate its dangers.

In Chapter 2, I walk you through creating a *Digital Family Policy,* which is a comprehensive document covering everything from online requests for credit card information to where your family stores devices while charging. Chapter 19 provides you with even more tools as you visit platforms and apps created specifically to help today's busy digital family manage their constantly changing needs.

Of course, different ages of children shape your choices and rules. Throughout the book, I discuss devices, apps, and family rules by age group whenever possible.

Birth to preschool

Children from birth to preschool age typically experience technology in the arms of their parents through applications on tablets or smartphones or time spent viewing television programming selected by their parents. At this stage, parents have far less to worry about in terms of outside influences through technology or difficulties limiting access and screen time. Some parents may opt out of this early exposure entirely, but the popularity of apps and products aimed at the age 3 and younger set suggests that most have not. For those parents looking to regain control of their tablets, see Chapter 16 for my discussion of tablets created specifically for children, some with a suggested starting age of birth.

Elementary

After children reach the preschool to young elementary age group, the variety of products available geared specifically toward them expands significantly. Many of the handheld gaming devices that I cover in Chapter 15 are created with this age group in mind, and many kids in this age group also enjoy the game consoles described in Chapter 6. This is the age when hidden screen and Internet time begins to become a concern for many parents as kids begin to take part in play dates in friends' homes and are given a bit more freedom to choose their own activities within the home. In Chapter 5, I deal with parents' struggle to fully understand where kids are plugging in to help you locate that often overlooked digital time. This is also the age group when you will need to begin discussion about online etiquette (Chapter 4), exposure to advertising (Chapter 9), and participation in social media created just for this age group (Chapter 11). There are also a vast number of educational websites perfect for this period of childhood, and Chapter 18 will help you make the best of those.

Tweens

Children who have reached the tween years will begin to enjoy a digital freedom for which their younger siblings are not quite ready. This means access to more websites, tools, and devices — potentially, including their first smartphone! It also means more interaction online with strangers and the danger that comes with that. In Chapter 3, I walk you through some of these dangers, including online predators and other potential consequences of oversharing from this age group. Likely to be interacting online with peers they know — and perhaps some they don't — tweens will need guidance regarding online chats (covered in Chapter 7), as well as the issue of cyberbullying (discussed in depth in Chapter 10). Should you decide that your tween is, in fact, ready for a smartphone, be sure to read Chapter 17.

Teens

After your child is age 13, the Internet becomes his oyster with online platform restrictions lifted on access to everything from Facebook to blogging platforms. Part III walks you through your child's entrance into the world of adult social media platforms as well as blogging and other opportunities to catch the entrepreneurial bug. Before cutting your kids loose on Google or Bing, searching for information they need, check out Chapter 8, helping you help them navigate search engines. And with access to smartphones now essentially a must-do, stop by that smartphone chapter again to find tips for talking to your teens about both texting and driving and the topic of sexting.

Fighting Foes You Know — And Those You Don't

Every parent worries about their children's well-being, and the constant connectedness of the digital age provides many more opportunities for parents to be concerned. Most parents agree that such issues as offensive material, digital overload, and the costs to keep a family digitally plugged in are concerning, but parents should consider other issues — some highly dangerous — when creating their Digital Family Policy. Throughout the book, I cover the following concerns that all parents should have.

Inappropriate content

Graphic images, inappropriate language, and adult content are only a click away, and most kids with unsupervised online access have stumbled upon this inappropriate content at least once in their online experiences. Children are naturally curious and can easily locate inappropriate content while searching for something else for a school project or to answer a question. Links to inappropriate content appear in confusing spam e-mails, and sometimes friends will text or message unsuitable material without parents knowing.

In Chapter 8 (on navigating search engines), I walk you through some ways to prevent this type of accidental access to inappropriate material. Using software and parental controls on home computers and other Internet-enabled devices can also help to protect your children from accidentally viewing inappropriate content. Some options for these types of controls are discussed in Chapter 3 as well as Chapter 17, which covers mobile device monitors specifically. Remember to discuss content guidelines when creating your Digital Family Policy, which I cover in depth in Chapter 2.

Screen time overload

Many families set guidelines for the amount of screen time their children can consume during the day. Even so, the typical teen and tween consume more than seven hours a day of entertainment media, from devices with screens from television viewing to smartphone texting to internet browsing on the home computer.

And although monitoring screen time in your own home is fairly easy, children also receive quite a bit of additional screen time at school, in friends' homes, and in less-obvious places, such as doctor's waiting rooms. In Chapter 5, you can read about some of the locations where kids may be plugged in without you realizing it, as well as strategies to limit this additional screen time. With so many opportunities for kids to stare at a screen, it's easy to see why screen time overload is a common concern for parents. Screen time rules are a critical piece of the Digital Family Policy, which I show you how to create in the next chapter.

Cost to stay connected

According to an iYogi survey, the average American family now spends more on monthly technology bills than on monthly utilities. Don't forget to include such topics as device replacement and updating of equipment into your Digital Family Policy to deal with requests for the "latest and greatest" before they occur. Explaining the family policy for replacing broken devices may also encourage the members of your family to be more careful with their gadgets. Chapter 2 covers planning where you would like your family to stay connected — in your home, that is — including appropriate placement of the home computer and an approved charging location for devices.

Online child predators

Many parents believe that their children are interacting only within their safe circle of friends when online, but the startling fact is that according to the Crimes Against Children Research Center at the University of New Hampshire, one in five U.S. teenagers who use the Internet has reported receiving an unwanted sexual solicitation while online. Even more frightening, many children don't understand the importance of not sharing their personal information online.

Online predators go where the children are online. For example, they may visit the same celebrity pages on Facebook or fan forums that are popular with young teens. They often pretend to be teens themselves and find ways to gain the trust of children online, messaging them privately and Friending them on social media platforms. Some experts have found that predators use social gaming, which I cover in Chapter 6, as a way to connect with potential victims through video and chat.

Despite the prevalence of online child predators, many parents aren't aware of the threat because only about 25 percent of children who have been approached by an online predator reported this encounter to an adult according to the Crimes Against Children Research Center. In Chapter 3, I cover the topic of online predators at length, providing you with tips on how your children can avoid them and also providing you with options for monitoring and protecting your children on your home computer. Your Digital Family Policy should include a section with procedures for reporting these encounters to adults — and if necessary, the appropriate authorities.

Cyberbullying

Cyberbullying occurs when one child targets another child using interactive technologies, such as texting, e-mailing, messaging, or social media platforms. The cyberbully may use hateful language or even post threats or warnings. At times, cyberbullies befriend the victim to gain personal or embarrassing information or photos, which they then share publicly as a way to harass or shame the bullying victim. Cyberbullying in extreme cases involves the creation of hate sites or even the hacking of victim e-mail or social media accounts.

As of this writing, 49 U.S. states have laws about bullying, and many states have updated these laws to include cyberbullying. Forty-five states have specific laws regarding electronic harassment making cyberbullying not just a family issue, but a criminal issue.

When creating your Digital Family Policy, set aside time to discuss cyberbullying with your children, including rules for reporting cases of being bullied as well as consequences should your child participate in online harassment. Be sure to read Chapter 10 during the creation of your Digital Family Policy because that chapter covers the topic of cyberbullying at length, including tips on how to speak to your kids about the topic.

Your children's digital footprint

A *digital footprint* is essentially a digital trail left every time you appear online, interact online, search online, and more. It may include tracking of your home computer's IP (Internet Protocol) address or your Internet browser's search history. It also includes saved chat message, e-mails, and shared digital images of you or your children. Most people understand that Facebook profiles and blog posts are part of their digital footprint, but they might not realize that comments on blogs, product reviews on retailer sites, and photographs in which they are tagged also leave a digital footprint.

Most children will have a digital footprint attached to their name before they really understand the implications of this digital footprint. Future employers and even colleges may search for the digital footprint of a candidate before making a decision about hiring them or accepting them into their school.

The 'Net's no invisibility cloak: IP addresses

Many people erroneously believe the Internet offers them a level of anonymity. After all, how can anyone see your true identity? However, just by connecting to the Internet, you share information about your computer, your geographical location, and the websites you visit because of your IP address.

An *IP address* is a string of numbers unique to your computer that identifies your computer on the Internet. Websites can tell when your computer visits that site based on this unique identifier.

So don't be lulled into thinking you or your children are invisible while surfing the Internet. Technologies exist that can track your online activity and potentially expose your personal information to others.

If you're curious to see your computer's public IP address, simply type **What is my IP address** into the search field at Google. Your computer's IP address will display above the search results!

When discussing online etiquette and rules as part of the creation of your family's Digital Family Policy, also take time to discuss not only the facets of a digital footprint, but also the future repercussions. I discuss your child's digital footprint in more detail in Chapters 3 and 4.

Identity theft

Most every adult has heard of identity theft, but very few parents realize that their children can also be the victims of identity theft. Children's Social Security numbers and other personal information are very enticing to identity thieves because kids have a financial clean slate. Predators then use this information to do everything from opening credit cards to purchasing homes.

Kits, software, and protection plans are available to help protect your family's identities online. And you can take steps to make your family less at risk for identity theft. Chapter 3 helps you understand child identity theft and how to prevent it from happening in your family. Including these steps in the rules section of your Digital Family Policy will help protect all members of your family from the danger of identity theft.

Advertising to your children

While parents typically approve the media their children consume, they may not realize that seemingly innocent educational websites and children's social media platforms often include a large amount of advertising aimed at children. Most parents are aware of ads that appear in sidebars and at the top of the page on websites, but advertisers trying to reach children also often mask these advertisements as special gaming opportunities or unexpected links within existing games and content.

For parents who wish to limit their children's exposure to consumer advertising, these somewhat deceptive advertising practices may come as a surprise. In Chapter 9, I discuss how to identify these less obvious forms of advertising as well as how to set rules for children regarding interacting with these advertisements and the dangers of doing so.

Chapter 2

Creating a Digital Family Policy

Keeping up to date on ever-changing technology can be a daunting task for parents who are navigating a digital world daily as well. However, the benefits of today's online tools and useful gadgets greatly outweigh the safety concerns associated with their use. The keys to safely exploring the modern digital landscape with your family are understanding the world in which our digital native children are being raised and setting appropriate guidelines that work for your family. Just as you would create a family plan for fire safety, a list of numbers to call in case of emergency, or a calendar of weekly activities, a Digital Family Policy should become ingrained in the fabric of your family — a living document that changes with innovation as well as the growth and maturation of your children.

As you read other chapters throughout this book, keep this chapter in mind. Here, I outline the key areas of focus for your family's Digital Family Policy, but other chapters cover many areas of the policy in much greater detail. Keeping your family's Digital Family Policy in mind as you read this book will help you begin to make decisions about your own policy creation.

Creating Guidelines by Age Category

One word that every parent hears far more than they'd like is the word "fair." Kids for generations have complained that their parents' rules are not fair and that one sibling is getting a better deal than the other. However, when it comes to technology, *fair* and *appropriate* may not be related. It makes the most sense for you to create different device rules according to age category rather than create one rule that applies to your entire family. Consider using the following age categories, which I outline in Chapter 1.

- ✔ **Birth to preschool:** This youngest age group is not at all immune to the digital world. Some children can operate a touchscreen device before they can even walk. With apps and devices created specifically for this demographic, you need to set specific guidelines for your little ones, paying close attention to screen time limits and appropriateness of content.

- ✔ **Young elementary:** Children in this demographic are often able to operate technology without parent supervision but still require this supervision to guide them to proper and safe use.

- ✔ **Tweens:** In many ways, tweens may appear to rule the digital world. This age group is catered to by tech companies with products created specifically for them and online worlds inhabited primarily by other tweens like them. This is also the age when most children receive their first mobile phone, opening up a whole new world of technology and connectivity. Your rules for tweens may require fewer restrictions but are likely to cover more devices.

- ✔ **Teenagers:** Teenagers want their freedom. They also want their technology. This is the age when kids are beginning to lay down their digital footprint and make online decisions that may affect their entire lives. Although most teenagers will be given many freedoms, they may also need much guidance.

Setting Screen Time Guidelines for Home and Away

The most basic place for your family to start when creating your Digital Family Policy is setting screen time limits. Be sure to include time spent watching television and movies and playing video games away from home, such as at friends' homes. To read more about the variety of places where kids are plugging in, see Chapter 5. Consider adding the following specifics to this section of your policy:

- Total amount of screen time allowed during the week and the weekend

- Type of screen time allowed during the week and the weekend (such as television during the week, but game consoles only on the weekend)

- Types of devices that may be used in friends' homes, including going online and game devices

- Changes in screen time and type allowed during special times, such as spring break

Establishing Mobile Phone Usage Rules

In Chapter 17, I cover mobile phones — smartphones and feature phones — in depth, including presenting a variety of options for limiting your children's phone capabilities. The average family's Digital Family Policy will include mobile phone usage rules after their children reach the tween age category, usually around the end of elementary school or the beginning of middle school. However, each plan is individual, and you may wish to keep mobile phones on the banned device list until your child is a bit older.

Although your family will likely set different mobile phone–related policies based on the age of your children, all these topics are worth discussing with each child in your home who does or ever will use a mobile phone. This is a good opportunity to remind your children that privileges and responsibilities related to phone use will change as they mature.

Emergency-only versus social use

When creating the mobile phone section of your Digital Family Policy, include specific rules about when and why your child's mobile device should be used. Be sure your policy answers the following questions:

- **When can the phone be used?**

  For example, is the phone for weekend use only or perhaps just after school? Can the phone be used at home or just when your child is not with you?

- **What are appropriate reasons for phone use?**

  Is the purpose of the phone simply to call home in the event of an emergency or change in schedule, or can the phone be used socially to chat with friends?

✔ **What constitutes an emergency?**

For example, is it appropriate use for your child to call to request that a forgotten homework assignment be dropped off at school, or is that an abuse of phone privileges?

Use of applications

If your child has a smartphone with access to downloadable apps, you need to include guidelines for app purchases and downloads in your Digital Family Policy. You may want to consider from the following options:

✔ No apps are allowed on the phone.

✔ Apps must be downloaded by a parent.

✔ Apps must be approved by a parent.

✔ App permissions must be approved by a parent before the app may be downloaded.

✔ Apps can be downloaded by the child but removed if they do not meet parental approval.

Be sure to also discuss who will pay for the apps on your child's phone.

Limiting when and how much to text

Text messaging has become a way of life for teens and some tweens, with some kids texting several thousand times per month. To keep texting from taking over your child's life — and your budget — consider including the following rules in your Digital Family Policy:

✔ **Where your child may text**

Consider setting boundaries, such as no phones at the dinner table.

✔ **What times of day your child may text**

You may want to restrict texting to only before or after school or perhaps just on weekends.

✔ **How many texts can be sent and received**

Some text plans allow you to restrict the number of texts and will block text functioning after that limit is reached.

✔ **Who will pay for texts**

Don't forget about overage charges.

Text charges can add up very quickly if you don't have a package with unlimited texting. If your teen texts often, consider upgrading your package or installing an app to block text functions.

Don't forget to include a conversation about texting and driving with all your children! For more information on how to have this conversation, visit Chapter 17.

Data content guidelines

Very few phone plans include unlimited data use, and overage charges can be very expensive. Monitor your child's data use by visiting your mobile service provider's website and setting up an online account.

As I discuss in Chapter 17, smartphones that include data plans are now far more common than call and text-only feature phones. This makes it very likely that your child's first mobile device will include data capabilities. When you write the phone section of your Digital Family Plan, be sure to set guidelines regarding both data content and data use.

Your data usage guidelines may include the following:

✔ No Internet browsing

✔ No Internet browsing without parental permission of specific content

✔ Use of public Wi-Fi only in pre-approved locations

✔ Restricting data functions to certain days or times of day

In Chapter 17, I also talk about parental controls and tools that you can use to limit your child's access to the data capabilities on their smartphone.

Appropriate use of camera functions

Any parent who has had a child snap a photo of them before they've had their morning cup of coffee knows that camera phones can be a cause for concern in the hands of children. Our phones tend to go with us everywhere, including locations where you would not otherwise take a camera, such as bedrooms and bathrooms. If your child's phone includes camera and video camera functions, include the following topics when discussing your Digital Family Policy:

✔ Remind your children to ask permission before taking photos and videos of people.

✔ Review locations where photography and videography are not appropriate, such as in classrooms, changing rooms at the mall, and bathrooms.

✔ Ask your child to not record conversations without people's knowledge and consent.

✔ Remind your children that even if a friend has approved having a photograph or video of them taken, that may not mean that they approve of that content being shared. Ask permission before sharing!

✔ Remind your children that a camera phone should never be used to bully or hurt other people.

Tell your children that after they share an image, *they can never take it back.* Think carefully before deciding what to put out into the world.

For more information on how to talk to your kids about cyberbullying, visit Chapter 10.

Some mobile device parental control software allows you to disable the camera function on your child's phone.

Contact list restrictions

When creating the mobile phone section of your Digital Family Policy, include a section specifically addressing your child's contact list. Address the following issues:

✔ Is your child allowed to add friends to contacts, or is the phone for family only?

✔ Does your child need to get parental permission before adding someone to their contact list?

✔ Does your child need to allow parental access to the phone's contact list at all times?

Guidelines for GPS and location services

Most mobile phones come equipped with GPS or location-determining capabilities. Many apps, including most social networking platforms, will request that your child provide location determining access. Create guidelines for each age group of your family regarding the use of these functions. Many safety experts agree that it is highly dangerous for children and teens to publicly disclose their location through their mobile phones. To read more about this concern, visit Chapter 3.

Even if you disable GPS functionality on a mobile device, rest assured that most emergency services are still able to determine your child's location through a working mobile phone.

Creating Rules for Internet Usage

With most families owning a personal computer and more than three-quarters of teenagers owning a smartphone (according to U.S. Census data), the vast majority of kids and teens have access to the Internet — and many of them unsupervised during this access. It is critical to set clear usage guidelines for Internet usage to protect both your kids and you.

Determine rules for sharing e-mail addresses and information

Children are faced with requests for e-mail addresses and contact information from the very first moment they attempt to create an account on a favorite website. Children younger than age 13 are asked to share parent e-mail addresses, while teens are able to use their own information to create accounts everywhere from educational sites to social media.

See Chapter 11 for information about the Children's Online Privacy Protection Act (COPPA).

As soon as your children are old enough to use the Internet without constant parental guidance — or they're old enough to have their own e-mail address — you should discuss your family's rules for sharing e-mail addresses and other identifying information. Most sites that require account creation to use the site also require the disclosure of an e-mail address. Consider discussing the following guidelines in your family's Digital Family Policy:

- ✔ Ask your elementary and tween children to receive parental permission before sharing an e-mail address with anyone requesting such information, including offline requests in locations such as activity and school forms.

- ✔ Set specific guidelines regarding when it's okay for your teens to share e-mail addresses, including the sharing of parent e-mail addresses. For example, is it always okay when filling out paperwork for after-school activities and sports, but requires parental permission in online contact forms?

- ✔ Consider creating a shared family e-mail account with a password controlled by parents. Use this e-mail address for online account creation on websites for kids.

When discussing this section of your Digital Family Policy, speak to your kids about the importance of protecting personal and identifying information, such as full name, birthdate, and address. Remind them to never share their Social Security number with anyone and to tell you should a website request that information. Chapter 3 covers the dangers of sharing information in much more depth.

Information shared online can never be taken back!

Set policies for credit card requests

Children and teens are faced with credit card requests for everything from app downloads to premium account creations to online purchases. Many teens are armed with a family credit card or know where to access your credit card information. You may even have saved your credit card location on common shopping sites, such as Amazon.com. Include a section in your Digital Family Policy with rules on the appropriate response should a site or mobile app request access to credit card information. Some guidelines may include

- ✔ Never allow your child to input credit card information. Require that parents are asked to decide on the account creation and be the ones to submit the information.
- ✔ Allow using credit cards online and on mobile devices only with prior parental permission.
- ✔ Allow the use of credit cards online only on approved sites.
- ✔ Allow using credit cards online only if the teen owns and pays for the credit card.

Create guidelines for search engine use

Search engines are a gateway to nearly endless information and entertainment, but they also connect your children to an often unfiltered world. Before allowing your kids to use search engines, set specific guidelines within your Digital Family Policy. Guidelines may include the following:

- ✔ No using search engines for kids below a certain age group
- ✔ Supervised use of search engines only
- ✔ No image searches
- ✔ Using search engines with parental controls only
- ✔ Using search engines for educational purposes only

Visit Chapter 8 to read more about setting filters on popular search engines and sites, such as YouTube.

Establish a list of approved and banned sites

If your children are spending time on the Internet without direct adult supervision, consider creating two website lists and storing them within your Digital Family Policy:

- **Approved websites:** If you would like to greatly restrict your children's Internet access, consider creating a list that contains the only sites your children are permitted to access. Bookmark these websites on your computer's browser or table to make access to these sites easy and direct. Allow your child to update the list as they get older and learn about new and appropriate sites.

- **Banned sites:** If you allow your children to explore the Internet with a bit of freedom but you prefer that they don't visit specific popular yet inappropriate sites, consider creating a banned site list within your Digital Family Policy. This list can be revisited both to remove and add sites as you and your family see fit. In Chapter 3, I talk about ways to block specific sites on your home computer.

Popular social media sites (such as Facebook) contain age restrictions within their terms of service. Use site age guidelines to help you create approved/banned website lists and to help you explain these rules to your children.

Rules for social media and chat capabilities

When creating rules for Internet usage, set specific rules about the use of social media and chat capabilities. Many sites, from online worlds to children's social media, provide kids with the ability to chat with strangers online. When creating the social media and chat section of your Digital Family Policy, include the following areas:

- Which social media and online world sites your children are allowed to participate in, by age group

- Restrictions and guidelines for the use of each of these sites, which typically contain various levels of capabilities and functions

- Guidelines for privacy settings on social media and other online accounts

- Rules regarding parent access to each child-owned account

✔ Guidelines for creation of friend and buddy lists, including whether parental approval is required before adding someone to a list

✔ Guidelines regarding chat functions on all platforms with this capability, including what level of chat, if any, is allowed

For more information about online chat functions, see Chapter 7. Part III introduces you to the world of social media, including platforms created specifically for children and tweens.

Not ready to allow your kids to create their own social media profiles? Consider a shared account, such as a family Facebook page, that you can all build and update together.

Deciding the Best Location for Your Family Computer

I think the many apps and programs available for parents to monitor their children's online activity are important, but nothing is quite as effective as actually spending time with your children while they are online. Not only does this give you a chance to demonstrate good online behavior as an example, but it also provides you with an opportunity to observe your children's online behaviors.

The conversation regarding the location of your family computer may be between you and your partner rather than you and your children. However, the guidelines for computer location should still be included in your Digital Family Policy. Many families still have a desktop computer that stays in one location all the time. With the rise of laptops and tablets, however, your family's computer might be a device that can be transported around your home and even outside your home. Consider the following rules for your family's computer to protect the safety of your children at all ages:

✔ Place the family's desktop computer in a highly trafficked area, such as the kitchen, family room, or homework area of the house.

✔ Require kids in certain age groups —preschoolers, elementary, and tweens — to only use computers and tablets with parental supervision.

✔ Do not allow Internet-connected computers and devices in children's bedrooms.

Setting Rules for Device Storage, Recharging, and Replacement

Much like deciding where to place the family's computer, setting the location of device storage and recharging stations should be made with safety in mind. Consider choosing a central location where all your family's devices can be stored and charged when not in use. You can easily find products that can charge multiple devices at one time, cutting down on cord clutter and outlet overload. Also consider a policy against storing and charging mobile devices in bedrooms, especially kids' rooms.

Even with specific rules about device storage, there is still a chance that a family member will lose or break a device. Before allowing your children to use a family device or receive a device of their own (such as a mobile phone), set guidelines within your Digital Family Policy for device replacement. Consider the following questions:

- If your child breaks or loses a device, will she be required to pay for it?
- If your child breaks or loses a device, will she be given a replacement?
- If your child breaks or loses a device, will she lose other digital privileges?

Even the most responsible kids make mistakes, and there are very few among us who have not misplaced something important. Be sure to set these rules prior to an incident occurring, when emotions may be running high.

Following Rules for Password Creation, Storage, and Sharing

Your digital family likely has passwords and pins for a variety of purposes, including the following:

- PIN passwords for phones
- Passwords to unlock tablets and computers
- App store PINs or passwords
- Passwords for website accounts
- E-mail passwords

To maintain these passwords, you may want to create rules about password creation and storage and include these rules in your Digital Family Policy.

Create safe passwords

A password may not seem like an important topic to kids, but passwords are the gateway to access personal information and should thus be taken very seriously. Discuss with your kids the following tips to create safe passwords:

- ✔ Include uppercase and lowercase letters.
- ✔ Include numbers as well as letters.
- ✔ Include other characters and symbols besides numbers and letters.
- ✔ Do not include a complete word.
- ✔ Do not include the child's name.
- ✔ Do not include other identifying information, such as a birthdate, an address, or a pet's name

Establish a password storage location

To manage a large number of passwords across family members and accounts, create a rule for safe password storage. Consider the following options:

- ✔ **Choose a safe location where you can keep all passwords written down.**

   This may not be a safe strategy in a public place such as an office, but you should be okay in your own home. Consider choosing a secure location, such as a filing cabinet drawer that can be locked.

- ✔ **Purchase software or an application that remembers your passwords, including different passwords across devices and platforms.**

During the passwords discussion in the creation of your Digital Family Policy, discuss family policies regarding which passwords you will require your children to share with you and which accounts, if any, they can maintain on their own.

Teach children the importance of password protection

After teaching your children tricks and tips for safe password creation and discussing rules for sharing passwords with you, also discuss the importance of protecting passwords from others. Children are often unable to comprehend that the friends they have today may not be their friends tomorrow.

Kids are likely to share personal information, including device and account passwords. See Chapter 3 for more on online safety and Chapter 4 for more on appropriate behavior online. When discussing passwords with your family, urge them to keep others from seeing their passwords and require them to never share their password with others, even their closest friends.

Setting Gaming Rules

Children as young as preschool age enjoy game console games, and handheld gaming devices are available for kids 18 months to 18 years. While you may want to include gaming in screen time limits and rules for appropriate activities when visiting friends' homes, there are two main areas regarding gaming that should be considered priorities when creating your Digital Family Policy: game ratings and multiplayer games online.

Game rating guidelines

In Chapter 6, I introduce you to the Entertainment Software Rating Board (ESRB) ratings. This ratings system allows you to read the age recommendations for all games available for game consoles and many games available for handheld gaming devices. These ratings also provide you with additional feedback focusing on specific areas of content, such as violence and sexual content.

Include specific game ratings guidelines for each member of your family, which can be applied across all devices. You may wish to include ratings exceptions on a game by game basis after previewing content or reading an in-depth game summary and ratings summary.

To enforce these game restrictions, consider setting the parental controls on each of your children's devices. To read more about how to implement parental controls, see Chapter 6.

Co-play and social gaming guidelines

Many game consoles, including handheld gaming devices, come equipped with the ability to co-play with one or even multiple players via a Wi-Fi connection. Be sure to set specific rules about these capabilities, including whether your children are allowed to play multiple player games with children online. Chapter 6 guides you to change settings that allow this type of interaction via game consoles.

Reporting Incidents to Parents

One theme that I repeat throughout this book is the idea that open communication within the digital family is the best tool for keeping the family safe online and making the most of this amazing digital world we live in. Rules such as device usage guidelines and content restrictions may seem like the most important piece of the Digital Family Policy, but the discussion that you have with your family regarding reporting of concerning or upsetting interactions may be the most important step in the creation of this document. Naturally, kids want to hide potentially upsetting or embarrassing information, but as the head of a digital family, you can ensure that your kids feel safe and comfortable talking to you about their concerns.

Whether someone says something off-color to your child in a chat room or your child accidentally clicks an inappropriate link, chances are that your child will be exposed to unwelcome content at some point. Establish family guidelines for what steps to take when this happens before allowing your children to use the Internet without direct adult supervision. Consider asking your child to take the following steps:

1. Do not click any links that appear questionable or inappropriate.

2. Immediately stop responding to the person who has said or done something inappropriate or questionable.

3. Do not close the screen or delete the content prior to showing an adult.

4. Get a parent or adult immediately, tell them what happened, and if possible, show them the content.

In Chapter 3, I talk about online predators at length, including information about how you may report this type of behavior. This chapter also introduces options for monitoring and prevention tools, which you may want to install on devices to help prevent access to inappropriate information.

Establishing Consequences

No family policy is easy to enforce without consequences that accompany each guideline and rule. As a family, decide what consequences are most appropriate for each section of your policy. Then, as the head of your digital family, be prepared to enforce these consequences. This may mean time away from devices, cutting back on allowances until broken devices are replaced, or taking a step back on the level of privileges. Whatever consequences you choose, be sure to communicate them at the same time that the policy is created to make them clear to all the members of your family. I strongly recommend creating a no-tolerance policy on dangerous behaviors, such as cyberbullying, sexting, and texting while driving.

Ask your children to sign your Digital Family Policy or create device-specific contracts, such as a contract for mobile phone use.

Chapter 3

Putting Safety First

○●●●●●●○●●●●●●○●●●●●●○●●●●●●○●●●●●●○●●●●●●○●●●●●●○●●●●●●

In This Chapter

▶ Setting digital device privacy settings

▶ Using available monitoring and protective products

▶ Being aware of digital footprints

▶ Helping children understand the dangers of oversharing

▶ Teaching kids about the risk of online predators

▶ Understanding the danger of identity theft

○●●●●●●○●●●●●●○●●●●●●○●●●●●●○●●●●●●○●●●●●●○●●●●●●○●●●●●●

Of the many concerns for parents raising kids in this digital age, safety concerns certainly top the list. You just can't directly supervise children all their digital time, but many tools are available to help keep children safe. With the right preparation, you can create a safe environment in which kids can enjoy and explore this digital frontier.

Most devices from mobile phones to game consoles as well as social media platforms like Facebook offer a range of privacy settings to protect users. Understanding and using such settings allows you to protect your children even when you're not with them.

Providing your children with guidance about what to share online and what not to share also guards them from oversharing, potentially putting themselves in harm's way. Sharing guidelines and discussing potential scenarios before allowing your children digital freedom may be all it takes to protect them from exposing themselves unwittingly to harm.

Later in this chapter, I discuss your child's digital footprint. Although you want to make sure your child knows how to not leave a negative digital footprint, you should also discuss creating a positive digital footprint. You want to be forward-thinking: What will potential future employers or educational institutions find when they conduct an Internet search of your child's name? Help your child understand how avoiding oversharing and including positive and appropriate content leaves a positive impression.

Also with an eye to the future, you need to recognize the very real danger of identity theft. The information your children share online can not only affect them, but also the entire family. With proper understanding of appropriate online behavior and possible use of monitoring services, you can guide your digital family safely away from identity thieves.

Using Device Privacy Settings

Just as families often create parameters for device usage based on such factors as time limits and appropriate age ranges, remember to discuss privacy settings when creating your Digital Family Policy (see Chapter 2). Your family may opt to create stricter guidelines around certain devices — say, your teen's phone that holds personal information — than perhaps home game consoles that don't disclose personal information. Likewise, you may set different privacy guidelines for your tween than you do for your teen who may be using his smartphone for more than just communication with family.

In general, look for privacy settings that affect the following things:

- Whether companies have access to your information, such as through third-party applications, and what they can do with that information
- Who can find you through the device or platform
- How people can contact you

Most digital devices — smartphones and tablets, for example — come equipped with a variety of settings to help families protect their privacy as well as the privacy of their children. Providing your tweens and teens with a smartphone is a great way to stay connected while allowing them freedom. And using smartphone privacy settings is a quick and simple way to gain additional peace of mind.

The trick to using these tools is finding and understanding them on each device. For example, the settings on your child's smartphone can help password-protect text messages and allow apps to locate the phone via GPS. After you decide on the safest settings for your family, be sure to include a device-by-device set of guidelines within your Digital Family Policy.

Like smartphones, tablets also provide some basic privacy settings to keep the information contained within the tablet private. Also like smartphones, tablet settings differ according to the operating system (OS) of each tablet.

Screen locks

Screen locks require anyone attempting to gain access to a phone or tablet to input a predetermined set of information. Setting a screen lock not only prevents those without the password from using your teen's phone but also from reading your teen's personal texts and e-mails.

Each OS provides users with a version of a screen-locking option, and each one is slightly different.

Android

To implement a screen lock on an Android OS device, take the following steps:

1. **Tap Settings from the main menu.**

2. **Tap Location & Security.**

3. **Under Security, tap Set Up Screen Lock.**

Android OS devices allow users to lock their screens using a variety of settings options, as shown in Figure 3-1.

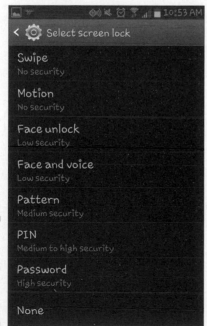

Figure 3-1: Select a screen lock setting on an Android device.

Windows

Windows phones allow anyone to use the Speech function to make a phone call without first unlocking the phone. However, the screen lock function does prevent unauthorized users from accessing private information, such as your child's e-mails or contact list.

To set a screen lock on a Windows Phone 7, take the following steps:

1. **Navigate to the Settings icon and tap Lock+Wallpaper.**

2. **Choose to turn on Password and enter a password in the New password text box.**

3. **Reenter the password in the Confirm password text box.**

4. **Select Done to save your settings.**

To unlock your Windows Phone 7, flick your start screen upward to reveal a keypad where you can enter your password.

iOS

Apple products — the iPhone, iPad, and iPad mini — operate on the iOS platform.

iPhone

You can set a simple screen-lock password on iPhones. Take the following steps to create a passcode on an iPhone:

1. **Select Settings and tap General.**

2. **On the General screen, select Passcode Lock.**

   The Passcode Lock screen appears.

3. **Slide the Simple Passcode setting to On and then tap Turn Passcode On. (See Figure 3-2.)**

4. **On the Set Passcode screen that appears, enter a four-digit numeric code and then re-enter it to confirm.**

5. **Press the Home button to return to your Home screen.**

Figure 3-2:
Set a
password
lock on an
iPhone.

iPhone users may also create a more intricate passcode than the standard four-digit numeric code. Here's how to make your iPhone's passcode setting a little more complex:

1. **Select Settings and tap General.**

2. **On the General screen, select Passcode Lock.**

   The Enter Passcode screen appears if you have Passcode Lock set up. If so, enter your simple password.

3. **Slide the Simple Passcode setting from On to Off (refer to Figure 3-2) and enter your old simple password.**

4. **On the Change Passcode screen that appears, enter your new passcode and tap Return.**

5. **Re-enter your new passcode to confirm.**

   The Passcode Lock screen appears.

6. **Press the Home button to return to your Home screen.**

iPad

Passcode Lock settings on iPads are very similar to the iPhone settings that I describe earlier. After you locate the Passcode Lock screen under the General settings, simply select Turn Passcode On to change the passcode settings on your iPad.

GPS settings

GPS capability is another setting to consider when setting up your teen's smartphone. GPS allows your teen's smartphone location — and, therefore, your child's location — to be tracked by everything from emergency services (such as the police) to the applications downloaded to your teen's gadget. Some parents take comfort in knowing their teen's location may be tracked through their phone in the event of an emergency, but other parents prefer that GPS be disabled to help protect against online predators. Find more on GPS and your child's safety in Chapter 17 and later in this chapter in the "Avoiding Online Predators" section.

Android

To edit the GPS settings on an Android phone, follow these steps:

1. **Tap Settings from the main menu.**

2. **Tap Location & Security.**

3. **Determine your preferred settings from the choices that appear on your phone, as shown in Figure 3-3.**

    You can choose from a standalone GPS service, or one offered by your carrier or Google.

Even if you choose to turn off your other location settings, the location of your Android phone can still be determined by emergency 911 services if the phone is turned on.

Windows

The Windows Phone also allows you to set your own preferences for location services.

1. **Navigate to the Settings icon and tap Location.**

2. **Select to turn off or turn on Location services.**

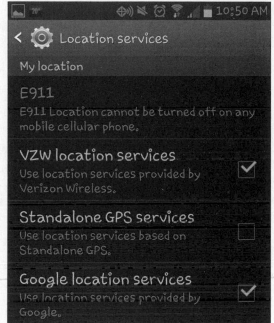

Figure 3-3:
Choose
location
setting pref-
erences on
an Android
phone.

iOS

On an iPhone, take the following steps to change the GPS capabilities:

1. **Select Settings and tap Privacy.**

2. **On the Privacy screen, tap Location Services.**

3. **Slide the Location Services setting to On for your device.**

   When Location Services is activated, you can use the On/Off slider to activate and deactivate Location Services for any listed application. (See Figure 3-4.)

4. **Press the Home button to return to your Home screen.**

Chapter 17 addresses more smartphone considerations, including setting smartphone use guidelines by age and using monitors available from your service provider. For example, many service providers offer the option to track everything from data usage and number of texts sent. They also typically allow account holders to block specific functions on your children's phones.

Figure 3-4:
Selecting
the Location
Services
settings on
an iPhone.

Cookie(s) patrol

Your family's web browser is another key location to ensuring the digital privacy of your family. Websites install *cookies* on your browser that track what you and your children do on that computer. Some cookies are helpful, such as those that offer the ability to save passwords so you don't have to re-enter information every time you visit a site. Other cookies, however, are placed on your computer to track all your actions on that web browser with the purpose of selling that information to advertisers.

You may wish to prevent cookies from being installed on the home computer used by your children so that online advertisers can't track the browsing habits of your kids. You can easily change the privacy settings on your web browser to not allow cookies to be installed. Typically, this setting can be found in the Tools section of your browser, but the location is slightly different in each web browser.

Chrome

To locate the privacy settings in Chrome, take the following steps:

1. **Click the Chrome menu in the upper right of your Chrome browser.**

2. **Select Settings from the drop-down menu, as shown in Figure 3-5.**

Figure 3-5:
Begin to
adjust
Chrome
privacy set-
tings here.

3. **Click the Show Advanced Settings link at the bottom of the page.**

   The Settings page expands to reveal numerous advanced settings. In the Privacy section, you can then opt in or out of allowing Chrome to

   • Use a web service to help resolve navigation errors.

   • Use a prediction service to help complete searches and URLs typed in the address bar.

   • Predict network actions to improve page load performance.

   • Enable phishing and malware protection.

   • Use a web service to help resolve spelling errors.

   • Automatically send usage statistics and crash reports to Google.

   • Enable AutoFill to fill out web forms in a single click.

   • Offer to save passwords entered by you on the web.

   • Send a Do Not Track request with your browsing traffic.

You can also elect to edit content settings by clicking the Privacy section's Content Settings button. As shown in Figure 3-6, you can choose cookie-related options, including blocking third-party cookies and site data, and designate whether images appear on web pages.

Another option is to clear browsing data by clicking the Privacy section's Clear Browsing data button. On the menu that appears (see Figure 3-7) you can delete cookies that have been placed on your computer's web browser.

Safari

The Safari web browser also allows users to edit security settings. From the Home screen of your iOS device, select Settings, and then Safari, as shown in Figure 3-8.

Figure 3-6: Content settings in Chrome.

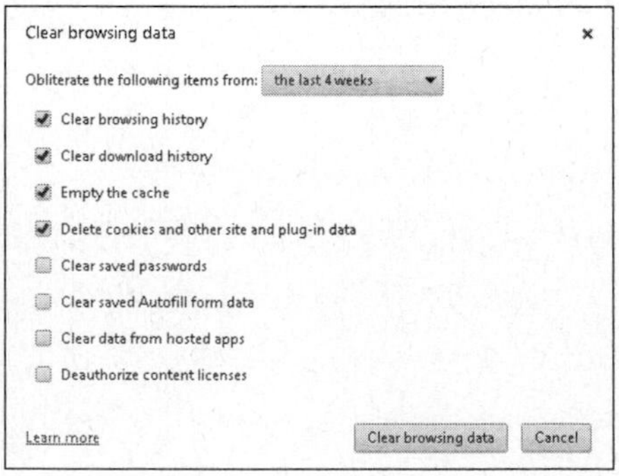

Figure 3-7: Clearing browsing history in Chrome.

Figure 3-8:
Locating
the Safari
settings on
your iOS
device.

From the Safari settings page (you might have to scroll down to see all options), you can

- ✔ **Enable or disable anti-phishing.**
- ✔ **Enable or disable private browsing.**
- ✔ **Set whether Safari accepts cookies.**

   Choose from the following:

   - *Never*
   - *From Visited*
   - *Always*

- ✔ **Enable or disable JavaScript.**
- ✔ **Clear browser history.**
- ✔ **Clear cookies and data**

Internet Explorer

To access privacy settings on the Internet Explorer web browser, take the following steps:

1. **Click the Tools button (or gear icon) in the upper right of your browser.**

2. **Choose Internet Options from the drop-down menu, as shown in Figure 3-9.**

   The Internet Options dialog box appears.

3. **Click the Privacy tab of the Internet Options dialog box. (See Figure 3-10.)**

Figure 3-9:
Start with
Internet
Options in
Internet
Explorer.

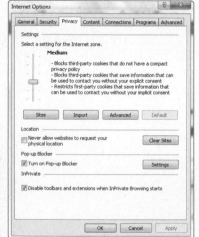

Figure 3-10:
Adjust
privacy set-
tings in IE.

4. **Using the slider, choose from the following settings:**

   • *Accept All Cookies*

   • *Low security,* which does the following:

     Blocks third-party cookies that do not have a compact privacy policy

Restricts third-party cookies that save information that can be used to contact you without your implicit consent

- *Medium security,* which does the same things as Low security but also restricts first-party cookies that save information that can be used to contact you without your implicit consent.

- *Medium High security,* which does the same things as Low security, but also blocks first-party cookies that save information that can be used to contact you without your implicit consent.

- *High security,* which does the following:

  Blocks all cookies from websites that do not have a compact privacy policy

  Blocks cookies that save information that can be used to contact you without your explicit consent

Also from the Privacy tab, you can elect to never allow websites to request your physical location.

Firefox

Firefox Internet browser users may change their privacy settings by taking the following steps:

1. **Click the Firefox button at the top left of your browser.**

2. **Click on Options in the window, as shown in Figure 3-11.**

3. **Choose the Privacy panel.**

Figure 3-11: Locating the options menu in your Mozilla Firefox web browser.

On the Privacy panel that appears, you can select the following privacy settings:

✔ Not allow websites to track your online behaviors.

✔ Select from the following histories that affect your browsing, download, form and search history, and cookie settings:

• *Remember history*

• *Never remember history*

• *Use custom settings for history*

✔ Alter the location bar settings.

Privacy in other online venues

I discuss privacy settings for gaming consoles in depth in Chapter 6. Understanding privacy options during online chats is covered in Chapter 7, and privacy settings on social media sites are covered in Part III. Keep in mind that social media platforms frequently change their privacy policies and default settings. Be sure to monitor the programs and platforms used by your family for updates that may affect your preferred settings.

Chapter 2 covers the creation of your Digital Family Policy in depth, and guides you through creating privacy setting guidelines.

Monitoring and Protecting: Tools for Parents

For many families, a Digital Family Policy is just the first step in providing children with a safe online experience. Some parents monitor activity and install protective software on devices.

When deciding whether monitoring tools and protective software are right for you and your family, keep in mind the ways to help your children stay safe online without taking this next step:

✔ Are you able to check the web browser history on your home's computers, as described earlier in this chapter?

✔ Have you Friended your children on social media sites, as referenced in Part III?

✔ Have your children provided you with the passwords to their accounts, as I discuss in Chapter 2?

✔ Have you installed basic antivirus and anti-malware software on your devices to protect your family from dangerous sites, links, and pop-ups, as described later in this chapter?

✔ Have you activated privacy settings on the browsers, devices, and social media used by your children and teens, as described earlier in this chapter?

✔ Have you created a Digital Family Policy and gone over that policy with your children, as covered in Chapter 2?

If you've taken these steps and would still like to implement additional safety measures, it's time to monitor your child's activity and deploy protective software to block and restrict use on your family's devices.

Monitoring tools can help you watch social media activity and provide you information regarding what your child is doing publicly. Other tools, however, can be installed on devices to provide parents with reports about what they are doing privately in chat locations and e-mails.

Protective software can block or filter keywords and site names to prevent access to certain websites and content. Programs offer different levels of coverage. Some simply block content the program considers inappropriate; others let you customize filtering and include time limits for computer use.

If your children use multiple devices in your home to access the Internet, you can block inappropriate sites on all devices connected to the same Internet router, including PCs and game consoles. These hardware-based solutions can apply Internet content filtering and Internet time scheduling to every Internet-connected device in your home. These types of solutions are more difficult to customize than software and subscription-based filtering tools, though.

And you can install parental controls on smartphones. See Chapter 17.

The following are some of the most popular monitoring tools and protective software:

✔ **Bsecure Online, Bsecure Family Safety** (www.bsecure.com) features social media protection, online media filtering, parental alerts for web and social media networks, text and e-mail alerts, whole home–filtering options, and integrated mobile filtering apps for Android and iOS devices.

✔ **ChildWebGuardian** (www.childwebguardian.com) screens page content for keywords and phrases, blocks blacklisted sites, allows for Internet use restrictions according to days and times, stores URLs of visited pages, sends reports via e-mail, restricts access to approved sites only, and allows gaming restrictions by day and time.

- ✔ **CyberPatrol** (www.cyberpatrol.com) provides parents with parental controls allowing for web filtering, online time limits, Internet activity monitors, chat and IM restrictions, and program blocking.

- ✔ **CYBERsitter** (www.cybersitter.com) includes remote monitoring, Facebook and Twitter activity recording, user-specific content filter controls, user-specific time schedules, different content filters for different members of the family/age groups, and the capability to block specific applications from accessing the Internet.

- ✔ **eBLASTER** (www.eblaster.com) records e-mails, social media messages, chat and IM, keystrokes, web browsing activity, applications run, and log on activity.

- ✔ **McAfee safeeyes** (www.internetsafety.com) filters web, video, and music content; and also creates reports that include Internet search activity, IM activity, and social network use.

- ✔ **Net Nanny** (www.netnanny.com) provides parents with the capability to filter Internet content, block adult content, set usage time limits, monitor social media activity, monitor IM and chat room use, mask inappropriate language, and receive cyberbullying alerts.

- ✔ **Norton Family** (https://onlinefamily.norton.com) provides families with smartphone monitoring; web monitoring and blocking; and capability to set time limits, monitor social network activity, track Internet searches, and receive e-mail alerts.

- ✔ **Avira Social Network Protection** (www.socialshield.com) scans activity and alerts parents to contact from strangers, potential cyberbullying, inappropriate content, and reputation risk.

- ✔ **Windows Live Family Safety** (http://windows.microsoft.com) provides family safety filters, website preference settings, and Windows parental controls.

- ✔ **iboss Home Parental Control Router** (www.iboss.com) offers a wireless router with filter functionality that acts as a firewall for all devices connected to the Internet through that router.

- ✔ **Identity Guard** (www.identityguard.com) offers a variety of identity-monitoring services along with Internet monitoring, public record monitoring, credit monitoring, and more. Identity Guard also offers kID Sure, a product designed for child identity–theft monitoring.

- ✔ **LifeLock** (www.lifelock.com) provides identity theft monitoring, credit- and noncredit-related alerts, monitoring for exposure of personal information, and comprehensive identity theft recovery services.

Leaving a Minimal Digital Footprint

A person's *digital* footprint is essentially a digital first impression. As I mention in Chapter 1, a child's digital footprint includes all information related to that child posted online. For example, Google indexes everything from tweets on Twitter to comments on Facebook. Not only do many employers use Internet searches to research potential employees, but many colleges and universities have begun to tap into online profiles when making decisions about applicants.

Many tweens and teens aren't aware that their actions online are tracked, recorded, and publicly available. Even those who have a vague awareness of their digital footprint probably don't remember what personal information they've shared online, especially if they're oversharing. Help your children to understand their digital footprint by searching online with them to find what information online is connected to their names and publicly available. If your children are just beginning to connect online, perhaps use your own digital footprint to show the importance of sharing only certain information.

Your kids may be leaving a breadcrumb trail, such as giving away personal ID information, without even knowing it or the potential negative consequences, including becoming a cyberbullying target, facing legal ramifications, losing a job, and more.

Identifying information

Although sharing embarrassing information or images online can be upsetting, a child publicly sharing too much identifying information is downright dangerous. Discourage your kids from sharing the following information publicly:

- ✔ Full birthday
- ✔ Phone number
- ✔ School name
- ✔ Names of immediate family members
- ✔ Address
- ✔ Current location
- ✔ Future location

Strangers can use this information to target children and pretend to know them using other information shared online, such as names of Friends and lists of favorites. Remind your children someone who "knows" information about them may still be a stranger.

And sharing location information can also make it easier for stalkers and predators to locate children and teens. I discuss online predators in more depth later in this chapter.

Finally, as I cover later in this chapter, sharing personal data also makes it easier for identity thieves to use your child's information.

Cyberbullying

Many tweens and teens feel comfortable sharing personal information from passwords to photographs with friends because they trust that they will never use that information to do anything hurtful. However, the shocking number of cyberbullying incidents has shown us that that is not always the case. Friends aren't always "friends."

Discuss with your children how they will feel if they share something deeply personal with a friend in writing via e-mail, text, or messaging, but someday down the road that person is no longer their "friend." Could that information be shared with others or used to harass them — or your family? I discuss cyberbullying in more detail in Chapter 10, including signs that your children are being cyberbullied and also how to report it.

Sexting and legal risks

Sexting — sending sexually explicit messages and/or photos from one mobile phone to another — is not only oversharing, but may also put your tween or teen at legal risk. Under both federal and state laws, creating, possessing, or distributing explicit images of a minor is illegal. A minor who takes and shares explicit images of themselves may be prosecuted under these laws and may even be required to register as a sex offender! I discuss sexting further in Chapter 17.

A precedent has been set in U.S. courts for attorneys to be able to use information posted online for everything from an alibi to proof of culpability. Teens should be aware of potential legal ramifications of publicly posting their location, images, and information about their actions.

Loss of employment or educational opportunities

Teens might understand that sharing may affect their potential employment, but they may not realize that their part-time or summer employer may have policies regarding social media that affect them in the here and now. Employees have been fired because of social media postings on Facebook and Twitter related to their job. Ask your employed teen whether his employer has a social media policy — and if so, what restrictions it includes. Some employers go so far as to require employees to turn over personal social media account names and passwords to those accounts.

Some colleges and universities also have policies related to social media use, dismissing students who have behaved inappropriately or in a threatening way online.

Stolen images

Images shared online are indexed by search engines just as text posted online is indexed. Despite safety precautions (such as image watermarks), many photographs posted publicly on personal social media sites or blogs are stolen. These images may then appear anywhere from other online sites to print ads halfway around the world without the permission of the photograph owner or those who appear in the photograph. Teens and tweens sharing images publicly need to be aware that after images are posted, there is the potential for them to be used without permission.

Risk of burglary

Sharing information about upcoming vacations or new home purchases can be fun, but discourage your children from sharing this information publicly via social media. Sharing such information — say, when your home will be empty for a week while you're basking in the tropics over the holidays — makes your home more susceptible to burglary. So does bragging online about new, large purchases. Children may unwittingly post other identifying information, such as your home address and phone number, making it easy (or at least, easier) for potential thieves to find your empty home or your new car in the driveway.

When discussing social media parameters as part the creation of your Digital Family Policy, be sure to include strict guidelines about the types of information your children should share publicly in relationship to your family and your home.

False sense of familiarity

Sharing large amounts of very personal information online as well as the common details of day-to-day life may make teens feel as if they really know their online Friends. Likewise, other people online may use this information to convince teens and tweens that their friendship is deep and real. The sad truth, though, is that there is no way to know whether the information being shared online is true and shared with honorable intent. And this false sense of familiarity may lead your teen to want to then meet online Friends in real life.

Help your children distinguish between online and real life friends when selecting both privacy settings and what to share online. Just as you would ask to approve what friends come into your home, ask for more information about the Friends your teen or tween has connected with online. For sites where your teen is more likely to share very personal and identifying information and images, such as Facebook, consider requiring that your teen Friend real life friends only. More information about the dangers of a false sense of familiarity are covered later in this chapter in a discussion about online predators.

Avoiding Oversharing

In a hyperconnected world, it takes just moments to share anything online: from what you had for lunch to your current location. Today's kids are growing up in a world where the private seems to be public, and people are plugged in around the clock, checking in online and updating social media statuses. This constant connectedness creates a vibrant sense of community and places unlimited resources at our children's fingertips, but oversharing personal information also presents potential dangers. With "safety first" in mind, remember to include a frank discussion about oversharing as part of your family's creation of a Digital Family Policy.

Although it's certainly important to show restraint to keep from alienating friends and upsetting Grandma, there are very real safety concerns related to oversharing. In 2010, Consumer Reports (`www.consumerreports.org`) conducted a survey that found that more than one-half of social media users post risky information online. Teens are far less likely than adults to believe that the amount of information they're sharing may be crossing a line.

Be sure to take the time to discuss motivation for sharing with your children. For example, are they likely to tweet pictures of the food they're eating because of an interest in cooking and recipe sharing? Do they share personal stories on their blog because they enjoy online journaling? Or has oversharing just become a bad habit? Such a discussion may prove enlightening for both you as the parent and for your children.

Also ask your children to consider the audience when sharing digitally. For example, does your teen use just one Facebook account to connect with both friends and family, or does she have a personal account to interact with peers and a family account to keep up to date on family happenings? Tweens and teens should consider that although their friends may enjoy seeing pictures of last Friday night's party, Grandma may be less interested in that photo album.

Teaching children the importance of restraint

To put it simply, just because you (or anyone, for that matter) *can* share every moment with the world, that doesn't mean you *should*. Just as you ask your children to follow an acceptable code of conduct offline, take time to discuss a code of conduct for online behavior. Begin a discussion with your family by first talking about the ways in which we share "whatever" with the world.

Here's a way to start the conversation ball rolling. If your teen has been digitally connected through a variety of platforms for some time, consider going through past posts and updates with your kids to discuss appropriateness and even remove some past information. Also, ask your children to have a discussion with their friends regarding how they feel about sharing personal information online. Your kids may be less likely to send an embarrassing photo, for example, to a friend who has no qualms about then sharing that photo via Facebook or Twitter.

Social networking sites

Start with the main venues, including

- Twitter
- Facebook
- Instagram
- Foursquare

Each of these social media platforms allows users to briefly and instantaneously share what is occurring in the user's life ("Awesome grilled cheese sandwich - #lunch!"), and each platform also allows uploading an associated image. Due to the instantaneous nature of these services partnered with the fact that they are all available on smartphones, users can quite easily share personal information quickly and across many settings. Kids may be sharing information reactively rather than thoughtfully.

If your teen's Foursquare, Twitter, and Instagram accounts (see Chapter 22 for more information) are linked to their Facebook account, for example, they may find that their Facebook page has become a play-by-play account of their day rather than a place to occasionally update a status, share photos, and participate in groups. For teens who are connected across multiple platforms, updates may be multiplied exponentially and become overwhelming to the audience.

Blogs

Many tweens and teens are also connected with the world through platforms (such as blogs and Tumblr, discussed in Chapters 14 and 22) that give kids a false sense of anonymity. Some kids, while hiding behind the assumed anonymity of the website profile, are likely to share private and personal information with far less restraint.

E-mail and texting

Also discuss one-to-one communication tools, such as text and e-mail, when discussing showing restraint with your kids. These platforms might seem private and protected, but there is no way to ensure that the communications won't be seen by anyone other than the intended recipient.

All in all, get your kids onboard, thinking hard about the connectivity between digital accounts when discussing the importance of showing restraint when it comes to sharing.

As a general rule, ask your children to consider the following before sharing information digitally:

- Is it potentially risky to share this information? If the answer is yes, you should not share it.

- Is there anyone who I would like to not be able to see this, such as my parents? If the answer is yes, consider not sharing it with anyone. After you share something digitally, there is no telling where it will go next.

- Will sharing this information hurt anyone? If the answer is yes, stop immediately.

✔ Is this something that my friends/family really want to know or see? If the answer is no, consider why you are sharing it. It may not be necessary.

✔ An hour from now, will I still be okay with this information being shared? If the answer is no, don't share it now. Even if you delete the information, it will still appear a variety of places including in e-mail updates and Google searches.

✔ Am I in an emotional state that may cause me to overshare and regret it later? If the answer is yes, wait and reconsider your post later.

Avoiding Online Predators

Online tools, such as social media networks and educational websites, can be a great resource for children and teens, but using them can put kids in the paths of online predators. In fact, according to the Crimes against Children Research Center (www.unh.edu/ccrc), one in five U.S. teenagers reports having received an unwanted sexual solicitation while online. Sites with chat rooms, instant messaging tools, and profiles posting contact information make it easy for kids to encounter strangers looking to take advantage of the anonymity of the internet to take advantage of young people. To protect your children from online predators, you need to first understand the risks.

Online predators locate children through a variety of online platforms including blogs, discussion boards, social networks, and chat rooms. They then use the communication tools on these sites along with texting and e-mail to contact these targets. Typically, online predators will draw in children through time and attention. They will claim interest in the same hobbies, music, shows, and movies as the children they are targeting, and appear sympathetic to the children's problems and concerns. They may even try to lure their targets through gifts. Eventually, they will begin to introduce inappropriate subjects and even content to the conversations, easing a child's inhibitions.

Talking to teens about predators

Most children will never encounter an online predator, but the risk is still very real. Teach your children that online predators exist and how to protect themselves. Here are some discussion points for talking to your children about online predators.

Anonymity

Children need to understand that people online can pretend to be anything and anybody. The children and teens they encounter on favorite social media and gaming platforms may be adults posing as young people. Because there is no way to really know who a person is that you have met online, set guidelines within your Digital Family Policy regarding Friend requests, chat platforms, and the sharing of personal information.

Oversharing

Include online predators in your discussions about what information is public and what information is private. Many children and teens feel comfortable sharing very personal information with strangers online because they are able to hide behind online profiles and personas. Children should understand that nothing online is ever really private, and they should use caution when sharing this information with strangers as it may be used against them in the future. This is another opportunity to reinforce that kids should never reveal personal and identifying information about themselves or their family publicly online, such as birthdate, phone number, and home address.

Private and offline communication requests

Prepare your children for potential requests from people they have met online to chat in private online rooms or even offline via text or phone. Set strict guidelines regarding these requests and encourage your children to come to you if someone online makes such a request.

E-mails and downloads

The Crimes against Children Research Center reports that one-quarter of children have been exposed to unwanted pornographic material online. Ask your children to never open e-mails or accept images or other documents to download from people they do not know in real life. Create a rule within your Digital Family Policy requiring children to notify you if they receive e-mails or images from strangers.

Secret keeping

Let your children know that a request from online Friends to keep a secret from parents or other adults is a red flag. Ask them to come to you if anyone online makes these types of requests.

Online persona

Discuss your child's online persona with them. The profile name and profile image they select for use online may catch the attention of online predators. Encourage them to use gender-neutral screen names that do not contain sexually suggestive words. I cover this topic in depth in Chapter 4.

Meeting in real life

Your Digital Family Policy should include a rule that your children should never agree to meet a person in real life whom they have gotten to know online. According to an ABC News report (http://abcnews.go.com), 100 percent of teens who became victims of sexual predators met the predator willingly.

Staying in the loop

As a parent, you also play a very important role in helping to protect your children. Even after you talk to your kids about online predators and set guidelines, here are steps you can take to ensure that your children are safe from online predators.

- ✔ **Monitor online conversations and e-mail accounts.** During the creation of your Digital Family Policy, prepare your children for the fact that accounts will be monitored for their safety. Maintain the ability to access your children's social media and e-mail accounts, and monitor periodically for communication from strangers and inappropriate content from previously trusted contacts.

- ✔ **Check online profiles.** From time to time, check to see what information your children have made available both to the public via their online profiles as well as to Friends. Ask them to remove private and identifying information, such as full birthdate and phone number.

- ✔ **Follow social media age guidelines.** Most social networking sites require that children be at least 13 years old to have an account. For your children's safety, do not let them use sites for which they are not the correct age. I discuss social media platforms more in Part III.

- ✔ **Restrict chat room use.** Young children should not be allowed to visit chat rooms and use chat functions on websites. As your children get older, you will need to create age specific chat guidelines within your Digital Family Policy to address different chat settings. Chapter 7 provides more information regarding chat platforms and children.

- ✔ **Keep your home computer in a public location.** In Chapter 2, I discuss home computer location and phone docking stations as part of the creation of the Digital Family Policy. Keeping your home computer in a highly trafficked area of your home — a family room or kitchen — rather than in a child's bedroom makes it less likely that they will engage in inappropriate conversations online or visit potentially dangerous websites and chat rooms.

✔ **Install and use parental controls software and monitoring tools.** A variety of tools are available to both monitor the use of your home's personal computer as well as protect your children through the use of parental control settings. I discuss these tools in depth later in this chapter.

✔ **Get hip to cyberslang.** Kids have their own crypto-shorthand. Know how to recognize these code words at a glance to help protect your children.

- A/S/L: A request to share age, sex, and location.

- ASLP: A request to share age, sex, location and a picture.

- CD9: Code 9 to indicate that parents are around.

- CFS: Care for secret?

- F2F or F/F: A request to meet face to face.

- FYEO: For your eyes only.

- GNOC: Get naked on camera.

- HSWM: Have sex with me.

- IPN: I'm posting naked.

- IRL: In real life.

- K: Kiss.

- KB: Kiss back.

- KOL: Kiss on the lips

- KPC: Keeping parents clueless.

- LMIRL: Let's meet in real life

- NIFOC: Naked in front of computer.

- NP: Nosey parents; a warning that parents may be nearby.

- P911: A warning that parents are coming.

- PAL: A warning that parents are listening.

- PANB: A warning that parents are nearby.

- PAW: Parents are watching.

- POS: A warning that parents are over the shoulder of the person typing.

- RUMOF: Are you male or female?

- TAW: A warning that teachers are watching.

- WTGP: Want to go private? (A request to move to a private chat room.)

- WUF: Where are you from?

- WYRN: What's your real name?

- 53x: Sex.

✔ **Keep communicating.** According to the Pennsylvania Attorney General's office (www.attorneygeneral.gov), only one-fourth of children nationally who say they received a sexual solicitation online also say that they told a parent about this unwanted communication. Keep lines of communication open and remind your children frequently that they can and should come to you with any concerns about online activity.

✔ **Watch for warning signs.** Here are some warning signs that may indicate that your child is communicating with an online predator. Your child

- Is withdrawn from the family

- Is receiving phone calls from an adult you don't know

- Has child pornography on his computer

- Receives mail or packages from someone you don't know

- Turns off the monitor quickly or changes screens/tabs when you walk into the room

- Spends large amounts of time online at night

If your child is the target of an online predator and receives sexually explicit photos or communications, contact your local police. Be sure to document any communication and save files and e-mails to turn over to the police. You can also report possible illegal online activity related to child pornography, predation, or other child sexual exploitation to the National Center for Missing and Exploited Children's CyberTipline at 1-800-843-5678 or www.missingkids.com.

Avoiding Identity Theft

Another potential safety risk online is identity theft. Everyday actions from using a mobile phone or laptop to visiting the pediatrician may put both your child and your family at risk for identity theft. In fact, according to the Federal Trade Commission (FTC; www.ftc.gov), 9 million Americans have their identity stolen every year, and an increasing number of these victims were children younger than 18.

Defining identity theft

Identity theft includes someone using another person's identifying information —
including name, credit card number, and Social Security number — without
permission. Identity thieves use this information to commit a variety of fraud
and theft crimes: for example, establishing accounts and obtaining credit
cards in the victim's name.

Here are some ways — some incredibly easy ways — how identity thieves
locate and steal this identifying information:

- Going through discarded documents in trash, such as bills, credit card
  statements, and bank statements.

  And "the trash" doesn't have to be what you take to the curb weekly. An
  Indianapolis TV investigative reporter helped bring national attention to
  pharmacies leaving lots of customers' personal info in their dumpsters
  instead of destroying it as they should have.

- Sending phishing e-mails pretending to be banks or other institutions
  (including AOL and PayPal) requesting that the recipient click through
  and provide information.

- Changing the victim's address so that billing and bank statements come
  to the identity thief.

- Skimming credit card information by using a special device in places
  where you scan or slide your card.

- Stealing your papers or wallet from your mailbox, car, briefcase/purse at
  work or other location.

- Lying to financial institutions and service providers to have them provide the thieves with your identifying information.

The cost of identity theft

According to the FTC (www.ftc.gov), in 2011 alone, identity theft cost
Americans $1.52 billion and financial losses are just one aspect of the cost of
identity theft. Victims also spend countless hours trying to recover losses,
repair credit, and regain trust. This same FTC report indicates that identity
theft victims spend up to 600 hours trying to restore their name and credit.
Most victims don't discover the identity theft until it has been occurring for
months, allowing thieves time to do extensive damage.

According to the identity-monitoring service Identity Guard (www.identity guard.com), the average debt incurred by a child identity theft victim is nearly $13,000, but the consequences of child identity theft extend far beyond initial monetary losses. Because many children don't discover that their identity has been stolen until they try to apply for college financial aid or open their first credit card account, their entire lives may be delayed while they deal with the aftermath of restoring their identity and credit. In fact, Identity Guard reports that one child identity theft victim reported having to take an entire year off of college because of identity theft.

Recognizing the risk of child identity theft

Most adults probably don't realize that children can also be victims of identity theft. According to *Bloomberg Businessweek* (www.businessweek.com), child identity theft has become the fastest growing type of identity theft. The FTC (www.ftc.gov) reports more than 50,000 known cases of child identity theft from 2010 to 2012. One study from AllClear ID (www.allclearid.com) estimates that as many as one in ten children in the United States are victims of identity theft.

Child identity theft often goes unnoticed because thieves use a child's Social Security number to open bank accounts and purchase homes. Adult identity theft victims might discover damage to their credit score while applying for a home loan or opening a credit card, but children may not find out about a stolen identity until they are an adult and applying for a college loan or renting their first apartment. At that point, their information may have been used for years without their knowledge.

Identity thieves targeting children can get identifying information from hospital birth records, schools, and even doctor offices. Add to that children who are active online may also be putting themselves at risk. The following tips can help decrease the risk of your child's identity being stolen from online activity:

- Remind your children to never share identifying information, such as their full birth date, online.
- Teach children to never share their Social Security number online.
- Teach your children to identify phishing e-mails and to not respond to or click through their links.

- Teach your teens to look for `https` in URLs at sites when shopping online to ensure that they're providing credit card information through a secure site.

- Ask your teens not to do any online banking or shopping on public computers, via their phones, or when using a shared Wi-Fi connection.

- Consider subscribing to both computer and identity monitoring services.

- Install antivirus software on your computer, tablets, and smartphones.

- Remind your children to protect laptops and phones against theft or loss, especially when transporting such devices in a backpack or school tote. A laptop with private account information goes missing about every 50 seconds.

- Ask your children to use password protection on all devices and remind them to log out of sites and devices.

- Teach your children to not click sidebar and pop-up ads when they are online.

- Ask children to not create e-mails and profile names that include identifying information such as birthdates, addresses, or Social Security numbers.

- Teach kids to come to you immediately if a site asks them to provide personal information.

- Remind children to never share passwords or store them in an easy-to-find location.

- Teach children how to create strong passwords and avoid reusing passwords for multiple accounts.

- Ask teens to not store sensitive information on laptops or phones.

- Ask your children to not accept Friend requests from people they don't know. Identity thieves use access to social media accounts to get password-protection answers, such as the victim's mom's maiden name or the victim's pet's name.

- Talk to your children about identity theft just like you talk to them about other risks.

Remind your children to never share *your* identifying information, either!

If any of the following events occur, consider checking to ensure that your child's identity has not been stolen by identity thieves:

- Your child receives unsolicited credit card applications.

- Your child receives unsolicited loyalty reward program applications.

- ✔ Your child's bank statements or credit card statements stop arriving.

- ✔ Your child applies for his first credit card and is turned down.

- ✔ Your child receives a credit card statement for an account that is not hers.

- ✔ Your child receives calls from a collection service.

- ✔ The IRS notifies you that a child you have listed as a dependent also appears on another tax return.

- ✔ Your child receives an IRS notification of overdue taxes, and your child has never had a job.

Chapter 4

Displaying Online Etiquette

●●

In This Chapter

▶ Understanding the importance of context

▶ Showing digital modesty

▶ Creating an appropriate profile

●●

*J*ust as adults follow different sets of etiquette guidelines at work and home, children speak differently with friends than with teachers. Similarly, online, appropriate tone and behavior varies from setting to setting. It's difficult enough for adults to navigate the tricky nuances of online etiquette, yet parents are responsible for helping their children do just that in a variety of online environments. By explaining the importance of context and tone to kids and setting some basic guidelines for online behavior, parents can help children feel comfortable and empowered across a variety of online settings.

Proper online etiquette begins with creating appropriate online accounts. Once again, as the head of your digital family, your guidance is essential as you steer your children toward judiciously creating their online profiles.

Using Context to Define Tone

The key to understanding what tone should be used in online communication is first understanding the context of that situation. Twitter? E-mail? Facebook? Texting? Different platforms and situations require different styles of interaction. Just as in offline life, different people also expect different styles of communication. These nuances may be difficult for tweens and teens to grasp, especially considering the rapid-fire digital communication to which they have become accustomed.

Google and some other free e-mail service providers require users to be at least 13 years of age to have an account.

Understanding the (often informal) social media atmosphere

Social media platforms invite informal communication, often with message length limits and casual terminology, such as "Friending" and "following." Read more about these and other aspects of social media in Part III. However, not all social media communication are equally relaxed. Certain social media sites invite more easygoing updates than others; the reason for site use will influence the tone and formality of communication.

Twitter

Twitter (see Chapter 12) is an informal platform that allows using only 140 characters per message. This restriction encourages users to share often-brusque snippets of information. (See Figure 4-1.) However, teens who tweet need to be reminded to keep their audience in mind when creating their Twitter status updates. Ask your tweeting teen to consider the following:

✔ Have you created a public account, which can be read by anyone? Chapter 12 guides you through selecting Twitter settings, including creating a private account.

✔ Are you followed by family members or just friends?

✔ Are you representing yourself only, or tweeting on behalf of others: say, a school club or an extracurricular group?

✔ Are you tweeting with companies or brands with customer service questions and feedback?

Twitter accounts that aren't protected can be seen by anyone. Remind your teen of this before they use this very public platform.

Figure 4-1: Many tweets use a very informal style.

bro

I seriously can't wait for Believe Acoustic. Just Justin and a guitar. Wow. Just like the Kidrauhl days :')

← Reply ⇄ Retweet ★ Favorite ••• More

12,836 RETWEETS   5,537 FAVORITES

4:48 AM - 14 Dec 12 · Embed this Tweet

Facebook

Like Twitter, Facebook (see Chapter 12) also often follows a "stream of consciousness" format with users posting status updates on a whim. To determine the right tone to use on their Facebook page, have your teens think about these questions:

- ✔ Are you friends with just peers or also family, coaches, and teachers?
- ✔ Do you have your own account, or are you posting to the family account?
- ✔ Do your privacy settings allow anyone to see your status updates, or are they hidden from anyone who is not your friend?

Despite the generally informal nature of social media, here are some general guidelines to ask your child to consider and that you may wish to discuss as part of your Digital Family Policy (see Chapter 2). Your teen may choose to ignore formal language constructs (such as spelling and punctuation), but they should avoid postings on all social media that contain

- ✔ Vulgarity
- ✔ Violence
- ✔ Sexual references
- ✔ Illegal activity

Your discussion with your teen about the difference between informal and inappropriate is the perfect time to remind him to assume that anything posted online is available to be seen by the public, including friends' parents, school staff, future employers, colleges, and law enforcement. Stress to them that it's safer to skip a questionable photo on Instagram or post on Foursquare than regret it later.

This is also a good time to remind your teen that in certain online locations, informal social media tone should be replaced by a more respectful and formal manner. Such settings include

- ✔ Online study groups
- ✔ Class blog or social media page
- ✔ Family Facebook page
- ✔ Extracurricular activity group or page

Demonstrating proper e-mail manners according to situation

It is perfectly acceptable for your teens to e-mail their friends using slang words and "text speak," but that kind of informality is clearly not appropriate in e-mails to teachers, coaches, and prospective employers. The best way to teach your kids proper e-mail etiquette is to demonstrate it for them. Be sure to include your children's e-mail address when appropriate when you communicate with coaches, tutors, and other adults in their lives. When you help your child get his first e-mail address, ask him to consider what might be different about his communications when e-mailing the following people:

- Friends
- Family
- Work
- After-school clubs
- Coaches

E-mail is just like sending a card or letter through the mail. Remind your children that they would write differently in a thank-you note to their grandmother than they would in a note passed to a friend in school. These same differences apply to e-mail composition.

Different e-mail manners make sense according to situation, but here are some guidelines that apply, especially for the first e-mail your child writes to a new contact. Remind them that just as they would when writing a non-electronic message, they should follow these guidelines:

- Include a subject line.
- Open with a greeting.
- Use standard spelling, capitalization, and punctuation.
- Write short paragraphs that are clear and to the point.
- End with a brief and appropriate closing.
- Be cordial but not joking.
- Use spellcheck before sending your e-mail.

Here's how an appropriately written introductory e-mail might appear:

> To: futureemployer@job.com
>
> Cc:
>
> Bcc:
>
> Subject: Babysitting Opportunity
>
> Mrs. Brown,
>
> I am writing about your request for a neighborhood babysitter. I am in the 10th grade at the local high school and have been babysitting for two years. I am certified in child and infant CPR and can share references if you would like. You can contact me at 555-3131 or this e-mail address.
>
> Thank you,
>
> Jill

After a person responds to your child's e-mail, continuing communication will likely be in shorter snippets with far less formality, but remind your kids that use of proper spelling, capitalization, and punctuation should continue.

This is a great time to remind kids that even though they are sending an e-mail to just one person, there is always a chance that the e-mail will not remain private. Here's a mantra you can share with them: *If you don't want it shared, don't type it!*

E-mail communication between friends will certainly be less formal in format and tone, but remind your kids that treating others appropriately applies across all situations, even e-mails. You may want to remind your kids that inappropriate e-mails, such as those used to cyberbully or send inappropriate pictures, will not be tolerated. Include consequences for inappropriate e-mailing behavior in your Digital Family Policy.

Teaching the Golden Rule in a Digital World

Every child learns the Golden Rule: Treat others the way you would like to be treated. However, in a digital world, children (and adults, for that matter) often feel as though they can hide behind online anonymity. With online behavior affecting everything from friendships to future employment, it's important to talk to your children about remembering their manners — especially online.

TIP

Stress to your children to never say something to someone online they wouldn't say to that person's face.

Bragging versus sharing: teaching kids digital modesty

Modesty is one area frequently of concern in the digital world where every detail of our lives can be shared instantly. Kids naturally want to share their happiness and success with friends and family, and there is no reason why they shouldn't. For example, kids may be quick to share a great report card, new job, or recent purchase. However, just as you would ask your child to share good news in person with modesty and not with the intent to brag, so should they share information online.

Ask your kids to consider the following in determining sharing versus bragging:

- ✔ How frequently are they updating their social media statuses?
- ✔ How often are they using social media status updates to share successes?
- ✔ What tone are they taking when sharing?
- ✔ How would they feel if their Friends' accounts were updated as frequently and in the same way as theirs?

Show your teens the following examples of Facebook status updates and ask them to decide which status they would rather see from their Friends as well as their own account. (See Figure 4-2.)

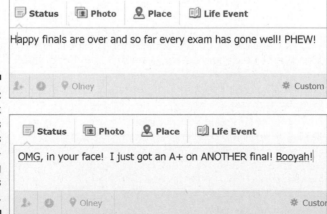

Figure 4-2:
Facebook status updates highlight-ing sharing versus bragging.

Keeping friends' secrets

Living in a digital world not only allows our kids to share their own information and thoughts instantly and with many people, but it also makes it easy to quickly share whatever has been sent to them. Texts and e-mails can be forwarded, private chats cut and pasted, and screenshots saved and shared with anyone. While reminding kids to share cautiously because *anything they share in writing through technology could be made public,* also stress the importance of keeping friends' secrets.

Keeping kindness in mind

Just as the ability to hide behind a screen causes many kids and teens to overshare, an online "cloak" can also make kids feel more comfortable saying mean or hurtful things to and about other people. The digital world has allowed playground gossip and bus ride bullying to move online and be shared instantly with an entire school rather than the handful of people within earshot. Remind kids that kindness counts online, and they should keep the following in mind:

- ✔ Stop and think before you type something mean and press Send.
- ✔ Don't forward mean e-mails, texts, or messages that you've received.
- ✔ Consider how you would feel if someone said something mean about you and shared it online.
- ✔ Sometimes mean behavior online can be considered cyberbullying, and that can have very serious consequences. Chapter 10 covers cyberbullying in depth.

Of course, your children will likely encounter kids and adults who don't exercise good online etiquette. In these moments, sure, it's tough for kids to keep their cool and not respond in kind with meanness. Remind your kids, though, to stay calm and just "walk away" if possible to avoid engaging in inappropriate behavior. At all times, kids should remember to report any behavior or interactions that might be dangerous or considered cyberbullying.

When your teen feels an interaction getting out of control, encourage them to take the conversation offline.

Creating an Appropriate Online Persona

With a child's digital footprint following teens as they seek jobs and entrance into college, they must think carefully about the online persona that they're creating. Posting appropriate profile pictures and wholesome activities, while using nonsuggestive online names, will help create and maintain a positive digital persona for your child.

Choosing suitable profile pictures

Teens often upload a profile picture quickly and with little thought, snapping a quick photo with a webcam or a phone's camera. A quick image search makes it clear, however, that the image your child chooses to associate online with their name can stick with them as part of their digital footprint.

While profile pictures are the most important because they are public, ask your teens to also think carefully before sharing any photos. Inappropriate pictures associated with their digital footprint may come back to haunt them!

Here are some important reasons why your kids select a suitable profile picture as they begin to explore all that the digital world has to offer:

- **Digital footprint:** As I mention throughout this book, the actions your child takes online — everything from product reviews on e-commerce sites to posts on Friends' social media pages — follow them into their future, creating a legacy that can be searched by future employers and educational institutions. Ask your kids to consider who might find their profile image in a quick search — and if they feel comfortable about the image they've selected to share with the world.

- **Safety:** Just as the information shared by your child in chat rooms (as discussed in Chapter 7) and on social media sites can be used by online predators to gain the trust of your child, profile pictures may also catch the attention of online predators. Ask that your kids do not use images that contain the following:

    - Sexually provocative images

    - Identifying information, such as full name, address, or birthdate

    - Illegal behavior

Selecting appropriate online handles

If your child is creating an account on a chat platform or online world that is frequented only by other friends their age, they may want to come up with a silly yet safe online name: a "handle." However, remind them that when creating more public and widely used names — including e-mail addresses — that they should choose a name they feel comfortable sharing. As I discuss in Chapter 3, kids should carefully select their online names for many safety reasons. Beyond safety reasons, however, they should keep in mind that this screen name may follow them for years and across platforms. They should carefully select a name that is

- ✔ **Easy to remember**
- ✔ **Free of identifying or private information (such as birth year or first name)**
- ✔ **Does not include their gender**
- ✔ **Safe to share with both friends and family**
- ✔ **Different from their e-mail address**
- ✔ **Free of vulgar or inappropriate words**

A handle is likely to be used for a long period of time, across many platforms, and using a random group of letters and numbers is unwieldy.

Remind your kids that not only is their screen name likely the first piece of information that others will see about them, but it also acts as a protective layer between the public and your child's private information. While it may make sense for your child to include their favorite activity or hobby as part of their screen name, this also provides strangers with personal information. The safest bet is to select a completely random screen name.

Ask your children to always use a screen name that's different from their real name — as well as different from their passwords.

Keeping positive

Your children can use their online persona to create a positive digital foot-print. Ask your teen to consider including the following information in their online biographies (see Figure 4-3) and profile information to give a positive first impression:

✔ Favorite after-school activities and hobbies

✔ Notable accomplishments, academic and extra-curricular

✔ Volunteer interests

✔ Educational and career interests

Even brief biographies give your teen the chance to make a great digital first impression!

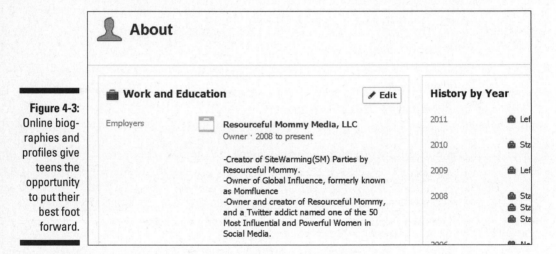

Figure 4-3:
Online biog-
raphies and
profiles give
teens the
opportunity
to put their
best foot
forward.

Chapter 5

Knowing Where Kids Are Turning On and Tuning In

In This Chapter
▶ Extending your Digital Family Policy beyond home
▶ Monitoring screen time during school hours
▶ Tracking hidden digital time

During the creation of your Digital Family Policy (see Chapter 2), you will likely set guidelines for how many screen hours each child in your family is allowed to have per day or week. The American Academy of Pediatrics (www.aap.org) recommends limiting the amount of hours because of several potential negative effects of too much screen time:

✔ **Behavioral problems:** Exposure to screen time more than 2 hours per day may cause children to experience attention and behavioral problems.

✔ **Obesity:** Children who experience more than 2 hours of screen time per day are at higher risk for developing obesity.

✔ **Impaired academic performance:** Excessive screen time, especially in children's bedrooms or locations where they complete homework, may lead to impaired academic performance.

✔ **Lack of play time:** The more time children spend in front of a screen, the less time they have for other play, including physical activities.

To implement rules regarding screen time limits, you need a complete understanding of all the places where digitally connected kids are turning on and tuning in. Long gone are the days of screen time being confined to the family room television and the home computer. Now some kids are connected around the clock with smartphones, tablets, handheld gaming devices, and more. With the help of friends' parents and the school community, you can gain a more complete understanding of your kids' digital lives.

Creating Rules for Usage in Friends' Homes

All kids know which friend's home is "the place to go" for everything from the snack food they aren't allowed to eat at home to the movies they aren't supposed to watch. In this digital age, that may often mean access to more screen time, different gaming devices, and other digital goodies that might be off-limits in their own homes. Communication is the key to finding out what your kids are consuming digitally when spending time in friends' homes.

Collaborating with friends' parents

Parents hosting children in their homes for play dates and after-school get-togethers typically find out from the guest's parents any specific likes or dislikes regarding food and activities as well as allergies or other rules to be aware of. Although you (understandably) can't enforce your own standards inside someone else's home, communicate with the other parents about what the children will be doing while together as well as about your family's rules for your children's screen time.

You may want to let your children's friends' parents know the following information:

- ✔ How much screen time you allow in one sitting
- ✔ What television, movie, and game ratings your children are permitted to watch or play
- ✔ What websites your children are allowed to visit
- ✔ Any devices that your children are not permitted to use

Likewise, be sure to find out from your children's friends' parents about any specific rules that they follow in their homes that you would like to respect when they are visiting.

Talk about your Digital Family Policy's rules (see Chapter 2) when first chatting with the parents of your children's friends, just as you would discuss allergies and other family rules.

Asking the right questions

Although you will likely include a conversation about digital time in friends' homes during the creation of your Digital Family Policy, the key to enforcing these guidelines is asking your kids the right questions. After your children are elementary school age, you will very rarely accompany them during time with friends, so having conversations with your children is the best way to determine how their time with friends is spent. Here are some questions to ask to conclude how much digital time your children spend with friends:

- ✔ What do you do when you go to "Johnny's" house?
- ✔ Do you ever watch television there?
- ✔ What are your friend's favorite shows?
- ✔ What video and computer games does your friend like to play?
- ✔ Do you ever play those games with him when you are there?
- ✔ Where is the computer in your friend's home?
- ✔ Where are your friend's parents when you are at his house?

When creating your Digital Family Policy, consider creating consequences for breaking digital policy rules when in someone else's home.

Being Aware of Extensive In-School Usage

Most teachers include time in a computer lab in their weekly lesson plans, but what you may not realize is that many classrooms today also have computers in the classroom and include computer time as part of daily lesson plans. A child who is allowed only 60 minutes of screen time per day may come home from school having already logged in 20 minutes of computer time. As parents, you may not even realize that one-third of your child's screen time has already been accounted for prior to their usage at home.

Talking to teachers about screen and Internet time

Any parent who has ever asked a child what they learned in school that day knows that sometimes it's tough to get a straight answer from kids about what happens during their school day. To get a complete picture of how much screen time your child is accumulating during the course of the school day, you may need to enlist the help of your children's teachers.

- ✔ **Request a daily schedule.** Most elementary school teachers have a standard plan that they follow each day, which may include classwork at dedicated learning stations. Many classrooms contain at least one student computer used during station rotations for activities, such as math drills and reading lessons.

- ✔ **Ask about computer lab time.** Your child's schedule of classes may also include time in a computer lab.

- ✔ **Inquire about free time activities.** As children complete their work or other activities, they are often permitted time to move around the room, locate a book to read, or begin a new activity. Some classrooms allow activities on the computer during this student free time as well as at the start and end of the day.

- ✔ **Ask about television viewing time.** You may not expect your child to watch television as part of their school day, but some teachers allow students to watch children's television programming during extended down time, such as the dismissal process or study halls.

- ✔ **Find out about device use throughout the school day.** Each school has its own unique device usage policy (discussed later in this chapter), which may allow students to use devices (such as smartphones) during certain times, such as study halls and lunch. Schools may also use technology throughout the school day as part of instruction. See the following section.

- ✔ **Share your family rules with teachers.** Acknowledging that classroom instruction practices and rules won't likely alter because of your family digital usage policies, you can still share with your child's teachers your family's rules regarding device use and screen time. Your child's teachers may be able to guide your children to activities other than computer use during free time, for example, if they are aware of your family's concerns and guidelines.

Understanding school technology use policies

Younger children may have very little control over their exposure to screen time, but older students may be allowed to bring a variety of electronic devices to school with them. The amount of access that kids have to these devices throughout the day will vary by school. Request a copy of your school's code of conduct, which should include the school's technology use policies, and be sure to find answers to the following questions:

- ✔ What devices are students allowed to bring to school?
- ✔ Are students allowed to keep the devices with them during class time?
- ✔ Are students allowed to use the devices during class time?
- ✔ Are students allowed to use devices during nonclass time, such as in the hallways before and after school, during lunch, and during study halls?
- ✔ What are the consequences for device use during restricted times?
- ✔ If a restricted device has been confiscated from a student, how and when can the parents get the device back?
- ✔ What devices are typically used in education throughout the school day?
- ✔ How has the school restricted access to certain websites?
- ✔ What are the consequences for school-owned devices that are used for restricted behaviors?
- ✔ What is the school policy should a school-owned device be broken while in the care of a student?

I cover using technology in education in more depth in Chapter 18.

School technology policies often apply to the entire school district and are typically posted on your district's website.

Finding and Tracking Hidden Digital Time

To accurately assess the amount of screen time your child is experiencing, you need to first find and then track hidden or unexpected screen time in your child's day. In a variety of locations, children may experience unexpected screen time. The following are just a few of the locations where kids may be turning on and tuning in:

✔ **Health professionals' offices:** Not only do dentist office waiting rooms often have a television with movies or even video game consoles, but dentists often also show movies to kids during teeth cleanings and even exams. And children's doctor's offices often use television and movie time to keep both the waiting children and their parents occupied while they wait to be seen.

✔ **Restaurants:** Many restaurants display sporting events or news channels in waiting areas or over bars, which may be seen from other areas of the restaurant.

✔ **Before or after care:** Children who attend before care or after care as part of their school day may be shown movies or television as part of the regularly scheduled activities of that child care facility.

✔ **Religious institutions:** Use of digital media in curriculum extends beyond the daily school curriculum and into many religious institutions that may show videos as part of their weekly lessons.

✔ **Airports and train stations:** Much like doctor's offices, airports and train stations often have televisions in their waiting areas.

✔ **Cars:** Many vehicles now come equipped with or offer screens that either drop down from the vehicle's ceiling or are installed in the back of headrests.

✔ **Hair salons:** Like pediatric dentist offices using television time to calm nervous children, hair salons created for young clientele often put televisions in their waiting rooms as well as at the cutting stations.

Most locations that provide children with access to computers or television do so in an attempt to make the children feel at ease during what otherwise could be an uncomfortable situation. With that said, if you are a parent who would like to limit your child's screen time, you may not wish for them to take advantage of these opportunities. Before going somewhere such as the dentist or a restaurant where your child may be given the chance to watch a movie or show, or play a computer, decide the following:

✔ Will you allow your child to watch the provided digital entertainment?

✔ Will this digital time count toward your child's screen time totals for the day or week?

If you decide to count this screen time toward the totals allowed in your Digital Family Policy, you may wish to offer your child the option to not partake of the television or movie viewing. In this case, provide the following:

- ✔ Other options for your child to pass the time such as reading a book, completing a puzzle workbook, or working on the evening's homework assignment

- ✔ Alternative locations to sit such as away from televisions in a restaurant or in a section of a waiting room that does not have a clear view of monitors

- ✔ Music to listen to in order to distract from the screens around the room

Part II

Navigating the Digital World Kids Live In

For a guide to talking to your children about cyberbullying, check out www.dummies.com/extras/raisingdigitalfamilies.

In this part . . .

- ✔ Gain an understanding of game system basics including multi-player game platforms and game ratings.

- ✔ Become familiar with popular chat forms and typical privacy and chat settings.

- ✔ Get to know more about the search engines your family uses including optional settings, filters, and sponsored content.

- ✔ Learn how advertisers target your children online and how to explain online advertising to your kids.

- ✔ Become aware of the dangers of cyberbullying and get the tools you need to have a conversation with your children about preventing and reporting cyberbullying.

Chapter 6

Decoding Gaming

· ·

In This Chapter

▶ Understanding gaming consoles

▶ Social gaming basics

▶ Explaining video game ratings system

▶ Integrating game ratings with your Digital Family Policy

▶ Using Parental Control tools

· ·

From game consoles to computer games to online game playing, most parents will encounter the world of gaming at some point in their children's lives. A 2011 study from NPD Group (www.npd.com) found that 91 percent of kids between the ages of 2 and 17 play video games, up 13 percent from a 2009 report by the same firm. Even if you consider yourself a gamer, you need to understand the game platforms on which your child may be playing at home or at friends' houses as well as new features you may not be familiar with, such as consoles you don't have in your own home or recent downloaded updates.

In this chapter, I show you gaming system basics including the top game consoles: PlayStation, Xbox, and Wii. I also walk you through the world of social gaming, including Wi-Fi–enabled gaming, Facebook games, and PC gaming. Finally, with safety in mind, I cover game ratings and how to use these ratings to create the gaming section of your Digital Family Policy (as discussed in Chapter 2).

Understanding Gaming System Basics

Video game consoles require a television or other monitor for display rather than being standalone, like a handheld device (think Nintendo DSi). First developed in the early 1970s, game consoles have become a standard fixture in most digital families. Each console type uses (typically proprietary) game cartridges or discs and may have a variety of interactive features, such as Wi-Fi capability or the ability to detect motion with a sensor connected to the console.

The primary game consoles on the market now are

- **PlayStation:** Sony (http://us.playstation.com)
- **Xbox:** Microsoft (www.xbox.com)
- **Wii:** Nintendo (www.nintendo.com/wii)

All three game systems allow users to engage in activities beyond playing game cartridges and discs. All three game systems have similar features, but each also has a variety of characteristics that makes it distinct. So, you need to understand the capabilities of each game system in your home so that you can adequately address each system function in your Digital Family Policy. For example, will your children be allowed to connect the game console to your home's Wi-Fi? Will they be allowed to download additional game components or play only game discs that you've purchased (or borrowed or rented)?

PlayStation

PlayStation 3 (PS3) is the latest version of Sony's PlayStation game system. Like most game consoles, PS3 capabilities extend beyond game disc play. However, the PS3 is the only game console with a built-in Blu-ray player. PS3 also gives families the capability to play many of the gaming industry's top games.

PS3 capabilities beyond game disc play include

- Blu-ray disc viewing
- Access to game add-ons via the Wi-Fi–enabled PlayStation Store
- Capability to stream 3-D and HD movies and shows through such services as Netflix, Hulu Plus, CinemaNow, and VUDU
- Capacity to watch sports through optional services, such as NHL GameCenter Live, NFL Sunday Ticket, and MLB.TV
- Access to Music Unlimited (a music-streaming service)
- DVD viewing
- Digital photo viewing and storage
- Internet access
- Digital music listening and storage
- Audio CD playback

Some PS3 features require a subscription or membership at an additional cost.

To troubleshoot PlayStation problems, monitor devices and services, and ask questions, visit `http://playstation.custhelp.com`.

Xbox 360

Xbox 360 is the most recent video game console from Xbox creator Microsoft. Through the built-in Wi-Fi, Xbox 360 owners may also use their console to do the following:

- ✔ View HD movies and stream television through such services as Amazon Instant Video, Crackle, EPIX, ESPN, GameSpot TV, Hulu Plus, Netflix, Syfy, TMZ, Verizon FiOS, and Zune Video.
- ✔ Listen to music via iHeartRadio, Last.fm, YouTube, and Zune Music Pass.
- ✔ Browse the Internet through Internet Explorer.
- ✔ Download additional games and game features.

Xbox 360 consoles also allow you to

- ✔ Listen to audio CDs.
- ✔ Store and listen to digital music.
- ✔ View DVDs.
- ✔ View and store digital photos.

For an additional cost, Xbox 360 owners may purchase the Kinect — a motion-sensing input device — which operates without controllers and instead uses a sensor to recognize your movements. Through the Kinect sensor, users can play game discs created for use with the Kinect and enjoy voice-controlled entertainment.

Xbox users may connect with game console support at `http://support.xbox.com`.

Wii

Like the Xbox Kinect, the Wii game console from Nintendo is motion-controlled, but unlike the Kinect, the Wii sensor requires Wii remotes. As one of the top game consoles, Wii offers some of the most popular games available.

Beyond game play, the Wii provides owners with the ability to

✔ View movies and television through such services as Netflix and Hulu Plus.

✔ Listen to audio CDs.

✔ View and store digital photos.

✔ View DVDs.

✔ Download classic Nintendo games and game add-ons.

✔ Access weather reports through the Forecast Channel.

✔ Browse the Internet through the Internet Channel.

✔ Read the latest news via the News Channel.

Wii owners may find answers to technical support questions at www. nintendo.com/consumer/index.jsp.

Wii U

The latest version of the Wii game system, Wii U (released in late 2012; see Figure 6-1) incorporates a Wii U GamePad controller that includes a front-facing camera, microphone, stereo speakers, motion control, a second video screen, and more. A GamePad allows players to view their gaming experience from multiple viewpoints simultaneously: one perspective appearing on the GamePad and the other appearing on the television screen.

Wii U also features Nintendo TVii, with which users can find, watch, and engage with TV shows, movies, and sports programming. You can use the GamePad to connect to other services, such as cable and satellite or video on-demand subscriptions.

Most games created for the Wii game console also work on Wii U.

PC gaming

Just like video game consoles, many video games are available for personal computers. In fact, many of the most popular game console games are also available for your home computer. Some games, such as massively multi-player online games (MMOGs), are more often available for PCs than for video game consoles.

Figure 6-1:
The Wii U
game
console
from
Nintendo.

Most games are playable on your PC without requiring additional add-on purchases, such as special keyboards, steering wheels, and joysticks. What you should check before purchasing a PC game, however, is that your PC meets the system requirements, especially memory requirements.

PC games can come on discs, much like the games you purchase for your video game console, or are downloadable via the Internet.

Introducing Social Gaming

With Wi-Fi–enabled game consoles, game applications available through social media platforms, and games available for play directly from your Internet browser, "social gaming" no longer refers to two friends playing a video game together in your family room. Instead, your kids now play with other kids or adults around the world, raising a variety of safety and privacy questions. When creating the gaming section of your family's Digital Family Policy, include specific questions relating to the social gaming opportunities that follow.

Wi-Fi–enabled PC and console gaming

PS3, Xbox 360, and Wii all allow players to interact virtually with other console owners around the world through your home's Wi-Fi connection.

The PlayStation Network allows users to play online, multiplayer games free. This network includes PlayStation Home, a social game platform that connects you to millions of other users through hundreds of games. Important to note, this service includes the ability to participate in both voice and video chat with other PlayStation Home account holders. Much like a standard social media platform, you can build a Friend list and send messages via your PS3 game console.

Similar to the PlayStation Network, Xbox 360 also allows users to play with other console owners through the Microsoft Wi-Fi–enabled social gaming platform, Xbox LIVE. Users can use their Xbox LIVE account to post to their Facebook account, including alerting Facebook Friends that they would like to play a multiplayer Xbox 360 game with them. You can also update your Facebook and Twitter statuses through Xbox LIVE and participate in video chats using Kinect.

Some Wii games can be played online with multiple people through the Wii's online features. These Wi-Fi Connection games are designed to allow the user to play with anyone around the world. And you can use a special Friend Code (a type of parental control) to allow only people you know to participate in the online game play.

Wii U features an online gaming community — Miiverse — through which users may interact with other Wii U users: playing games, chatting, and posting messages. You can also use Wii U's GamePad controller to video chat in real time with other Wii U users.

PC gaming allows for many online gaming opportunities both via purchased games and free, online-only games. Multiplayer games, MMOGs, and MMORPGs (Massively Multiplayer Online Role Playing Games) are very popular in the PC game realm, allowing players to interact with other players around the world. Many games allow players to use webcams, microphones, and headsets to interact vocally and visually with other players.

Because their capabilities vary from platform to platform, set rules according to each game console when discussing Wi-Fi–enabled gaming during the creation of your Digital Family Policy. Be specific about features that may include a variety of levels of use, such as chat with or without video, or online play with anyone or just friends. Also include specific rules regarding pay-to-play options your child will encounter during Wi-Fi–enabled console gaming, such as the ability to download online-only games or console game add-ons.

Many families allow their children computer time for homework and other school-related tasks, so set clear rules in your Digital Family Policy regarding accepted uses of the computer at specific times. For example, are your children allowed to play PC games after completing their homework? Are PC games allowed only on the weekend? Also note whether children have permission to purchase and download PC games online as part of their PC gaming time.

Facebook games

More than one-half of Facebook's one billion account holders report playing Facebook games. As I discuss in Chapter 12, these game applications require access to your Facebook account — and thus might be a privacy concern. Include an area in your Digital Family Policy to address Facebook games; specifically, rules about participating in games, gaming with other Facebook users, and paying for in-game features that require a fee for access.

Types of Facebook games

The enormous variety of Facebook games and game types can make creating specific Facebook gaming rules very difficult for parents. Some of the most popular categories of Facebook games are

- **Board games:** Think checkers, chess, and Mahjong.

- **Sports games:** From fishing to baseball and football, sports games can be played solo or with a Facebook Friend.

- **Arcade-style games:** Arcade-style games are reminiscent of shooting games and original arcade video games.

- **Puzzle games:** Games focusing on strategy, logic, and quick reflexes fall into this category.

- **Role-playing games:** Role-playing games (RPGs) allow the player to take on the role of a character to complete tasks and journeys during the course of the game.

- **Betting games:** These games allow users to "bet" on games, such as bingo, poker, slots, and sports.

Paying to play Facebook games

Playing games on Facebook is free. However, some Facebook games have within-game options that require payment for access. For example, many games — including some role-playing games and betting games — allow users to pay money for the chance to win virtual rewards. Some games also require a fee to add features or tools to your game experience. For example, in the popular Facebook game Farmville, you can purchase items (such as virtual tractors) that help in game play. Be sure that your Digital Family Policy includes specific rules regarding paying for these game features.

In the United States, you can't currently bet with and win actual money on Facebook. However, Facebook users in the UK can gamble through adults-only, highly regulated betting game apps.

Protecting your account's privacy

Participating in Facebook game play requires allowing game applications to access information in your Facebook profile. You might also have to set a list of permissions for that game application, such as posting in your Friends' News Feeds on your behalf. For many parents, this is a privacy concern. You can, however, restrict the permissions you grant a Facebook game application while still being able to play that game.

When you choose to play a game, a permissions screen appears (see Figure 6-2), telling you the various permissions that particular game is requesting: for example, your e-mail address or your location.

Figure 6-2:
Facebook
game
permissions
screen.

You may edit specific game permissions after the game has been installed. To do this, follow these steps:

1. **Go to** www.facebook.com **and sign in to your account.**

2. **From the drop-down menu in the upper-right corner, choose Privacy Settings.**

3. **Click the Edit Settings link to the right of the Ads, Apps and Websites section. (See Figure 6-3.)**

4. **Click the Edit Settings button to the right of the Apps You Use section (see Figure 6-4).**

5. **Click Edit next to each game application to change what that game application may do through your account.**

Figure 6-3:
Edit settings
for Ads,
Apps and
Websites.

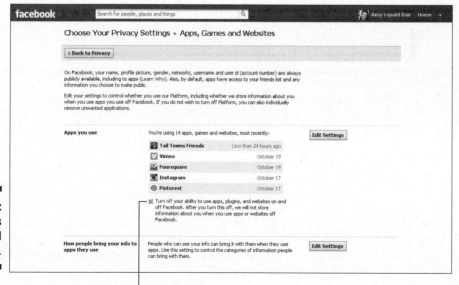

Figure 6-4:
Edit settings
for installed
applications.

Disable Facebook Platform

Even if you choose to not allow your children to participate in Facebook gaming, their accounts might still be accessed by Facebook game applications due to their Friends' activity.

To control which applications may access your account through your Friends, follow Steps 1–3 of the preceding list, click the Edit Settings button for the How People Bring Your Info to Apps They Use section (refer to Figure 6-4), and select what information you choose to share with apps being used by your Facebook Friends. (See Figure 6-5.)

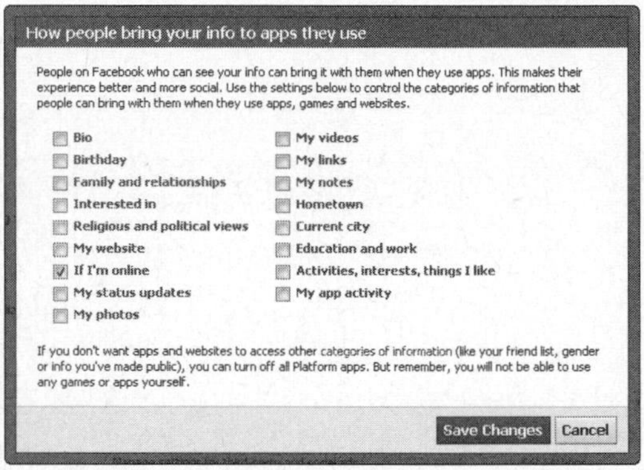

Figure 6-5:
Edit how
people bring
your info
into apps
they use.

How people bring your info to apps they use

People on Facebook who can see your info can bring it with them when they use apps. This makes their experience better and more social. Use the settings below to control the categories of information that people can bring with them when they use apps, games and websites.

- Bio
- Birthday
- Family and relationships
- Interested in
- Religious and political views
- My website
- ☑ If I'm online
- My status updates
- My photos

- My videos
- My links
- My notes
- Hometown
- Current city
- Education and work
- Activities, interests, things I like
- My app activity

If you don't want apps and websites to access other categories of information (like your friend list, gender or info you've made public), you can turn off all Platform apps. But remember, you will not be able to use any games or apps yourself.

[Save Changes] [Cancel]

Even though changing these settings will control what information from your accounts can be provided to game applications used by your teen's Friends, she may still receive Facebook game invitations from her Friends on Facebook. Your teen can block all game invitations from Friends, though.

The first option is to block game application invites from specific Friends by doing the following from the Privacy Settings menu (see the preceding steps):

1. **Click the Manage Blocking link next to the Blocked People and Apps section (refer to Figure 6-3).**

2. **In the Block Invites From field, type the name of the Friend whose invitations you would like to block (see Figure 6-6).**

The second option is to block specific game applications from contacting you or receiving nonpublic information about you from Facebook. From the Blocked People and Apps section (see the preceding steps), find the Block Apps field, and type the name of the application whose contact and access to your nonpublic information you would like to block (refer to Figure 6-6).

If you would like to allow your children or family to have a Facebook account, but you don't want that account to have access to Facebook games and applications, you may choose to permanently opt-out of the Facebook apps platform. Disabling Facebook game applications makes that Facebook profile completely inaccessible to all apps, including games.

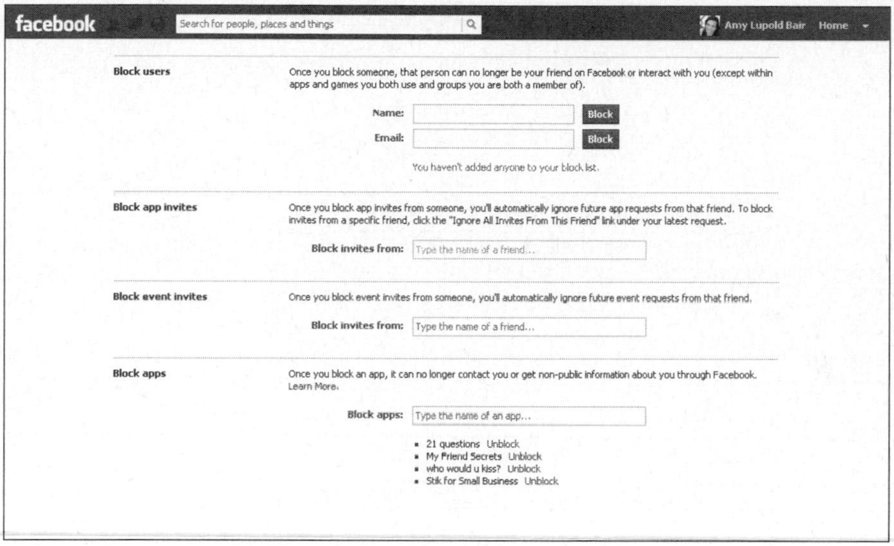

Figure 6-6:
Block
application
invitations
from
specific
Friends.

To disable the Facebook apps platform, do the following:

1. **Click the Edit Settings link next to Ads, Apps and Websites (refer to Figure 6-3).**

2. **In the Apps You Use field, click the Turn Off link next to the red X (refer to Figure 6-4).**

3. **In the Turn Off Apps, Plugins and Websites pop-up that appears, shown in Figure 6-7, click the Turn Off Platform button.**

Figure 6-7:
Disabling
the
Facebook
application
platform.

After you turn this platform off on any account (you or your child), you won't be able to use the Facebook integrations on third-party apps or websites. And, the following will also occur:

✔ You won't be able to log into websites or applications via Facebook.

✔ Your Facebook Friends can no longer interact and share with you using apps and other websites.

✔ Instant personalization is turned off for your account.

Protecting the privacy of your Friends

Protection is a two-way street. After you add a game application to your Facebook page, it may be able to access the public information of your Facebook Friends. To edit the application's access to your Friends' information, take the following steps:

1. **Click the Edit Settings button of the Ads, Apps and Websites section (refer to Figure 6-3).**

2. **Click the Edit Settings button next to the Apps You Use section (refer to Figure 6-4).**

3. **Click Edit next to the name of the game application you'd like to edit.**

4. **Click the X to the right of Access Your Friends' Contact Information (see Figure 6-8).**

Following these steps for each game application with access to your account will restrict that game application's access to your Friends' Facebook accounts.

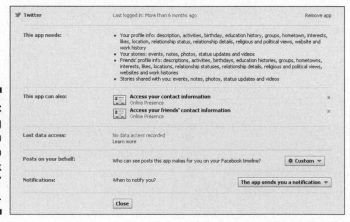

Figure 6-8:
Removing
application
access to
Facebook
Friends'
information.

Understanding Game Ratings

The primary game rating system in the United States and Canada is the Entertainment Software Rating Board (ESRB), which is a nonprofit, self-regulatory body that assigns content ratings for video games and mobile apps based on age and content ratings. Founded in 1994 by the Entertainment Software Association, the ESRB (www.esrb.org; shown in Figure 6-9) works to empower parents to make informed decisions about the video games they purchase for their children and allow to be played in their homes. The ESRB doesn't aim to prohibit certain games from being purchased and played, but rather hopes to provide concise and impartial information to parents and other consumers.

The three-part ESRB rating system includes

- ✔ **ESRB rating:** An assigned rating category that suggests the age-appropriateness of that particular game

- ✔ **Content descriptors:** Inform parents why the rating category was selected for that particular game

  These descriptors also inform the consumer what content included in the game may be of interest or of concern.

- ✔ **Interactive elements:** Cover interactive features of the game, including capabilities, such as location sharing

Figure 6-9: ESRB home page.

Content descriptors do *not* list every type of content found in the video game. The absence of a content descriptor does not guarantee the absence of that content within the game.

Games are *not* required to have an ESRB rating, but many stores that sell video games will sell only those games that do contain an ESRB rating. Game console manufacturers also require games for their systems to include an ESRB rating.

The ESRB rating symbols rate only the content created by the game publisher — not online interactions or content created by individuals.

When assigning a rating, ESRB raters look at any content that reflects both the most extreme content in the video game and the overall frequency of this extreme content. Raters also consider factors such as the degree of player control and any other unique elements to the games, which are inherently interactive.

Seven ESRB rating symbols suggest the age appropriateness of video games. The categories are

 ✔ **Early childhood (EC):** Video games receiving this rating are suggested to be suitable for children ages three and older. This rating indicates that the game does not contain material that parents find inappropriate for children.

 ✔ **Everyone (E):** Games content may be suitable for everyone ages 6 and older. The games may contain minimal cartoon, fantasy, or mild violence, and/or infrequent use of mild language.

 ✔ **Everyone 10+ (E10+):** These games have more cartoon, fantasy, or mild violence, mild language, and/or minimal suggestive themes than those with an E rating. Games in this category are recommended to be suitable for ages 10 and older.

 ✔ **Teen (T):** These games have content that may be suitable for ages 13 years and older. They may contain violence, suggestive themes, crude humor, minimal blood, simulated gambling, and/or infrequent use of strong language.

 ✔ **Mature (M):** The game may contain intense violence, blood and gore, sexual content, and/or strong language. These games may be suitable for those age 17 years or older.

 ✔ **Adults Only (AO):** The game has content suitable only for those age 18 years or older. Games receiving this rating may include prolonged scenes of intense violence and/or graphic sexual content and nudity.

Each ESRB rating symbol is easily recognizable. Locate ESRB ratings by looking on either the front or the back of nearly any video game. Be sure to show your children which symbol corresponds with each rating.

 Video game manufacturers may use a Rating Pending (RP) symbol to advertise a game prior to receiving an ESRB rating for that game. Games shown (in an ad or online video) with the RP symbol may not yet appear for sale in stores.

Searching for game ratings

For information on a rated game, you can search ESRB rating summaries for nearly all video games rated by the ESRB since July 1, 2008. This supplementary information provides a content description highlighting the types of content characteristics that parents look for when selecting or approving a video game for their children. To locate these ESRB rating summaries, simply search by video game title on the homepage at www.esrb.org (refer to Figure 6-9).

When searching for a game title, you can search by game platform, too, because some games are available for multiple devices. The game platform choices available are

- All Platforms
- Mobile App/Tablet
- Nintendo DS/DSi/3DS
- PlayStation 3
- PlayStation Vita/PSP
- Wii/Wii U
- Windows/Mac
- Xbox 360
- Other

When searching for a game rating, use the advanced search option to filter your search by rating category and by content. Filtering content choices allows you to include or exclude the following content types:

- ✔ Violence
- ✔ Blood/gore
- ✔ Sexuality
- ✔ Nudity
- ✔ Language
- ✔ Substances
- ✔ Gambling
- ✔ Humor

After you search for a specific game, you see a rating chart (see Figure 6-10) that includes the following information:

- ✔ Title
- ✔ Platforms
- ✔ Rating
- ✔ Content descriptors
- ✔ Other
- ✔ Company that manufactures the game

Figure 6-10: ESRB ratings search results page.

If the game you've searched includes a rating summary, a short synopsis of that summary will appear in the search result. Click the search result for that game to read the full rating summary, as shown in Figure 6-11.

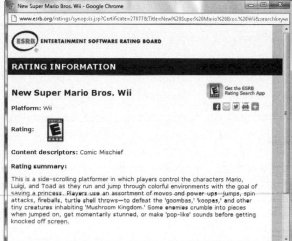

Figure 6-11:
Example of
an ESRB
Ratings
Information
summary.

Discussing the ESRB in your Digital Family Policy

Nearly every game available for purchase at major retailers in the United States and Canada will include an ESRB rating. For parents, this is an invaluable tool to not only inform their decisions about the games played in their homes, but also to include in the Digital Family Policy. When creating the video game section of your Digital Family Policy, establish which game ratings are allowed for each member of the family or age range. Just as you may not allow your elementary school child to watch every PG movie that is released but rather make decisions on a case by case basis, you may want to include the option of evaluating games based on content descriptions if they fall within a certain rating category.

When creating your Digital Family Policy, go over each game rating (http://www.esrb.org/ratings) with your family so that all family members understand the symbols used to rate video games. These ratings are easily found on games, and children will be accustomed to seeing them. Discussing the full description of each game rating will help your children understand the details of each rating category. Visit the ESRB Family Discussion Guide for tips on how to chat with your family about game ratings:

www.esrb.org/about/familyguide.jsp

You may also wish to discuss with your children how the ESRB assigns each game a rating. Explaining to your kids that the ratings are the result of a careful process and are assigned by experts may make it easier for them to trust the ratings and follow the ratings rules in your Digital Family Policy. In fact, each ESRB rating is the result of the work and recommendations of at least three specially trained experts who come together to agree on the rating for the game. Rating video games is their full-time job, and to avoid outside influence, they don't have ties to the video game industry.

Placing the ESRB at your fingertips

ESRB rating summaries are available through mobile devices for parents interested in learning more information about a game's rating while visiting a video game retailer. To access the ESRB rating summaries, download the free ESRB Rating Search App for iPhone, Android, and Windows Phone. This app is available by searching *ESRB* in your phone's app store or marketplace. Use the ESRB Rating Search App to search by game title by saying the game title, taking a photo of the game box, or entering the game title into the search field (see Figure 6-12).

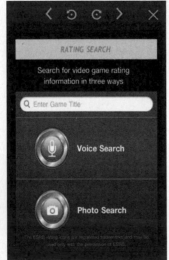

Figure 6-12: The ESRB Rating Search application.

You can also access the rating summaries on your mobile device through the mobile website at www.m.esrb.org. The ESRB mobile site allows you to

- Search games by title.
- Search games by platform.
- Access the ratings guide.

✔ Read the FAQ.

✔ Contact the ESRB.

The ESRB can't enforce its ratings nor require age identification at the time of purchase, but many retailers have store policies that require age verification for purchase of sale or rental of games rated M (Mature) and AO (Adults Only). You may wish to include rules about game acquisition within your Digital Family Policy to safeguard against the purchase or rental of games with ratings that you deem inappropriate for your family.

Understanding Parental Controls

All major game consoles come with parental controls, accessed via password, to manage everything from online purchases through Wi-Fi to the game ratings that may be played on that console. Each console allows you to create general parental controls for the entire family as well as individual accounts per child with different settings.

Wii

Using your Wii Remote and the A button selector, do the following:

1. **Turn on the console and go to the Wii Menu.**

2. **Select Wii Options and then Wii Settings.**

3. **Click the blue arrow to the right to gain access to the Wii System Settings 2 menu choices.**

4. **Select Parental Controls and then choose Yes (see Figure 6-13).**

Figure 6-13: Selecting Parental Controls in the Wii Settings menu.

5. **Create a 4-digit PIN and then select OK.**

6. **Select a secret question to answer — and the answer — (in case you forget your PIN) and then select OK.**

7. **Select Game Settings and PIN.**

   Here, you can select the game ratings allowed to be played on your Wii console.

8. **Select OK and then select Confirm.**

9. **Select Other Settings to set limits for additional features, including**

   • *Internet Channel:* Restrict use of the Internet browser.

   • *News Channel:* Control access to the News Channel.

   • *Online Communication and User Created Content:* Control the sending and receiving of messages from the Wii console and in online game play. This area may also be used to restrict access to user-created content: that is, any aspect of a game that has been created by a user.

   • *Use of Points:* Wii Points are used in the Wii Shop Channel to purchase game downloads. Use this section to require a 4-digit PIN before the use of points. You may want to include a section in your Digital Family Policy (see Chapter 2) to address who funds the points on your Wii account. Can your children earn access to these points? Will they use their own money to fund this account?

10. **Select Settings Complete to complete the process.**

If you forget your PIN, contact Nintendo Technical Support at 1-800-255-3700.

PS3

The following content can be restricted via the Parental Controls settings on the PS3:

✔ **Games:** Restrict games by ESRB rating level.

✔ **DVDs:** Restrict DVD viewing by standard movie ratings (PG, PG-13, and so on).

✔ **Blu-ray Disc:** Restrict viewing Blu-ray discs that exceed a certain rating category.

✔ **Website Browsing:** Restrict the capability to launch the Internet browser, and also use a web-filtering service to check the appropriateness of displayed websites. Fees may apply for using this filter.

✔ **PlayStation Network:** Restrict chat usage and set monthly setting limits.

Here's how to access the PS3 Parental Controls:

1. **Turn on your console and go to the XMB home menu.**

2. **Go to Settings and select Security Settings.**

3. **Select Change Password.**

   From here, you change the password required access restricted content.

   You can also set the following:

   - *BD Parental Control:* Select this to change the Blu-Ray disc content limits.

   - *DVD Parental Control:* Change the restriction level for DVD viewing.

   - *Parental Control:* Restrict game play according to ESRB rating.

   - *Internet Browser Start Control:* Require a password to launch the PS3 Internet Browser.

If you forget your PS3 Parental Control password, choose Settings⇨System Settings⇨Restore Default Settings to reset the password to 0000. Then, you'll need to reset all Parental Control settings.

Xbox 360 parental controls may be customized according to game, movie, and television content access. Settings can be altered for both the Xbox 360 console and the Xbox LIVE network. Controls may even be set to control how long each family member may use the console, with time limits set according to both daily and weekly limits.

Xbox 360

To turn on Xbox 360 Parental Controls, do the following:

1. **Turn on your Xbox 360 console and go to Settings.**

2. **Select the Family square and then select On to use the Parental Controls feature.**

3. **Set the four-digit pass code.**

   - *Console Controls:* Set limits for the entire console.

   - *Game Ratings:* Limit game play by ESRB rating.

   - *Video Ratings:* Limit the viewing of videos according to rating.

   - *Access to Xbox LIVE:* Limit access to the Xbox LIVE platform.

   - *Family Timer:* Set time limits by individual accounts.

4. **Select Done.**

Did you forget your Xbox 360 pass code? Call 1-800-4myxbox to reset your number.

Chapter 7

Preparing Kids for Online Chats

- -

In This Chapter

▶ Discussing chat functionality with kids

▶ Preparing children for chat options

▶ Understanding ways to block chat functions

▶ Comprehending potential chat room dangers

▶ Setting family guidelines regarding online chats

- -

*W*ith social media infiltrating nearly every aspect of the Internet, many online places our children visit — everything from finding information to playing age-appropriate games — also contain the option to interact with other users. While many of us parents got caught up with our friends after school by talking on the phone, today's digital kids are just as likely to meet up in a chat room to discuss the events of the day. Your job is to empower children to make wise decisions about social interaction through chat functions, including rules about online interaction in your Digital Family Policy, which I show you how to create in Chapter 2.

For the purposes of this book, I will primarily cover IM and chat rooms, but I will also touch on safety guidelines and Digital Family Policy rules that apply to message boards and forums as well.

Anticipating Chat Requests

Internet users can have conversations with other site members in a variety of ways:

> ✔ **Message boards and forums:** Unlike chat rooms and instant messaging (IM), message boards and forums (see Figure 7-1) are ongoing, but not live, conversations around a specific topic or question. Users may post a question or comment and not receive a response for hours, days, or

even weeks. Typically, message boards are moderated, and posts to the board may be placed in moderation before appearing as part of the ongoing conversation. Messages that are inappropriate are typically removed quickly or simply not approved for posting.

✔ **Chat rooms:** Some chat rooms, especially those that are available during only certain hours of the day (rather than around the clock) are also monitored like most message boards. Unlike message boards, though, chat room posts appear in real time, and conversations occur live. Chat rooms created specifically for teens and children by trusted sites and brands are more likely to be moderated and monitored than member-created rooms or those open to all ages.

There is no way to verify that the people using chat rooms specifically for kids are actually children.

An example of a teen chat room is shown in Figure 7-2.

✔ **IM and private chat:** IM and private chat between one user and another are live conversations that occur privately between two or more people. Many sites and platforms, such as those listed here, have a chat or IM function.

- Online games

- Virtual worlds

- Children's social media sites, such as those covered in Chapters 11 and 21

- Facebook

- Gmail

- Wi-Fi–enabled game consoles

Figure 7-1: A typical message board where users post questions and responses around a topic.

Forum	Last Post	Threads	Posts	Moderator
Disney Trip Planning Forums These forums focus on topics important to planning your Disney World vacation.				
Welcome to the DIS This is the place to start if you would like to learn more about the DIS. Please read our forums guidelines	**Hi everyone!** by Maleficent53 Today 12:14 PM	18,576	183,877	The DIS Moderator Team, lovetoscrap
The DIS Unplugged Podcast Discussion forum for the official Disney podcast of the DIS - the DIS Unplugged. Listen to new shows each Wednesday at podcast.wdwinfo.com	**Exciting (not THAT exciting)...** by OKW Lover Today 01:33 PM	20,187	444,227	The DIS Unplugged Team, *NikkiBell*
Theme Parks Attractions and Strategies Discuss touring plans and strategies for the Disney World theme parks on this board.	***** New Official February...** by cubsblue Today 01:46 PM	315,220	4,391,119	danny1649, Cyrano, Brian_WDW74
Disney Resorts Ask questions and share information on the Walt Disney World resorts. **Sponsored by The Walt Disney World Swan & Dolphin**	**Disney's BOARDWALK INN and...** by Jasperann Today 01:46 PM	222,584	2,801,717	CanadianGuy, The DIS Moderator Team, Lynne M
Disney Restaurants Ask questions and get suggestions on all the dining possibilities around Walt Disney World. Be sure to check out our Disney dining area and restaurant menus	**Victoria & Alberts Queen...** by quixoticvalue Today 01:43 PM	215,596	2,236,330	Tricia1972, Mackey Mouse, TDC Nala, Pumbaa_, pumba
Orlando Hotels and Attractions Discover the "Other Side of Orlando", including the great deals available at hotels all around Orlando. **Sponsored by: DreamsRES - A service of Dreams Unlimited Travel**	**beach** by swilshire Today 01:42 PM	38,901	265,428	The DIS Moderator Team
Adventures By Disney A forum dedicated to Adventures by Disney vacations and reviews. **Sponsored by Dreams Unlimited Travel**	**Thoughts on the Tasmania...** by paddles Today 06:49 AM	2,276	30,446	DisneyKevin, sayhello

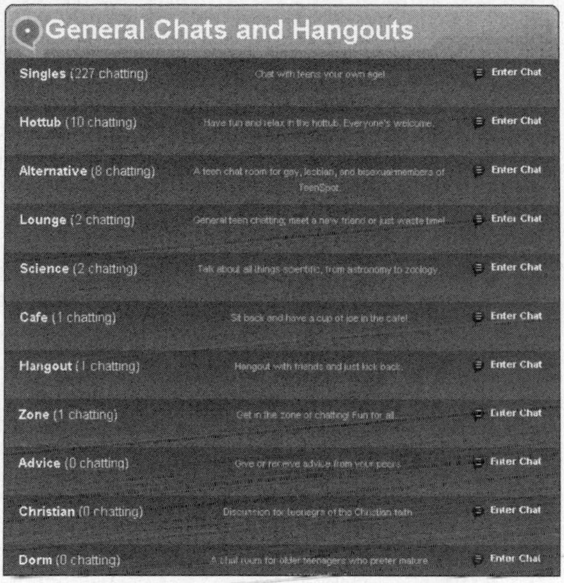

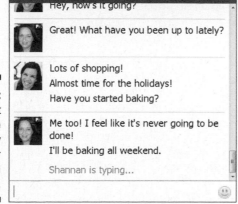

Figure 7-2:
One example of a chat room specifically for teens found at Teenspot. com.

These chat opportunities are different from a webpage or platform created specifically for the purpose of hosting online chats or forums. (See Figure 7-3.)

Figure 7-3:
Instant message functionality on a popular social media site.

Not all chat rooms for kids are moderated, so be sure to approve a chat room before your children use it.

Even if your child is not initiating chats, you should prepare kids to anticipate chat requests if they are going to sites that contain an interactive function. Not all sites contain chat functions that work in the same way, and chat requests may be coming from a variety of sources.

Chat requests from other users

One type of chat request is from other users on the same site. These chat requests are often unsolicited and may be unexpected. Typically, the other users will need to request permission to interact with your child by asking to be added to a buddy or Friend list. Prepare your children to expect these types of requests and include answers to the following questions in your Digital Family Policy:

- ✔ What should your child do if he receives a Friend or buddy request from someone he doesn't know?
- ✔ Does your child need to receive parental approval before adding someone to a friend or buddy list?
- ✔ Does your child need to give parents access to the list of people with whom they chat?

Not everyone online is who they say they are! Remind your children that they may receive chat requests from adults pretending to be children.

Chat requests from site administrators

A second kind of chat request is from site administrators or group moderators. Some children's sites use characters within the online world to communicate with the children using that site. The purpose may be to guide new users through the site, suggest an activity to an inactive user, or introduce new site functionality. Figure 7-4 shows an example of a Bearville.com administrator engaging a child user as she enters the online world to begin playing.

Site administrators may also initiate a chat as a customer service function to see whether the user has any questions or needs help using the site. Prepare your children to receive these sorts of messages, and be sure to discuss how you would like your child to respond to such chat requests.

Figure 7-4: Bearville. com uses a site admin- istrator to engage a site user.

Understanding Chat Options

After you make your child aware of potential requests to participate in chatting and IM, discuss with her the various options for how to respond to such chat requests. Most chat rooms and IM services are completely unsupervised, so empower your children with the tools they need to stay safe while enjoying all that technology has to offer.

Declining chat requests

If your child is using a site with chat functionality, he will likely receive chat requests from other users. Remind your children that they have the right to decline a chat request without needing to respond to the person making the request. Ask your children to come to you if they receive a request to chat and aren't sure how to decline a request on that particular platform. Most platforms allow users to simply click an X to hide the message, or click the Decline button to keep one user from contacting another. (See Figure 7-5.)

Figure 7-5: Declining a chat request in Yahoo! Mail.

Decline Add Request

If you decline this request, morganlaganaax5746 will not be able to see when you are online.

☑ Block all future chat messages from morganlaganaax5746

(Note: You can also learn more about how about how to protect yourself against chat abuse or contact Customer Care to report threats or harassment).

Decline   Cancel

Using prepopulated responses

Some popular social media and online world sites for children allow users to use pre-approved phrases to communicate with other users rather than allowing children to type anything they like in chat rooms. These prepopulated chat functions prohibit children from saying inappropriate things to one another, including sharing private information that may put them at risk. Some online worlds and children's social media platforms allow only this type of chatting, and others offer it as a setting to parents who are setting up their children's accounts.

If your children would like to visit a site that allows users to chat with one another with pre-populated or limited chat, consider the following:

✔ **Create a parent account.** Many sites for children allow parents to make a parent account, which typically has access to the child's account. This allows parents to modify settings in the child's account, track the child's behavior on the site, and even limit playing time. See Figure 7-6 for an example. In Chapter 21, I talk about parent accounts on specific social media sites for children.

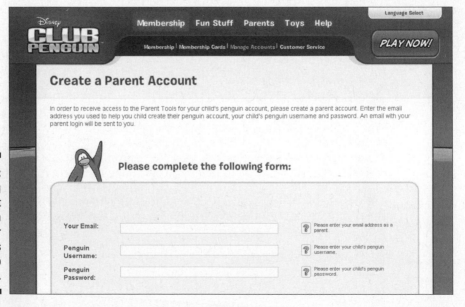

Figure 7-6:
Creating a parent account on the popular children's site, Club Penguin.

✔ **Select the chat settings of your child's account.** Most children's social media sites that allow children to chat with other users also allow parents to select the chat settings. Club Penguin, for example, allows the options of Standard Safe Chat (filtering the child's messages) and Ultimate Safe Chat (only allowing users to select from a pre-determined set of messages and responses). See Figure 7-7.

✔ **Create chat rules.** If you decide to allow your children to use pre-populated chat options on the websites they use, include rules in your Digital Family Policy about online chats. Include rules about whom your child may chat with while online and what to do when unwanted chat requests appear from another user.

TIP

Prepopulated chat programs are a great way to introduce your tweens to the world of chatting online while still controlling the content that they're sharing.

Creating a chat platform profile

As I discuss in Chapter 4, make sure that your children and teens create online profiles that don't put them in harm's way. When your children select a user name and create a user profile for a chat platform profile, insist that they consider the following:

Figure 7-7:
Pre-populated message options on Club Penguin.

✔ Do not create a user name that's sexual or suggestive in any way.

✔ Do not include information in the user name that identifies who you are offline, such as your real name.

✔ Do not include personal information in the user name, such as e-mail address, birth year, or Social Security number.

✔ Do not upload a profile photo that's sexual or suggestive in any way.

✔ Do not upload a profile photo that includes identifying information, such as a name on a jersey, your school name, or a house number or street name in the background.

Selecting privacy settings

Many sites and programs that include a chat function also provide users and parents with the ability to select from a variety of privacy settings. For example, PS3 owners may use the PlayStation Network to restrict chat usage on all sub-accounts via a parent or guardian master account. Another popular online communication service, Skype, allows users to control who can contact them, including who is able to do the following:

✔ Send an IM

✔ Call a user

✔ Send a video

✔ See a user's online status

If you don't want your child to be contacted by unauthorized users, but you can't disable chat function entirely — or don't wish to — search the privacy settings of the platform for options to simply hide your child's account from users who are not Friends or approved contacts.

Blocking chat functionality

Some platforms allow users to turn the chat or IM feature off completely. This prevents other users from contacting your child to request a friendship or begin a chat. Of course, this also prevents your child from initiating chats with other users. If you would like your child to use websites with chat functions but not receive chat requests, look for settings regarding these features when creating the account, such as the settings on Build-A-Bear's Bearville shown in Figure 7-8.

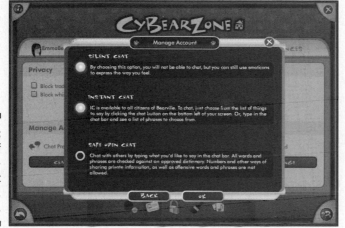

Figure 7-8:
Turning off
chat func-
tions at
Bearville.
com.

Sometimes changing settings on a child's account must be approved first by a parent, including any attempts to change the settings back to their original status.

Participating in open chat

Another option for kids using platforms that include chat and IM functions is to engage in open chats with no restriction. This is the type of online chatting that you are likely most familiar with: the format for sites aimed at adults.

These chats are typically not moderated and likely contain no filters for language and appropriateness. Depending on the age of your children, you may include rules about open chatting in your Digital Family Policy.

Making chat requests

During the discussion of your family's rules regarding IM and chat, cover what your family's expectations are regarding chat requests. Many kids use IM and chat platforms to communicate with their friends, but be sure to have specific rules about initiating conversations with people your children do not know in real life. Remind them that even if their friends chat with this person as well, a stranger is still a stranger. You may wish to cover this topic during the discussion of Friend and buddy list rules in the creation of your Digital Family Policy.

Comprehending Potential Chat Room Dangers

I discuss safety concerns in depth in Chapter 3, but pay close attention to the risks specifically associated with participating in chat rooms, message boards, and private chats. Consider the following, and discuss these potential issues with your kids:

✔ **Sharing information:** Even after you talk with your children at length regarding the sharing of personal information online, conversations in chat rooms can quickly become familiar, and kids may be tempted to share personal information with online "friends."

✔ **Others sharing your information:** As I mention in Chapter 3, kids may share information, believing it is just being seen by one person, but then have that information shared with others or even posted publicly. Remind your kids that *anything they type via chat may be shared.*

✔ **Cyberbullying:** The assumed anonymity of Internet users often gives people an excuse and a venue to say things that they would not say otherwise, including hurtful and mean statements. Kids can be bullied by people they know and also strangers, who can use information shared in chat rooms to bully kids. For more on cyberbullying, read Chapter 10.

✔ **Online predators:** Chat rooms and message boards are one of the top places where online predators seek child victims. They use the personal information provided by kids and watch their online discussions in order to introduce conversation and engage with them, playing the role of a sympathetic listener or pretending to relate to kids. Read more about online predators in Chapter 3.

✔ **In-person meetings:** Online Friends commonly discuss meeting in person. Kids need to be reminded that they don't really know the people they are talking to online — and should never agree to meet them in person.

Establishing Rules for Chat and IM

If your family decides that your children may participate in online chats and IM, set guidelines for the use of these platforms and include these guidelines in your Digital Family Policy. Here are some thoughts to guide the creation of chat rules:

- ✔ **Strangers are strangers.** Remind your children that people in chat rooms are always strangers, even if they have chatted with that person for a long time. There is no way for your children to know whether the person they are talking to is who they say they are. Your children should always consider them strangers and apply the rules they would normally follow for interaction with people they don't know.

- ✔ **Don't share personal information.** Require that your children never share personal or identifying information in public chats or with people they only know online including name, address, name of school, phone number, and location.

- ✔ **Never meet an online acquaintance.** Tell your children that it's never okay to meet someone in person with whom they chat online.

- ✔ **Practice good online manners.** Ask that your children follow the same rules for interaction that they follow with people in person including manners and courteous behavior. For more about online etiquette, visit Chapter 4.

- ✔ **Use the same manners everywhere.** Remind your children that they need to follow the same home chat and IM rules regardless of whether they are at a friend's house or public location, such as school or a library computer. Chapter 5 discusses screen time at friends' homes in more depth.

- ✔ **Speak up.** Require your children to report any suspicious or bullying behavior to you immediately and ask that they save the body of the chat in case you need to report it to a chat room administrator or other authority. Chapter 10 covers this topic in more detail, and Chapter 3 deals with online predators, including how to report suspicious behavior.

- ✔ **Follow platform-specific rules.** Decide upon rules specific to the various types of chats, including video chat, text, and voice. For example, you may create different rules for a kids' only online world with monitored text chat than you would for a video chat platform, such as FaceTime.

- ✔ **Keep it public.** Ask that your children never accept a request to enter a private chat room with someone they only know online. They should report to you if someone has asked them to do this. They should also avoid member-created chat rooms, which are less likely to be moderated.

- ✔ **Choose your chat room carefully.** Encourage your children to pay attention to chat room names when they are joining a conversation because the name of the room may indicate the tone of the chat taking place.

- ✔ **Do not click links or downloads.** Remind them to not click any links or downloads shared with them in chat rooms and messaging platforms.

- ✔ **Keep the folks informed.** Ask your children to let you know if they have begun to chat with someone on a regular basis and form a relationship with someone that they only know online.

✔ **Set the rules.** Establish rules about what to do if a user continues to request chats after being denied or if a user says something inappropriate: for example, using the block or ignore features in the messaging program.

You will likely need to create different rules for different age groups of children in your family. Most young children who are old enough to read can safely enjoy restricted chat with pre-populated greetings and responses, while children a bit older may be able to safely enjoy open chats on safe, child-only platforms while using appropriate chat profiles with appropriate privacy settings

Just because a chat room says it is for kids, there may still be adults chatting, and the content may not be appropriate.

Before allowing your children to participate in any chat platform, be sure that they know how to do the following:

✔ **Keep a history.** Change the chat settings so that chat history is saved. This may be needed in the future should you need to report a chat or user.

✔ **Report a suspicious chat.** All chat platforms have steps that users can take to report suspicious activity. If your child is old enough, he may be able to report suspicious or inappropriate behavior without your help. Younger children may need you to help them decide whether content should be reported and locate how to do this. Figure 7-9 shows an example from Bearville.com of how to report a user for inappropriate behavior.

Figure 7-9: Reporting suspicious activity on Bearville. com.

✔ **Block a user.** Chat platforms allow users to block specific users, keeping them from reaching out again to your child's account. Each platform does this a bit differently, so be sure to help your child find the steps they will take to block a user in the event that they need to do so. Figure 7-10 is an example of how to block a user on the Skype online calling, video messaging, and text IM program.

Figure 7-10:
Blocking
a user on
Skype.

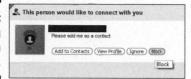

Even after discussing the safety concerns of online conversation and your family's rules as laid out in your Digital Family Policy, you might still be concerned about your children and online chatting. Consider installing monitoring software on your family's computer that can help you capture all chat and IM activity. You can even have activity logs and Friend/buddy lists e-mailed to you. Some monitoring software includes chats on gaming and social media platforms as well as voice, video, and text chatting. For more information about available monitoring software, read Chapter 3.

Chapter 8

Search Engines, Image Search Results, and Sponsored Links

Children are naturally curious, and in this digital world, that means turning to the Internet for answers to their questions. Gone are the days of paging through dusty old books to write reports. Kids use search engines to not only satiate their own curiosity but also to create school reports, write papers, and craft science projects. With Internet search engines an integral part of most families' daily lives, you need to understand how these tools select the information they provide. Let this chapter be your guide as you look at ways to protect your children from links that could be dangerous to computers and other devices, and protect your children also from inappropriate material.

Selecting a Search Engine

The key to understanding which search engine is right for your family's use is to first understand how each of the most popular search engines works.

Google (www.google.com) and Bing (www.bing.com) are the two top search engines. Each tool uses proprietary software that "crawls" the Internet looking for new pages and information to collect and add to platform indices. The information in these indices is then organized according to a unique algorithm that decides what each page is about. When you, the user, enter a query in the search box on a search engine page, the tool's software tries to find the most relevant pages that are indexed.

Search engines do not, in fact, search the web — they search the pages that have already been filed into the search indices of each tool.

Both of the top two search engines locate answers to your search requests in essentially the same way.

Google

Google uses a patented and trademarked system — PageRank — to determine which results are most relevant to the search query. PageRank assigns a numerical weight to each website, which then influences how close to the top of the list that site appears in search results.

Google also allows users to filter search results based on specific criteria. (See Figure 8-1.)

Filter options menu

Figure 8-1:
Google
search
result filter
options
menu.

The search filter options are as follows:

Web	Images	Maps
Videos	News	Shopping
Applications	Books	Places
Blogs	Flights	Discussions
Recipes	Patents	

To see all your search filter options, select More from the menu shown in Figure 8-1.

Bing

Bing uses its "best match system," which sorts search results according to what Bing believes is most relevant to the search term used. Like Google, Bing allows users to filter search results according to a variety of filters, as shown in Figure 8-2.

Filter options menu

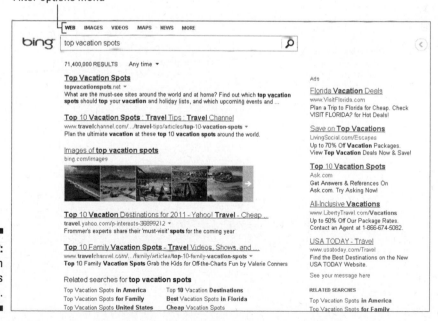

Figure 8-2: Bing search filter options menu.

These filters include the following:

Web	News	Entertainment
Events	Movies	Images
Maps	Social	Math
Friends' Photos	Videos	Local
Weather	Dictionary	

To see all your search filter options, select More from the menu shown in Figure 8-2.

Bing also provides the following search features:

- ✔ **Deep Link:** Users can preview a website without having to click the link in the search result.

- ✔ **Explore Pane:** Users can search the search results.

- ✔ **Instant Answers:** Using this feature provides users with quick, most relevant answers to a search query.

When discussing search engines during the creation of your Digital Family Policy, discuss not only the specific search engines, but also the types of search features that your family feels are appropriate for each member of your family. I discuss image searches in particular later in this chapter and provide special areas of concern for some parents.

Understanding how search results differ by user

Both Google and Bing retain information on your browser regarding past searches and use this information to influence future search results. Both search engines can integrate social media into their search results, allowing information from Friends to shape the results provided in response to a search query. Google not only uses past searches to influence future results, but also takes into account which search results you've followed (clicked) in the past.

Some parents prefer that search engine results not include personalization, such as the influence of social media and past search activity. Perhaps multiple users within your family are using the same Google account, or you're concerned that past search results preferences will manipulate the current results of a search for a school report.

As a preventive, you can sign in to your Google account and disable personalization within the search engine to keep personalized results from appearing in future searches.

1. **Click the gear symbol in the upper right of the Google search results page.**

2. **Choose Search Settings from the drop-down menu. (See Figure 8-3.)**

3. **Under Personal Results, select the Do Not Use Personal Results radio button. (See Figure 8-4.)**

4. **Click Save.**

Figure 8-3: Finding Google search settings.

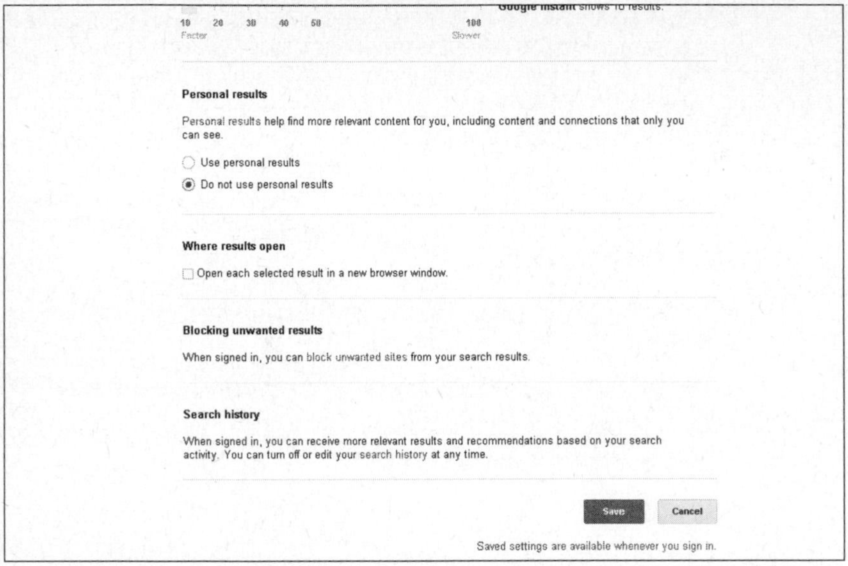

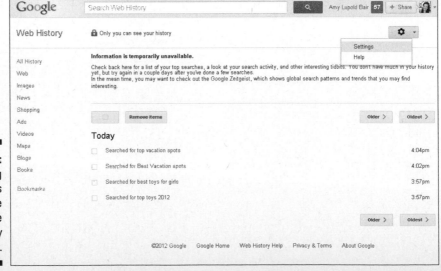

Figure 8-4:
Remove
personaliza-
tion from
Google
search.

You can also choose to turn off your Google Web History to disable history-based search customizations while signed in to your Google account.

1. **Click the gear symbol in the upper right of the search results page, but this time, choose Web History from the drop-down menu (refer to Figure 8-3).**

   The Web History page appears.

2. **Select the gear symbol again and click Settings. (See Figure 8-5).**

Figure 8-5:
Locating
settings
within the
Google
Web History
page.

3. **On the Settings page that appears, click the Pause button, to the left of Web History Is On. (See Figure 8-6.)**

Even if you're not signed in to a Google account, your search results on Google will still be personalized based on past search information, thanks to a cookie on your computer's web browser. To disable this personalization, take the following steps:

1. **Go to** www.google.com/history/optout.

2. **Click Disable Customizations Based on Search Activity. (See Figure 8-7.)**

Figure 8-6:
Pausing
Web History
on Google
search.

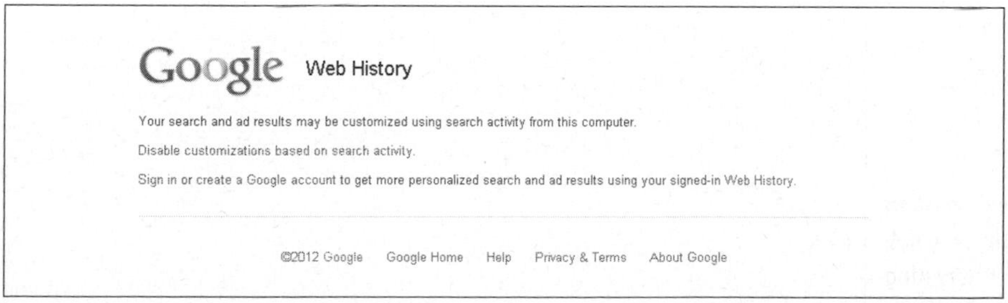

Figure 8-7:
Disabling
Google
customized
search.

To disable personalized search results on Bing, take the following steps:

1. **Click the gear symbol in the upper right at** www.bing.com. **(See Figure 8-8.)**

2. **Select Search History from the left sidebar. (See Figure 8-9.)**

3. **In the Turn On/Off section, select the Off radio button.**

Figure 8-8:
Locating
personaliza-
tion settings
on Bing.

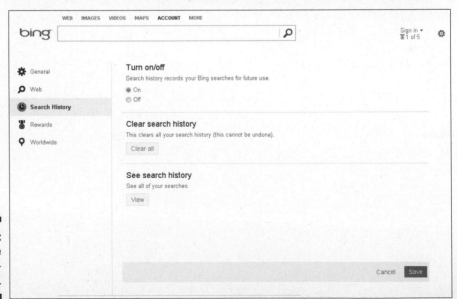

Figure 8-9:
Disable
search his-
tory on Bing.

From this page, you can also view and clear all Bing search history.

Because many families share digital devices — and, therefore, search history — discuss the option of disabling search history on these shared devices and accounts to keep the actions of one family member from affecting the search results of fellow family members. You may also want to create separate browser accounts for each family member, or perhaps for parents and children.

If you disable search history on a particular browser or platform, though, you won't be able to view your child's search history.

Distinguishing Sponsored Results from Unsponsored

Even with personalized search results disabled and such tools as PageRank and the Bing Best Match system in place, children may not realize that some of the results in response to their search queries actually appear because the site owners have paid an advertising fee, not because they're the most relevant results for that search.

Just like it's smart to help kids identify advertising content on websites they visit (see Chapter 9 for more information about advertising to kids), helping your children see the difference between paid and unpaid search results can help them determine the most useful information for their projects, papers, and other search purposes.

Recognizing sponsored search results

On Google search results pages, topically related paid links appear on the right side of the search results page but also at the top of the list of search results.

Depending on the search query, shopping results may also appear within the search results or sidebar without the user first selecting the shopping search filter. (See Figure 8-10.) These shopping results sometimes appear because of sponsored content.

Ads   Shopping search filter

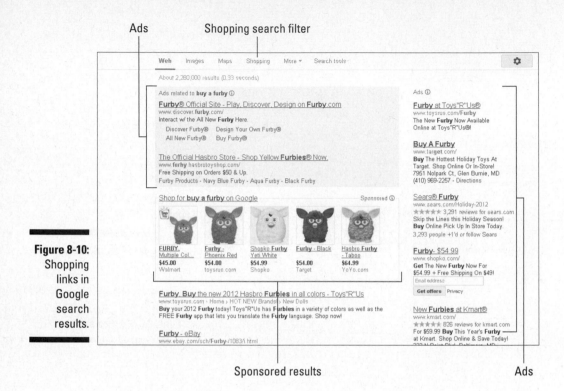

Figure 8-10:
Shopping
links in
Google
search
results.

Sponsored results   Ads

All paid search results on Google are clearly labeled as either sponsored or as an ad, as shown in Figure 8-10, making it much easier for parents to help kids distinguish between organic search results and results that appear as a paid advertisement.

Organic search results are those that appear because of the Google PageRank and Bing Best Match systems that were explained earlier in the chapter. These organic searches provide the user with the most relevant links in response to the user search. Paid and sponsored results appear only because an advertising fee was paid to the search engine. These results may not be relevant, and they exist with the purpose of self-promotion, so they may not be as useful as the organic searches and may also take you to offers and solicitations rather than information.

During the creation of your Digital Family Policy (see Chapter 2), you may wish to discuss rules for clicking these paid search results.

Similarly, when searching Bing, paid search results also appear above and to the right of organic search results. (See Figure 8-11.) As you can see in Figure 8-11, all paid links on Bing are clearly marked with the word *Ads*.

Ads

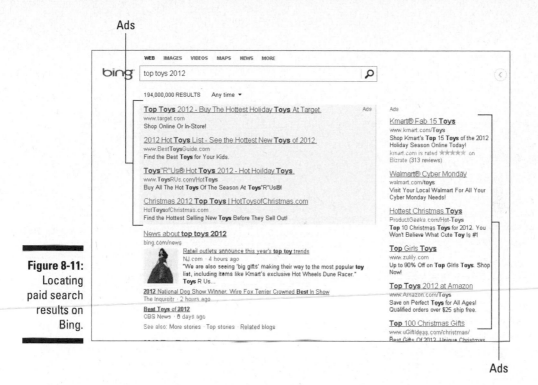

Figure 8-11:
Locating
paid search
results on
Bing.

Ads

Changing sponsored link settings

Google allows users to change advertising personalization settings. If you're
signed in to your Google account when searching the web through Google,
you will be provided with ads based on your account history. Even if you
sign out of your Google account before searching, you will be shown ads that
Google believes are relevant to you based on page content or search terms.
To opt out of personalized ads, take the following steps:

1. **Go to** `www.google.com/ads/preferences`.

2. **Click the Ads on Search link from the left sidebar. (See Figure 8-12.)**

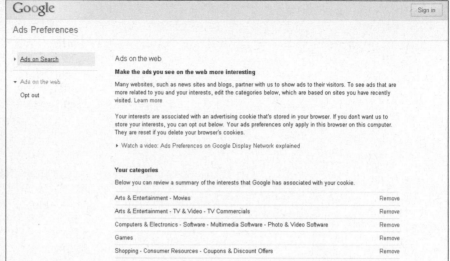

Figure 8-12:
Locating person-alized advertising settings on Google.

3. **Click the Opt Out link from the left sidebar.**

4. **Under the Opt Out section (center of the page), click the Opt Out button. (See Figure 8-13.)**

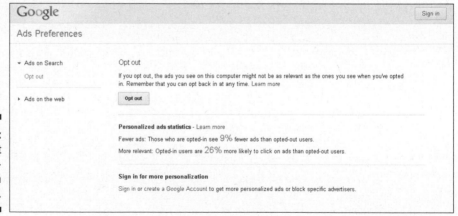

Figure 8-13:
Opting out of personal-ized ads on Google.

Using Kid-Safe Search Filters

Not only do major Internet search tools offer filters and settings to protect your family, but a variety of supplementary tools are available that you can use to monitor and screen the search results that appear to your children. Additionally, search engines have been created with kids in mind to provide them with a safe way to search for the information they need and the answers to the questions they have.

Google SafeSearch

SafeSearch by Google screens sites and removes certain sites from search results based on preferences and settings. Parents can use SafeSearch to prevent adult content from appearing in search results. To use the SafeSearch filter on your family's computer, take the following steps:

1. **Go to** www.google.com/preferences.

2. **On the Search Settings page (as shown in Figure 8-14), select the Filter Explicit Results check box.**

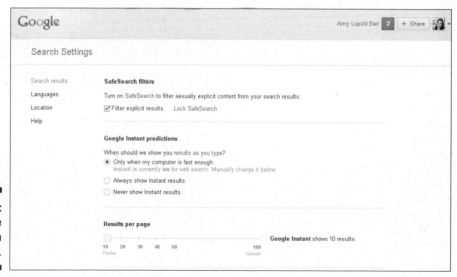

Figure 8-14: Enable SafeSearch on Google.

3. **To lock the SafeSearch setting, click the Lock SafeSearch link to the right of the SafeSearch Filters check box. (See Figure 8-15.)**

   You might be asked to sign in to your Google account to complete these steps.

Figure 8-15:
Lock
SafeSearch
settings on
Google.

4. **On the SafeSearch Filtering page that appears, confirm by clicking the Lock SafeSearch button.**

   You will receive a confirmation page, and Google will appear differently on your computer, making it possible to tell from across the room whether your children are searching the web via a SafeSearch-enabled Google page.

To verify that your child is using SafeSearch, look for the colorful spheres in the top-right corner of all search pages, as shown in Figure 8-16.

Figure 8-16:
Verify that
Google
SafeSearch
is enabled
on your web
browser.

Bing filters

Bing also allows users to change search preferences to filter by content. To change the search settings on Bing, take the following steps:

1. **Click the gear symbol in the upper right at** www.bing.com. **(Refer to Figure 8-8.)**

2. **Select your SafeSearch settings from the following radio buttons, as shown in Figure 8-17:**

   - *Strict:* This selection filters out adult text, images, and videos from the search results page.

   - *Moderate:* This selection filters out adult images and videos but not text from your search results page.

   - *Off:* This setting completely turns off filters from search.

3. **Click the Save button in the lower-right corner of this screen to save your settings.**

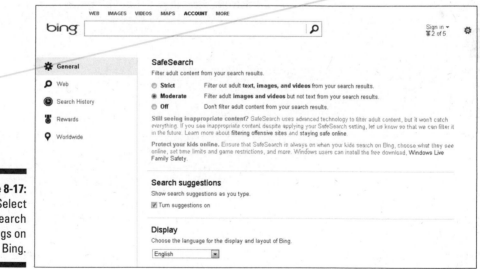

Figure 8-17: Select SafeSearch settings on Bing.

Additional Kid-Friendly Search Options

A variety of platforms, tools, and applications have been created with the express purpose of allowing kids to safely search the Internet. The following are some of the options for parents who would like to allow children to browse the internet without close supervision, but still feel confident that their children are not being exposed to inappropriate content:

- **Ranger Browser,** a free application available for both Android and iOS, replaces the standard web browser on the tablet or phone, and provides the following safety features:

  - Provides five levels of filtering

  - Gives parents the option of setting use time limits

  - Records all visited websites for parents to view

  - Allows parents to both allow and block specific websites

- **KIDO'Z** (www.kidoz.net), a tool available for phones (both Android and iOS), tablets, and computers, provides a free trial, but to fully access the tools, parents must purchase a license of use. A KIDO'Z subscription includes access to the KIDO'Z Browser, prepopulated with thousands of kid-friendly content from sites that were created for kids.

- **Ask Kids** (www.askkids.com) is the child-friendly version of Ask.com, a free search engine designed specifically for children ages 6–12. Ask Kids uses a proprietary search engine to filter content around a variety of core educational topics. This safe browser is intended to be a resource for kids needing to search the Internet for educational purposes.

- **KidsClick!** (www.kidsclick.org), a search engine created by librarians hoping to catalog sites and age-appropriate information for kids, allows children to browse by topic or use a search engine. The search results include not only a description, but also the suggested reading level.

- **Awesome Library** (www.awesomelibrary.org), a web-based search engine designed to provide kids with a safe place to find educational resources, provides kids with only carefully reviewed search results.

- **Dib Dab Doo and Dilly Too** (www.dibdabdoo.com) provides kids with a Google-based search engine that contains safety filters. This site also provides a catalog of pre-screened links on topics ranging from news to nature.

- **CantUFind.com** (`www.cantufind.com`) uses a prescreened directory of resources to allow children to search the Internet or browse a directory according to categories.

- **Sweet Search** (`www.sweetsearch.com`) designed for use by students, provides search results that have been evaluated by experts before appearing on the site.

- **Quintura Kids** (`www.quinturakids.com`), a children's search engine, handpicks the sites that appear in search results and rechecks sites from time to time for safety. Search results appear not only in a traditional list format, but also in a tag cloud of suggested terms to help kids refine their search and find more relevant information.

- **KidRex** (`www.kidrex.org`), a free browser-based search engine powered by Google Custom Search, uses Google SafeSearch to provide results that focus on kid-related web pages. KidRex also maintains its own database of inappropriate keywords and websites to help filter and provide safer search results for kids.

Allowing Image Search Results

Image searches can be some of the most concerning for parents because rather than a site title and link, kids are immediately exposed to the images that appear within the search results. Image searches, however, can be very useful to kids for everything from a science project to how to complete a level on a favorite video game. When creating your Digital Family Policy, be sure to include specific guidelines for using image searches, including which search tools may be utilized and if kids are permitted to use image searches without adult supervision.

Previewing image search results

Even with safety filters in place, inappropriate content can indeed slip through and appear in your child's search results. For this reason, consider previewing image search results either on behalf of your child or with your child before allowing them to click through the image to the site itself. When searching for images on both Google and Bing, users are provided with thumbnails of the images, as shown in Figure 8-18. This affords parents the opportunity to screen results.

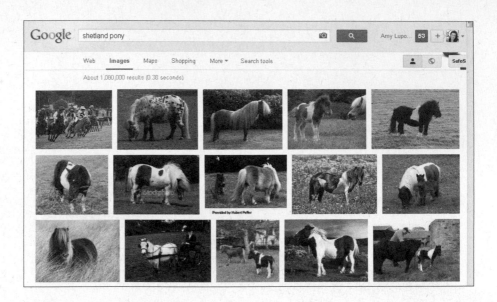

Figure 8-18:
Google and
Bing image
search
preview
screens.

Employing alternative image search tools

Just as there are alternative text search engines for kids, some sites allow kids to search for images in a safe environment. The following are three options:

- ✔ **Pics4Learning.com** (www.pics4learning.com) provides a safe (and free) image library that gives kids access to copyright-friendly photos they can use for school projects.

- ✔ **Picsearch** (www.picsearch.com) uses family-friendly filters to remove all offensive material from image search results.

- ✔ **KidsClick!** (http://kidsclick.org) not only provides kids with text search results but also provides an image search. The results have been carefully filtered to be safe for children.

Chapter 9

Becoming Aware of Online Advertising

*T*he digital world is an amazing place for today's children, offering nearly unlimited educational resources, opportunities to connect with enhanced content, and endless entertainment. Most parents would say that their kids are even better at navigating the online world than they are, but what both kids and parents may not realize is how advertisers have creatively found ways to expose even the youngest consumers to marketing messages while they enjoy online content. For parents looking to limit their children's exposure to advertising, make identifying hidden marketing a priority as well as educating your kids about the potential dangers of clicking ads marketed to then.

Screening for Sidebar Advertising

As of this writing, federal legislation requires that websites aimed at children must obtain parental consent before gathering identifying information (such as name and e-mail address) from any user younger than age 13. I cover this legislation — the Children's Online Privacy Protection Act (COPPA; www.coppa.org) — in further detail in Chapter 11. Despite this legislation, though, websites have been able to find loopholes allowing them to gather information about your children's online habits to be used for marketing purposes. For more information about how to protect your children's privacy via web browser settings and privacy software, visit Chapter 3.

Even with the existence of COPPA, children are still subjected to a variety of advertising while visiting some of the most popular children's pages on the web. Just as you would watch a new television show for the first time with your children or ask friends' parents about a popular movie in theaters before allowing your kids to go see it, you should stop by the websites that your children frequent to screen for potential advertising aimed at your kids. One of the most obvious locations where websites sell advertising space is in the right sidebar of the page, as shown in Figure 9-1.

To know what types of advertisements to display for your children, most sites install tracking programs — "cookies" or "beacons" — on your home computer. The information collected about your children's online behaviors helps marketers know which advertisements to show your children while they are online. Some studies have shown that more tracking devices are placed on home computers as a result of visits to websites for kids and teens than as a result of web browsing by adults. These tracking devices are also used to create a profile of your child, which is then sold to advertisers. The types of information collected about your children include

- ✔ Age
- ✔ Preferences based on web browsing
- ✔ Hobbies
- ✔ Shopping habits
- ✔ Race
- ✔ Location

Figure 9-1: Many children's websites feature sidebar advertising.

Sites are not allowed to sell data sharing your child's name and e-mail address.

When visiting the sites that your child frequents to monitor sidebar advertising, note whether the site displays consistent ads sold to one advertiser or whether the sidebar location has been sold to an ad network that serves advertisements to the site based on cookies placed in your web browser. Ads that are the result of an ad network — rather than a static ad from one sponsor — typically include text in a corner of the advertisement related to the network. Many ad networks rely on tracking devices to choose which ads to display, so sites displaying this type of sidebar ad are potentially more likely to place beacons and cookies on your computer or web browser.

You can block cookies via your web browser to prevent sites from tracking your child's online activity.

Unexpected Pop-up Ads

Even if you prescreen websites for advertising content prior to allowing your children to visit those sites, they may still experience unexpected pop-up advertising. You can take steps, though, to avoid exposing your kids to unanticipated advertising.

Defining pop-up ads and how they work

Pop-up ads are a form of Internet advertising specifically designed to catch the website user's attention, distracting them from whatever else they're doing. (See Figure 9-2.) They may appear when your child clicks from one page to another or search for a particular term, or they may even appear as a special game or feature of the website your child is visiting. That action, which may even just be logging on to the site, triggers the pop-up ad to appear onscreen. Pop-up ads are used by many advertisers because they are more likely to both catch the user's attention and to get them to click the advertisement.

Unlike ads that appear in the margins around the page's content, pop-up ads appear in a new browser window that floats over the page being viewed. The advertising windows can appear in a variety of sizes, but they typically are smaller than the browser window. Pop-up ads obscure the website the user is trying to view, forcing them to engage with the pop-up window to either close it or move it out of the way. At times, the advertisement may contain graphics that appear to guide the user to close the window, when it actually tricks the user into clicking through the ad to another site. These types of pop-up ad tricks make it more likely that kids will click through without realizing the potential dangers.

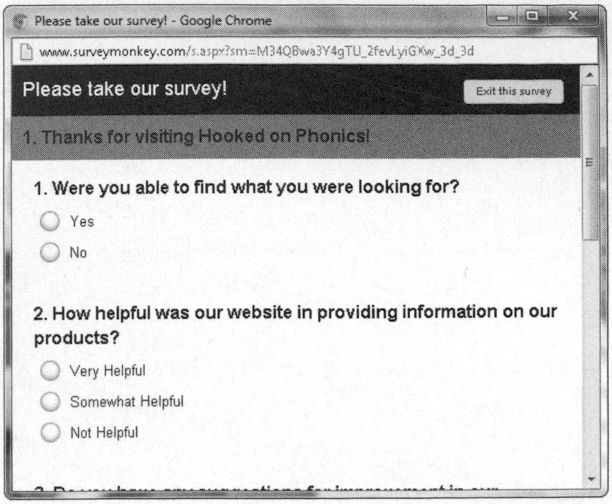

Please take our survey! - Google Chrome

www.surveymonkey.com/s.aspx?sm=M34QBwa3Y4gTU_2fevLyiGXw_3d_3d

Please take our survey!   Exit this survey

1. Thanks for visiting Hooked on Phonics!

1. Were you able to find what you were looking for?

○ Yes

○ No

2. How helpful was our website in providing information on our products?

○ Very Helpful

○ Somewhat Helpful

○ Not Helpful

Figure 9-2:
Children's
sites have
annoying
pop-up ads.

Pop-up advertisements also sometimes appear behind the active window. These ads are referred to as "pop-under ads" and are not noticeable until you close the browser window you are using, making it very difficult to tell which site caused the pop-under ad to appear.

Pop-up advertisements may be from legitimate companies, but they may also be phishing scams hoping to collect information from unsuspecting web users. These scams may ask kids to share protected information, such as their names, ages, and e-mail addresses. Because some websites use pop-up browsers legitimately to request approval or confirmation to begin a requested task, some children may not be able to determine whether the request is coming from the website they are using or from a site hoping to scam them into sharing their information.

Although some websites cause pop-up windows to appear when visited or when users take certain actions, sometimes pop-ups appear because of a virus or cookie on your computer. To read more about how to disable cookies and change your browser settings, read Chapter 3.

Changing settings to avoid pop-ups

You may know from experience that certain sites your children go to cause pop-up ads to appear. If that's the case, ask your kids to avoid those sites to protect your computer and private information. Better yet, disable pop-up ads from appearing on your computer, regardless of what site your kids go to.

To disable pop-up advertisements from appearing when using the Internet Explorer (IE) web browser, take the following steps:

1. **Open IE and click the Tools menu (or gear icon) in the upper-right corner.**

2. **Choose Internet Options from the drop-down menu.**

3. **On the Internet Options dialog box that opens, click the Privacy tab.**

4. **Select the Turn on Pop-up Blocker check box, as shown in Figure 9-3.**

5. **Click OK to dismiss the dialog box.**

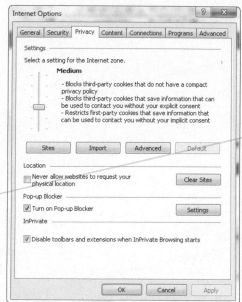

Figure 9-3:
Turn on
Internet
Explorer's
pop-up
blocker.

To enable pop-up advertising blockers in Mozilla Firefox, do the following:

1. **Click the Firefox menu in the upper-left corner of your Firefox browser.**

2. **Choose Options from the drop-down menu and then choose Options again.**

3. **In the Options dialog box that appears, click the Content tab and then select the Block Pop-up Windows check box, as shown in Figure 9-4.**

4. **Click OK.**

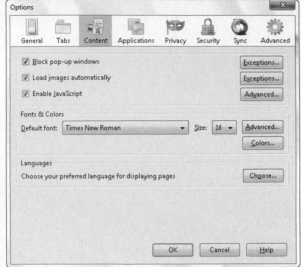

Figure 9-4:
Adjust your
content
settings.

The Google Chrome Internet browser also includes settings that allow you to block pop-up ads from appearing in your web browser. To activate these settings, take the following steps:

1. **Locate the Google Chrome tool bar and click the Customize and Control Google Chrome button (just under the 'x' Close button) in the upper-right corner of your web browser.**

2. **Choose Settings from the drop-down menu.**

3. **Select Show Advanced Settings.**

4. **On the Settings page, in the Privacy section (you might have to scroll down), click the Content Settings button. (See Figure 9-5.)**

5. **Within the Content Settings window that appears, in the Pop-ups section, select the Do Not Allow Any Site to Show Pop-ups radio button; and then click OK. (See Figure 9-6.)**

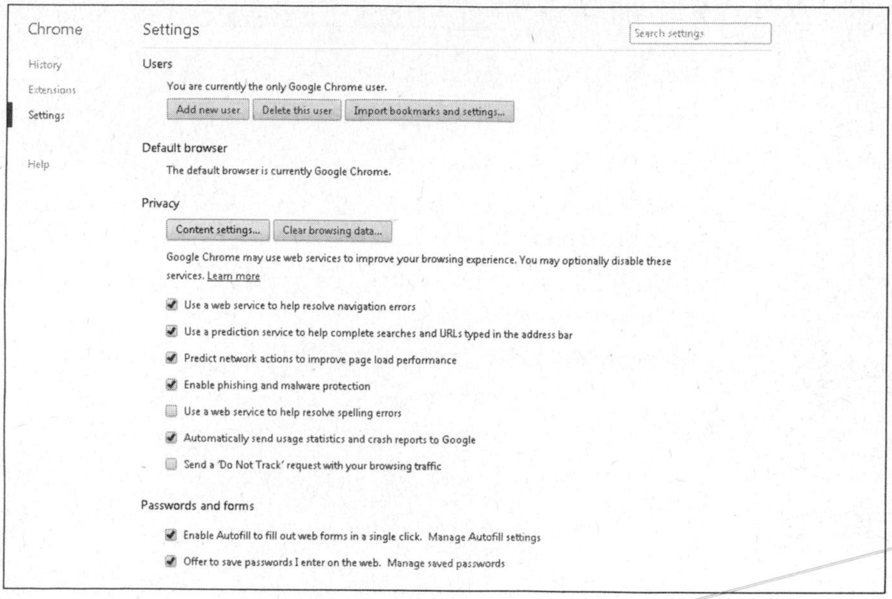

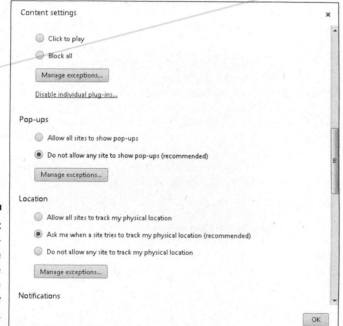

Figure 9-5:
Adjust your
content
settings.

Figure 9-6:
Block pop-
up ads here
via Google
Chrome
Privacy
settings.

To block pop-up ads on the Safari web browser, take the following steps:

1. **Choose Edit⇨Preferences.**

   The General dialog box appears by default.

2. **Click the Security tab.**

3. **In the Web Content section, click the Block Pop-up Windows check box. (See Figure 9-7.)**

   You can also set other Security preferences here including enabling plug-ins, Java, and JavaScript.

4. **After you set preferences, simply close the dialog box.**

Figure 9-7: Set Safari to block pop-ups.

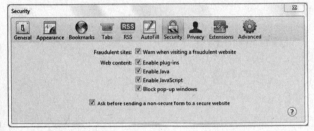

Along with using your web browser preferences to prevent pop-up ads from appearing during Internet use, you can also purchase security programs to block pop-up ads from appearing on your computer. These programs are often included within other protective software such as those that I discuss in Chapter 3. Typically, such software not only blocks pop-up ads, but also erases spyware or adware that has been installed on your computer without your knowledge.

Even if you elect to block pop-up ads on your home computer, still take some time to discuss pop-up ads with children of all ages. Remind them that clicking these ads may harm the computer and that pop-up ads should be closed immediately. If they're unsure how to close a pop-up ad safely, have them come to you for help before proceeding.

Include rules regarding pop-up ads in your Digital Family Policy (see Chapter 2) even if you disable pop-up ads on your web browser.

Teaching Kids about Text Link Ads

It's fairly easy to show kids where to find most of the advertising content on sites targeted to children. However, some sites also use text link ads to earn money on their site, and kids may click these links without realizing that they're actually clicking on advertising.

Identifying text link ads

Advertisers pay web page owners to link back to their own sites via keywords. For example, a site selling bicycles for kids may pay a site to link the words "best kids' bikes" to their site. The goal of the text link ad is not necessarily for your children to click that link. Instead, those purchasing the concealed advertisement are hoping to capitalize on the popularity of the site containing the text link ad to increase their own site's rankings in search engines.

Many sites require you (or your kids) to click links to access all aspects of the site, such as moving from one page to another or beginning a new game. Because digital natives are so used to recognizing and clicking text with hyperlinks, it may be difficult for them to distinguish between links that transport them to additional site content and those that take them away from the site they are on to a new site. Although most advertising on websites is clearly labeled — *Sponsored Content* or *Advertisement* — text link ads are almost never labeled, making identifying them even more confusing.

Help your children recognize the difference between a hyperlink that leads them to additional site content and a text link ad by looking at how sites typically lead kids from one site feature to another. Sites typically draw the user to more content through the use of graphics or buttons, such as the featured games shown in Figure 9-8. When simple text is used, this text tends to appear in list or bullet form rather than being found within additional text that's not identified as additional site content. (See Figure 9-9.)

Figure 9-8: Graphics leading to additional site content.

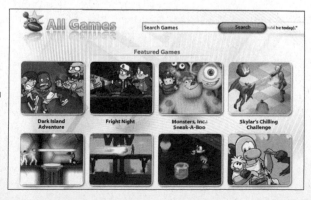

Figure 9-9:
List of links
to additional
site content.

Some children's websites display a pop-up warning (see Figure 9-10) notifying the user that they have clicked a link that will take them to a new site and asking them to verify that they meant to do this. Prior to allowing your kids to visit a site, discuss your family's policy regarding what to do if they see one of these pop-up warnings. Unless your child has previously clicked a link taking them to this site and knows that it is safe, it may be best for them to opt to stay on their current site and ask you before clicking through again. This pop-up warning may be an indication that they unknowingly clicked a text link advertisement.

Figure 9-10:
Pop-up
warning
window
indicating
that you are
leaving your
current site.

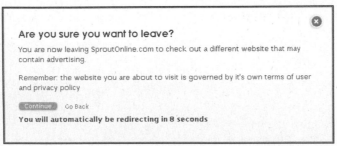

Finally, point out text link ads to your kids to help them understand that some hyperlinked text on a website is there for the benefit of an advertiser — not because it adds in any way to the user's experience. Images such as the one shown in Figure 9-11 (see the links at the bottom) are a great way to show kids how text link ads appear on many sites.

Text link ads

Figure 9-11:
An example
of a text link
advertise-
ment within
site content.

Seeing the dangers of clicking links

Certainly many text ad links that appear on sites aimed at kids are harmless, but potential dangers are associated with kids clicking links. One possibility is that the link is actually part of a phishing scam.

Phishing scams are designed to trick the victim into providing identifying information that can then be used to steal money, steal the user's identity, or target them for similar fraudulent crimes. These types of links may take you to a page offering a special download or opportunity that will then lead you to turn over your information under false pretenses. The pages and downloads often claim to be helpful and may target your children by claiming to offer special opportunities or features, when they are really simply trying to steal from you. Phishing links may even take your children to sites that appear to be legitimate favorites but are really copycat sites. See Chapter 3 to read more about identity theft and ways to protect your family.

Another potential danger comes in the form of malware. *Malware* — malicious software — infects your computer to steal information stored on the computer or disrupt the functioning of your computer. Some text link ads cause malware to infect your computer when someone clicks them. Antivirus and antimalware software can help to protect your computer from these dangerous computer viruses.

- ✔ **Bitdefender Antivirus Plus:** www.bitdefender.com, $49.95
- ✔ **Norton AntiVirus:** www.norton.com, $49.99
- ✔ **Webroot SecureAnywhere Antivirus:** www.webroot.com, $39.99
- ✔ **AVG AntiVirus:** www.avg.com, $39.99
- ✔ **BullGuard Antivirus:** www.bullguard.com, $29.95

A third potential danger that results from clicking text link ads is viewing inappropriate content. Sites containing adult content sometimes attempt to trick teen users into visiting their site by purchasing text link ads on sites targeted toward teens and disguising the link to inappropriate content within unrelated keywords. Popular brand names for kids — things like *My Little Pony* and *Pokemon* — are used in the titles of adult content sites as well as in text link ads to trick kids into clicking on these links. Include rules within your Digital Family Policy regarding what to do should your children accidentally navigate to a site with inappropriate content, including rules about future visits to the site containing the inappropriate link.

During the creation of your Digital Family Policy, discuss phishing scams and malware in relationship to links within website content. Consider including a rule in your Digital Family Policy that asks your kids to come to you if they clicked potentially dangerous or damaging links or have approved a potentially dangerous download. You may need to scan your computer to check for potential damage and make repairs.

Preventing phishing and malware

As I mention in Chapter 3, most web browsers offer protection from both phishing scams and sites containing malware. Phishing typically surfaces as unsolicited e-mail pretending to be from banks or other institutions (including AOL and PayPal) requesting that the recipient click through and provide information.

Internet Explorer provides users with protection against phishing and malware as part of their default settings. Within the Internet Options Security menu, users can verify that they will be prompted before downloading potentially unsafe content. Discuss with your children that they may see this type of prompt, as shown in Figure 9-12, and that they should not proceed with the download.

Figure 9-12:
Internet
Explorer
warning
pop-up
window.

Within the Mozilla Firefox web browser, users may elect to block sites that have already been reported or that may be trying to install unauthorized downloads. To activate these protective settings, take the following steps:

1. **Select the Firefox menu in the upper left of your web browser.**

2. **Select Options and then Options again.**

3. **In the Options pop-up window, click the Security tab. (See Figure 9-13.)**

4. **Select the following check boxes:**

   - *Warn Me When Sites Try to Install Add-ons*

   - *Block Reported Attack Sites*

   - *Block Reported Web Forgeries*

5. **Click OK to save changes.**

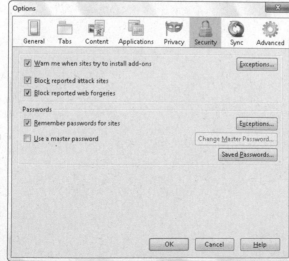

Figure 9-13:
Changing
security
settings
in Mozilla
Firefox web
browser.

To activate this protection within Google Chrome, do the following:

1. **Select the Chrome menu in the upper right of your web browser.**

2. **Select Settings and Show Advanced Settings.**

3. **Under Privacy, select the Enable Phishing and Malware Protection check box. (See Figure 9-14.)**

To enable phishing protection within your Safari web browser, take the following steps:

1. **Choose Edit⇨Preferences.**

   The General dialog box appears by default.

2. **Click the Security tab.**

3. **In the Fraudulent Sites section, click the Warn When Visiting a Fraudulent Website check box. (Refer to Figure 9-7.)**

4. **After you set preferences, simply close the dialog box.**

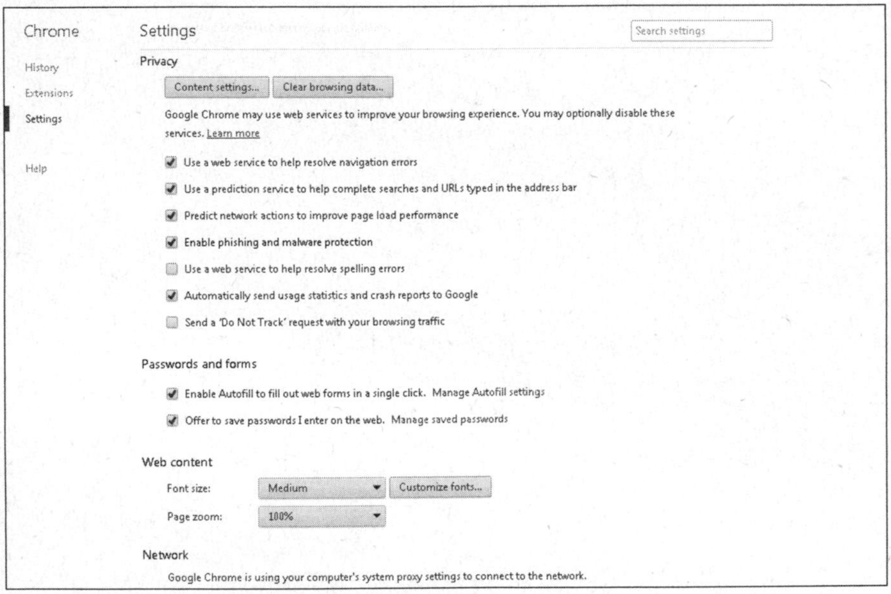

Figure 9-14:
Enable phishing and malware protection in Google Chrome.

Reporting something phishy

If your child accidentally navigates to a suspicious site, you can certainly report that site while you're online. To do so via Internet Explorer, take the following steps:

1. **Open the Tools menu (or gear icon) in the upper right while still on the suspicious site.**

2. **Choose Safety from the drop-down menu.**

3. **Click Report Unsafe Website.**

Those using the Mozilla Firefox web browser can report a potentially dangerous site by taking the following steps:

1. **Open the Firefox menu (upper left of your web browser).**

2. **From the drop-down menu, choose Help and then submit feedback.**

To report a potentially dangerous site via the Google Chrome browser, take the following steps:

1. **Click the Google Chrome menu icon (upper right of your web browser).**

2. **Choose Tools from the drop-down menu.**

3. **Select Report an Issue to send the link, screenshot of the site, and the description of the potential dangers of the site.**

Recognizing Advertising Disguised as Special Features

One of the amazing aspects of living in this digital age is the access our children have to vibrant interactive content. Favorite characters and stories now come alive onscreen through interactive games and video content. These enriched content features are a wonderful resource, but they are also sometimes the source of disguised advertising and marketing content.

Unlike text link advertisements, special feature advertising is less dangerous in terms of potential phishing scams, downloads containing malware, and inappropriate content. However, for parents looking to limit their children's exposure to advertising, this type of marketing may be of concern because of both its prevalence and popularity with kids.

One type of marketing hidden with special content is an "advergame." (See Figure 9-15.) Trusted and popular websites hoping to promote a new feature or product create these new online games with the purpose of introducing this product to their users.

Figure 9-15: An advergame on a popular children's website can hide marketing.

Unlike a traditional advertisement, advergames provide the site user with a gaming experience rather than asking them to passively view an ad. Users connect with the characters within the game, which then begin to appear in DVDs for sale or products for purchase. Although some advergames simply introduce users to a new character that will be available for purchase, others very directly feature a known product, such as a favorite cereal brand or an action hero. Still others hide the marketing messaging or product images within the game rather than introduce them directly.

If your children are playing on branded websites (such as those owned by popular children's networks Nickelodeon and Disney), they are already playing games created with the intent of furthering a connection to favorite characters and their related products. However, you may want to include a discussion during the creation of your Digital Family Policy regarding what to do if newly featured advergames request that users provide information (such as your child's e-mail address) before continuing with game play.

Another hidden form of advertising is the video ad, as shown in Figure 9-16. Some video ads are promoted within existing web content as a special feature and ask users to click to view the video. Although the video appears to be a special new feature, video ads are intended to promote a product or service to the site user. Other types of video ads appear prior to allowing access to a website's regular content. Show your children that these video ads can typically be closed after a certain period of time (so that you continue directly to the website) by clicking the video screen. If you are concerned about your children's exposure to advertising, you may wish to include a rule in your Digital Family Policy that prohibits your kids from visiting websites requiring them to watch video advertising prior to gaining access to the website.

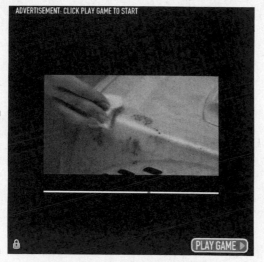

Figure 9-16:
Video ads allow users to close the screen before viewing the entire ad.

Along with video ads and advergames, many sites aimed at children and teens hide advertising within interactive content, such as surveys and quizzes, that can be forwarded — and that often capture protected information, such as your teen's e-mail address. Other times, advertising may appear as special offers, such as ringtone downloads, that pop up on sites frequented by children and teens. See Figure 9-17 for an example.

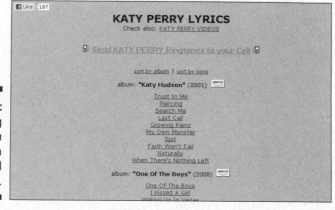

Figure 9-17:
Advertising hidden within a special offer.

To protect your children — as well as your computer — ask that they *never* click this additional content without your permission and that they never fill out any associated forms without your permission. Explain to them that this "free" content is actually sponsored by advertisers looking to gain access to your children and their information. Consider adding this rule to your Digital Family Policy.

And at the end of the day . . .

Be sure to discuss each advertising type covered in this chapter with your children, and show them the examples I have here throughout the chapter. Remind them that although some ads include the word "advertising" or "sponsored ad" in small print, not every ad is labeled this clearly. Kids need to understand that not all content on a website is related to that site or is safe to click. When creating your Digital Family Policy, don't forget to create specific rules regarding clicking advertising content, even on trusted websites. In particular, be sure to warn your children about ads that ask them to download a file or provide information, such as an e-mail address or a credit card number.

To help your kids understand advertising aimed at them, check out Admongo, a site created by the Federal Trade Commission to teach children about advertising. This site is located at www.admongo.gov. This site is targeted to kids ages 8–12 and includes helpful information for parents, too.

Chapter 10

Talking to Your Kids about Cyberbullying

According to the Cyberbullying Research Center (`www.cyber bullying.us`), nearly 20 percent of students in the United States between age 11 and 18 have been cyberbullied. Girls are more likely to be cyberbullying victims than are boys, and social media users are more at risk than nonusers. Although being a victim of cyberbullying can be a passing unpleasant experience for some teens, some young people have been pushed to the point of taking their own lives because of the overwhelming victimization they faced at the hands of cyberbullies. With nearly all children and teens spending time online, include a conversation about cyberbullying not only during the creation of your Digital Family Policy (see Chapter 2), but also as a regular part of talking to your children about online safety and appropriate behavior.

Defining Cyberbullying

Cyberbullying comprises any digital communication, typically from one minor to another minor, with the purpose of frightening, threatening, embarrassing, or harassing a person. The most common form of cyberbullying is sharing a private text message, e-mail, or instant message (IM) with someone else or through a public posting. Cyberbullies' tools are computers and smartphones, and they plague victims via text, e-mail, IM, chat rooms, social media, and blogs. Examples of cyberbullying behaviors include

✔ Using websites to rank or rate peers according to things such as looks and popularity

✔ Publicly blocking someone's participation in an online group

✔ Tricking someone into sharing embarrassing information with the purpose of sharing it digitally with others

✔ Creating a website with the purpose of harassing someone

✔ Creating a fake social media account to pose as another person and post untrue things about that person

✔ Sending threatening or mean e-mails, text messages, and IMs in chat rooms

✔ Posting embarrassing pictures of someone on a social media website

The effects of cyberbullying can be far more devastating for victims than traditional bullying:

✔ Cyberbullies often remain anonymous, making victims unsure of how to protect themselves and whom to trust.

✔ Victims often receive bullying messages via their home computer, taking away their feeling of safety within their own home.

✔ Victims may be affected both at school and online, taking away two primary locations where teens socialize and interact.

✔ Cyberbullies can reach a large number of people easily and instantly, making it possible for the entire world to see the behaviors and shared information about the victim.

✔ Because cyberbullies don't face their victims, the bullying behaviors are often more extreme than traditional bullying.

✔ Cyberbullies can attack their victims frequently on multiple technology platforms simultaneously.

Many states have laws regarding cyberbullying, but current laws vary by state. To see where your state stands regarding cyberbullying legislation, visit www.cyberbullying.us/Bullying_and_Cyberbullying_Laws.pdf.

Cyberharassment

Cyberharassment is beyond typical cyberbullying. The person harassing the victim digitally may be doing so with a specific goal, such as getting the victim to do or admit to something. The methods are often the same as cyberbullying in general and include sending harassing or threatening digital communications.

Some U.S. states consider cyberharassment to be an incident of cyberbullying that includes at least one adult. Although most cases of cyberbullying happen between two minors, there are known cases of adults harassing a minor online. Your kids should understand that any occurrence of these types of behaviors should be reported to you immediately. Some states include cyberharassment under existing harassment laws.

Be sure to discuss cyberharassment with your teens when discussing cyberbullying and your family's consequences for such behavior. Include these consequences in your Digital Family Policy and enforce a zero-tolerance policy.

Both the definition of cyberharassment and any laws regarding cyberharassment differ by state.

Cyberstalking

Some behaviors considered as cyberbullying may fall under the category of *cyberstalking* — when someone uses the Internet, e-mail, or other digital forms of communication or devices to stalk another person. This may include some of the same harassing and threatening behaviors as cyberbullying in general, but typically resembles offline stalking (such as constantly watching the victim or repeatedly trying to contact the victim). Cyberstalking often begins when a teen tries to end either an online or offline relationship. The cyberstalker may react to this attempted severing of communication by sending repeated, sometimes threatening, messages via text, e-mail, and social media. Some cyberstalkers even enlist friends in harassing the victim digitally.

Cyberstalking is a very serious and often dangerous situation, and teens should report potential cyberstalking immediately. Like offline stalking, online stalking often moves from online threats to actual physical acts of violence. Some cyberstalking is at the hands of online predators who your teen may not know in real life. See Chapter 3 for more information about online predators and how to report contact from a potential online predator.

Cyberstalking often stems from an offline relationship that has ended badly.

Teens who are the victims of cyberstalking should take the following steps:

- ✔ Make it clear in writing to the stalker that you do not want to receive contact from the person.
- ✔ Keep an unedited record of all communication from the potential cyberstalker.

✔ Keep a record of any contact with your Internet service or phone service provider regarding the issue.

✔ Change privacy settings to block contact from this person. See Chapter 12 for more information about Facebook settings, and Chapter 3 for information about additional privacy measures. I discuss blocking later in this chapter.

✔ Contact local law enforcement.

Recognizing the Signs of Cyberbullying

Even with the creation of a Digital Family Policy, parental supervision, and safety settings in place, your children may still be the victims of cyberbullying. Keep a keen eye for signs that your children may be falling victim to a cyberbully.

Technology use decrease or increase

Suddenly withdrawing from technology is one of the first indicators that your child may be uncomfortable with a situation online. If your previously tech-connected teen has suddenly stopped using his computer or phone, talk with him about this sudden change in behavior. On the other hand, if your child is suddenly spending much more time online, that may also indicate he is the subject of online bullying.

Emotional distress

Some victims of cyberbullying show signs of emotional distress without any apparent cause. Your child may suddenly become sullen, edgy, or quick to cry. She may seem anxious and unhappy for no reason. For some cyberbully victims, these behaviors may increase right after they use a computer or smartphone. If your child appears to be emotionally distressed, talk to her immediately and help her communicate clearly what she is experiencing so that she can get help.

Change in behavior or mood

Tween and teen years are an emotionally challenging time, but sudden and noticeable changes in behavior or mood are a red flag that your child may be facing something more than standard teenage angst. Watch for moodiness, agitation, or sudden shyness. Changes in behavior may include no longer participating in favorite activities or finding other friends. A previously well-behaved child may start acting out or get in trouble at school. Your child may alter sleeping or eating habits or show signs of depression. Some victims of cyberbullying may even fear leaving the house.

Drop in grades/performance

Victims of cyberbullying often avoid attending school and may begin cutting classes, exhibit behavior problems in school, or ask to stay home because of illness. Trips to the school nurse may increase, and their grades may drop as they fall behind in schoolwork. If you notice any of these behaviors, discuss them with your children's teachers, coaches, and school administrators; they may also have noticed the same change in behavior.

Secretive or withdrawn behavior

Children who are being subjected to cyberbullying may suddenly become socially withdrawn. A child who typically likes to spend time with friends may appear to be pushing all friends away. Victims of cyberbullying may also act secretive when they receive a text message or spend time online. Watch for examples that they are trying to hide information, such as leaving the room when a text message is sent to their phone or clicking a different tab on the computer when you enter the room.

Protecting Children from Cyberbullying

Discussions about cyberbullying should happen in all homes, hopefully before an incident of cyberbullying makes the discussion necessary. However, for many tweens and teens, cyberbullying is an uncomfortable topic. For kids who have already been victims of attacks online, discussing cyberbullying can be even more anxiety producing.

The key is to make it clear to your children that you are available to talk and willing to take their concerns seriously. Be sure to include your teen in deciding how best to handle any potential cases of cyberbullying and assure him that you are working toward the same goal. Also include information in your Digital Family Policy regarding what steps the family can take should a child become the victim of cyberbullying, including limiting social media activity, changing social media accounts, or parents monitoring technology use.

You can also read the other chapters in this book to become more familiar with the types of technology that cyberbullies use to reach their victims, such as chat rooms and social media.

Report cyberbullying

Although not all schools have policies regarding students and cyberbullying, contact your child's teachers and school administrators if you believe that your child is being cyberbullied. Many schools offer resources to help parents navigate this unfamiliar territory and may even assist parents in contacting local police if the bullying behaviors reach a criminal level.

Contact the police immediately if your child receives a physical threat or otherwise threatening communications.

For more information about which states currently have laws to prosecute cyberbullies, see

`www.cyberbullying.us/Bullying_and_Cyberbullying_Laws.pdf`

Be sure to save all communications that you believe are evidence of cyberbullying. You may also want to capture screen images of online cyberbullying on blogs and social media, because the cyberbully may remove or change those pages before the police can see them.

Many states have legislation against cyberbullying. Know your state's laws regarding cyberbullying, including state-by-state guidelines for reporting.

Use blocking features

Many incidents of cyberbullying occur via social media, where blocking features can help teens avoid contact from the people who are doing the bullying. Facebook allows users to choose who can see their information, including status updates, Wall posts from Friends, and photos. Your teen can make nearly all her information visible to Friends only and can even block certain users by their account name or e-mail address. Twitter also allows users to protect their status updates and individually approve who can see those status posts. Additionally, Twitter allows users to block other users, prohibiting them from sending messages via Twitter to the blocking user, as shown in Figure 10-1. To learn more about privacy and blocking features on Facebook, see Chapter 12.

Parents may also work with their phone service providers to block contact from specific phone numbers, both via text and voice. For more information about partnering with your phone service provider to create a safer environment for your children, see Chapter 17.

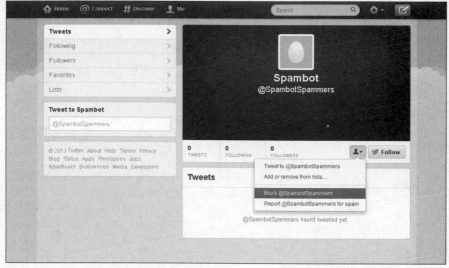

Figure 10-1:
Block
unwanted
users on
Twitter.

Preventing Your Child from Cyberbullying

Your children becoming the victim of a cyberbully is bad enough, but imagine how hard it would be to consider that your child may be the perpetrator. To help prevent your child from being a cyberbully, know the signs that she may be engaging in this activity online, as well as what to do if she is.

Signs that your child may be a cyberbully

Teens who are taking part in online bullying activities may also show changes in behavior, just as victims do. Watch for the following changes in behavior:

✔ Your child may stop using the computer when you come into the room or quickly change screens or tabs.

✔ A child may sharply increase time spent on the computer or on a smartphone.

✔ Your child may appear anxious or secretive when using these devices, and may become anxious, upset, or excessively angry when you take away access.

✔ Your child may be spending more time with a new group of friends or perhaps no longer interact publicly with a long-time friend.

Anxiety or secretive behavior around technology may also indicate that your child is being cyberbullied. See the earlier section, "Recognizing the Signs of Cyberbullying."

Ongoing dialog

Unlike most parents, digital natives do not know a world free of social media and smartphones, and they may not understand why parents find some online behaviors confusing and disconcerting. Cyberbullying is often a group occurrence with more than one child playing a role and different participants contributing varying levels of bullying behaviors. By keeping an ongoing dialog with your children, you not only gain insight into this online world in which your kids live, but you may also discover warning signs that your child's online group is participating in these types of activities. Use these conversations as a chance to discuss the following topics:

- ✔ Help your kids understand the difference between harmless joking and mean, harassing behaviors that others find hurtful.

- ✔ Continue to talk to your kids at every age about what is appropriate to share online, and what is not — including friends' secrets and personal communications. See Chapter 4 for more about how to be a good friend online.

- ✔ Teach your children how to stand up to their friends to discourage bullying behaviors online. Help them understand the importance of not standing by while others are being bullied.

- ✔ Help your kids find the words to tell their friends that they refuse to participate in these bullying actions.

- ✔ Encourage your kids to talk to teachers, coaches, and friends' parents if they don't feel comfortable coming to you with concerns about their own online behavior, which may have potentially crossed the line into cyberbullying.

Consultations with teachers, coaches, and others

Most children spend less time each day with their parents than they do with their teachers, coaches, and school administrators. To get a clearer picture of your children's daily lives at school, stay in touch with the adults in their lives for input if you believe that you're seeing signs of cyberbullying in your child's life, either from the role of the victim or the bully.

Although you may not see some of the signs that your child is interacting inappropriately through digital communication, your children's teachers may be seeing these behaviors. For example, your teen may be caught texting in class, spending more time in the computer lab, or arguing with a former friend during school hours or sports practices.

Find out through your children's teachers, administrators, or guidance counselors whether your children's school has a cyberbullying policy or speaks to students about cyberbullying.

Ask your child's school what its policy is regarding cyberbullying.

Having Age-Appropriate Discussions about Cyberbullying

Just as your Digital Family Policy includes different rules for children of different ages, your family discussions about cyberbullying will change based on the ages of your children.

Elementary school children

Instead of focusing on specific aspects of technology that may not yet be part of your child's life, discuss appropriate interactions in general and apply them to socializing online. The following topics can help you prepare your elementary-age children to not only avoid becoming cyberbullies themselves, but to also be aware when cyberbullying is occurring around them:

✔ As I discuss in Chapter 4, show your children that the same characteristics that make a good friend offline also make a good friend online. A great place to start is with the Golden Rule: "Do unto others as you would have them do unto you."

✔ Talk with your kids about how feelings can be hurt when people share secrets or tease one another. Most elementary-age children have learned about offline bullying, so ask your children to apply that same awareness to online behavior.

✔ This is also the perfect age to talk to your children about being a good digital citizen, including reporting (to parents, teachers, trusted adults) when they believe their friends may be in danger rather than staying silent when bullying occurs.

✔ Be sure to point out to your children that your family has included consequences for cyberbullying in your Digital Family Policy.

To help protect your elementary-age children, keep online socializing to a minimum and primarily on sites created specifically for children their age. See Chapter 21 for examples of age-appropriate social media sites for children.

Middle school children

Middle school children are far more likely than elementary school children to have either been victims of cyberbullying or to have participated in cyberbullying themselves. Middle schoolers are beginning to use digital communication tools more often as well as participate in social media. To help protect your middle schoolers, take the following steps:

- ✔ Monitor their early social media use to help teach them about appropriate and inappropriate behavior.

- ✔ Give your kids clear guidelines about what to do if they see behavior online that they believe is bullying.

- ✔ Reinforce the basic rules of good online behavior from Chapter 4 and the Digital Family Policy from Chapter 2, and talk about specific guidelines per device.

- ✔ Middle school children likely know someone who has used their smartphone or online accounts to do or say hurtful things, so discuss the ramifications of these actions and how the victim may feel after such an attack.

- ✔ Explain to your kids what cyberbullying involves and that it is serious enough to sometimes involve the police.

- ✔ Brainstorm examples of behaviors that may be included in cyberbullying, and discuss what makes those behaviors cyberbullying.

- ✔ Establish and share clear codes of conduct for using each digital device, and be sure to remind kids of the consequences of breaking the code of conduct as laid out in your Digital Family Policy.

This is another opportunity to remind your children of the dangers of oversharing and the importance of not sharing passwords, even with friends they trust now, as I discuss in Chapter 3.

High school children

By the time your teens reach high school, they likely have an active, independent online life that involves frequent use of texting, e-mail, and social media. For teens, a smartphone can be their main connection to their friends. Discussions with teens regarding cyberbullying may include the following points:

✔ In discussing the ramifications of cyberbullying as related to your Digital Family Policy, remind your kids of the consequences, which may include losing access to these devices.

✔ Remind your teens of the differences between offline bullying and cyberbullying and the often severe effects of cyberbullying on the victims.

✔ Help your teens understand the potential long-term effects of participating in cyberbullying, including possible legal ramifications (possibly expulsion or being arrested).

✔ Use current news stories about cyberbullying to encourage discussion about the seriousness of cyberbullying and how frequently it occurs.

✔ Ask your teens to include you in their social media Friend list so that you have access to what others are posting on their public pages.

✔ Discuss the differences between cyberbullying, cyberstalking, and cyberharassment, and set clear guidelines for how your teens should respond if they feel they have experienced any of these types of behaviors.

✔ Encourage your high school–age kids to take any threats or threatening language made online just as seriously as if they received the threats face to face.

✔ Ask your teens to ask any questions they have about cyberbullying and help guide both your discussions and your decisions about related family rules.

✔ Assure your teens they can always come to you if they feel they have been bullied or believe they may have crossed a line with their own online behavior.

Use your Digital Family Policy to help enforce rules across age groups in your home against cyberbullying.

Part III

Grasping Social Media's Effect on Your Family

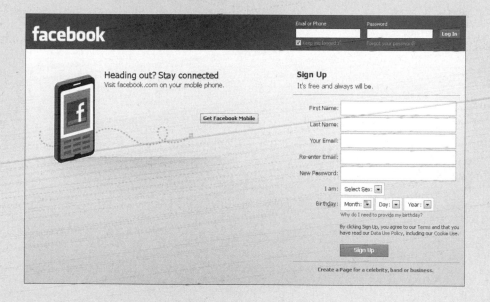

Visit www.dummies.com/extras/raisingdigitalfamilies to read how the Child Online Privacy Protection Act affects your family.

In this part . . .

✔ Get to know social networking platforms created specifically for children including understanding how they differ from adult social networks.

✔ Learn about the settings on two popular adult social networks that may help protect both the safety and privacy of your teens.

✔ Understand how to create a YouTube profile and get to know the variety of settings you can use to restrict your children's access to inappropriate content.

✔ Discover the world of blogging and how your children may turn this online hobby into a business.

Chapter 11

Introducing Social Networking for Children

Many kids are anxious to join the world of social media, which they may see their parents or even older siblings enjoying. However, with most sites requiring users to be at least 13 years old to have an account, kids can't join popular social media sites, such as Facebook and Twitter. Just because your kids aren't old enough for top social media sites doesn't mean that they're left out in the social media cold, though. Sites created specifically for teens and even children younger than 13 allow your kids to dip their toes in social media waters, preparing them for future online interactions while providing entertainment.

Many social media sites — including Facebook, Twitter, and Instagram — require users to be at least 13 years old. Even though the terms of service require users to be at least 13 years old, many Facebook users are much younger. Ask your kids to make sure they have not set up an unauthorized account.

Understanding How Social Platforms for Children Differ from Adult Networks

There are many positive reasons for kids younger than 13 to engage in social media platforms created specifically for their age group. Not only do these platforms act as social media training wheels for kids who are growing up in a digital world, but they may also foster the following:

- Development of personal interests and identity

- Practicing social skills

- Sharing personal achievements

- Supporting friends' achievements

- Collaboration on projects and group goals

- Interaction with teams and clubs

- Awareness of social good and causes

- Increased technical literacy

- Interest in community service and giving back

With potential benefits of allowing kids to engage in age-appropriate social media in mind, think about how social media platforms for kids differ from those created for teens and adults. Due to the U.S. FTC's Children's Online Privacy Protection Act (COPPA), which I cover in more detail later in this chapter, sites that are aimed at children younger than 13 must follow strict guidelines. These platforms typically include the following unique characteristics:

- Parental approval for the child's account creation

- Moderated interactions between users, including deleting banned words and cyberbullying

- Parental notifications of child account activity

When you think of social media use, you likely imagine platforms such as Facebook, where social interaction and sharing is the primary purpose. However, kids younger than 13 may be socializing online on platforms that you typically would not associate with social media.

The following platforms often also have online chatting capabilities (see Figure 11-1), Friend lists, and even ways to share files and images:

Figure 11-1:
Social
media
component
of a popular
online world
for kids.

Wanna be friends?

Goodbye

✔ Handheld gaming devices

✔ Game consoles

✔ Classroom project sites

✔ Online virtual worlds

Researching and Monitoring Platform Safety

Even though social media sites created specifically for children typically follow rules in place to protect children, you should research each platform before allowing your children to create an account. You should also use the parental monitors created by each site to keep an eye on your children's activity and select appropriate account settings.

Online ratings systems and reviews

Unlike the Entertainment Software Rating Board (ESRB), which I cover in Chapter 6, there is no official ratings system for social media, including social media for kids. The best source of ratings and reviews for these platforms is Common Sense Media at www.commonsensemedia.org. Common Sense Media is a not-for-profit organization that rates and reviews movies, TV shows, songs, books, video games, apps, and websites. All site reviewers are trained to adhere to child development guidelines when writing their evaluations.

Common Sense Media's reviews (see Figure 11-2), including those of social media for children, contain the following main ratings guidelines:

- ✔ **Age:** Ranging from ages 2 to 17, this category also includes color coding to help guide parents.

- ✔ **Quality:** This rating lets parents know whether the quality of the content is worthwhile.

Figure 11-2: Common Sense Media provides myriad data in their reviews to help guide parents.

Common Sense Media also provides a rating in each of the following additional categories:

- ✔ Positive messages
- ✔ Violence
- ✔ Sex
- ✔ Language
- ✔ Consumerism
- ✔ Drinking, drugs, and smoking
- ✔ Privacy and safety

Additionally, many technology blogs review new sites when they are released, providing information about the quality, usability, and safety of the platform. In the quickly changing social media landscape, sites change often. Read updated reviews of your children's favorite sites from time to time to stay up to date on changes and how they affect your child's experience online.

Examining privacy policies

Every social media site for children contains a page with the site's privacy policy. Before you help your child create an account, locate the privacy policy link (usually at the bottom of the web page) or the privacy conditions within the site's terms of service.

Read the entire privacy policy carefully, looking specifically for information about the following:

- ✔ Compliance with the Children's Online Privacy Protection Act (COPPA)
- ✔ Details about age guidelines for users
- ✔ A list of what information the site will collect about your child
- ✔ Specifics regarding how the site will use that information, including whether they will share any of it with advertisers
- ✔ A description of how the site is moderated and by whom
- ✔ Site rules regarding parent accounts and ways that parents may monitor and/or restrict their children's site usage
- ✔ Advertising policies, especially any use of third-party cookies, that will be placed on your computer's web browser

> ✔ Rules about closing an account, including whether you can remove your child's information from the site after an account has been created
>
> ✔ Particulars about account holder's ability to change privacy settings

Even with privacy settings in place, anything your children post online could end up being seen and shared. *If they don't want something to get out, they should not post it anywhere on the Internet.*

Sometimes social media account holders who have been added to Friend or buddy lists by your child may share your child's posts and information with their own lists.

Accessing Your Children's Profile Information

There is certainly no way to completely guarantee your child's safety, even on the most carefully reviewed websites with stellar privacy policies. Having said that, no parent wants to monitor their child's every action online, and that type of supervision misses the point of allowing our children to grow and learn using the amazing technology at their fingertips. However, I recommend maintaining access to your children's profile information not only to protect them from sharing too much or inappropriate information, but also to guide them as they craft their early digital presence.

As I mention earlier in this chapter, sites created for children younger than age 13 require parent permission before the child user may create a new account. Many sites also allow parents to create a parent account, though, which acts as a master account for all child accounts within that family, allowing parents to change settings, monitor usage, change profile information, and more.

To access great safety tips, authenticate your child's account, or create a master account, locate the Parents section of the social network platform. Figure 11-3 shows the Parents link on the popular site Everloop.

Figure 11-3:
Social networks for kids typically have a section for parents.

Understanding COPPA

The Children's Online Privacy Protection Act, most often referred to as COPPA, is a law passed in 1998 that allows parents to control what personal information companies can collect about children younger than age 13. COPPA also regulates the following:

- ✔ What must be included in a site's privacy policy

- ✔ Rules for seeking verifiable consent from a parent or guardian before allowing a child younger than 13 to use a site

- ✔ Responsibilities of website owners to protect children's privacy and safety online

In December of 2012, the Federal Trade Commission (FTC) updated COPPA regulations to remain up to date with changes in technology. Changes include the following:

- ✔ Requiring sites to get parental permission before collecting a child's photographs, videos, and location information (all popular components of social media)

✔ Requiring advertising providers (such as Google Ads) to obtain parental permission before tracking a child's online activity in order to tailor advertising to that child's online behavior

✔ No longer allowing apps for kids to permit third parties to collect personal information from the children without parental consent

✔ Extend COPPA regulations to cover IP addresses and mobile device identifiers

The changes do not, however, make app stores liable for the apps that they sell to children, which likely collect information about the children who use those apps.

Establishing family rules regarding parent access to accounts

Although many sites for children include the option for parents to create a master account to monitor child accounts, not every account has this feature. Also, if your child has his own e-mail address, he may be able to circumvent the rules in place regarding parent verification of accounts.

Prior to allowing your children to enjoy social media sites created for them, set rules for your family specifically regarding parent access to your children's online accounts. Include a section in your Digital Family Policy regarding what your children are expected to share with you. Consider keeping a list of the following:

✔ Account names by site and child

✔ Account passwords by site and child

✔ Approved settings by site and child

Consider creating your own user account on sites that your children frequent so you have a better understanding of what they are experiencing online.

Creating Social Networking Rules

Because social media for children expands beyond simply social media websites to include interactive functions on platforms such as gaming consoles, online worlds, and handheld games, it is important to create very specific rules regarding social networking in your Digital Family Policy. For each individual platform, create rules about the following areas:

✔ Parent access to accounts

✔ Sharing accounts among your children

✔ Days and times when kids are allowed to use social media

✔ Requirements regarding requesting permission before making changes to account settings

✔ Multiplayer game setting guidelines

✔ Instructions for when parents need to be notified of unwanted or inappropriate online contact

✔ Specific chat setting rules

Make these platform-by-platform and age group-by-age group guidelines clear to your children. Equally important, include associated consequences with each rule.

Chapter 12

Helping Kids Use Adult Social Networks

Social networking — people interacting on digital platforms — has become the way lots of folks, from your child's best friend to the Pope, interact in the twenty-first century. Facebook and Twitter are the two most popular social media sites.

Even though the vast majority of Facebook users are older than 25 and the average age of Twitter account holders is 37, many children and young adults view these platforms as their own — an appropriate place to interact with their friends as well as the brands and celebrities they love. Because neither site actively enforces a specific age restriction (more on that in a bit), the choice for when (or *if*) your children use either platform is in your hands.

This chapter provides you with a basic understanding of the two most widely used social media platforms to help shape your family's social media policy. It is important for your kids to understand social media and potentially even participate as social media use becomes more commonplace within schools, activities, and even workplaces. Many teens also simply want social media accounts as a way to interact online with friends as well as the brands and celebrities they love. However, social media can also become highly addictive and a place for kids to encounter digital dangers, such as online predators. Set very clear guidelines within your Digital Family Policy (see Chapter 2) regarding social media use.

Understanding Facebook

Facebook is a social networking platform on which users can connect with friends and family online to share everything from what they're doing in that moment to photo albums from a recent family vacation. Users not only use Facebook to connect with friends and family, but they also interact with favorite brands, celebrities, and other users with similar interests.

Even though Facebook is a social network used by one-half of the U.S. population (according to Facebook itself), you might want to implement a variety of privacy settings for your child's account that aren't necessarily as important for your personal page. Likewise, some general settings and guidelines might be helpful when discussing your family's Facebook policies.

At times, it may seem as though Facebook has its own language. Some basic terms to understand include

- **News Feed:** The list of updates posted by members of your Friends list or brand pages you have chosen to "Like."

- **Like:** How you indicate that you have enjoyed a status update from a Friend and also the way you connect with brand and celebrity pages.

- **Pages:** Accounts held by brands, companies, and celebrities rather than individual users.

- **Profile pages:** Accounts held by individual users.

- **Timeline:** The collection of all the information you have shared on your Facebook profile, including status updates and images.

- **Status updates:** Information posted by individual account holders. These status updates appear in the News Feeds of Friends.

- **Wall:** The main page of the account holder's profile or page. Friends can post to each other's Walls.

- **Group:** How Facebook users with similar interests can interact in a virtual room with the ability to share information, documents, and pictures visible only to other group members.

- **Messages:** How Facebook users interact privately. When both users are online at the same time, the messages platform may appear as an instant message format. When a user is not available, the message platform appears more like e-mail.

Knowing the recommended user age

The Facebook Terms of Service (TOS) lay out a variety of rules and regulations for the site covering everything from appropriate uses for status updates to rules for cover photos. One regulation is the recommended user age. Any new user creating an account has to declare being age 13 or older. Some parents allow their children to create a personal account before age 13, but if you do, you're breaking the Facebook user agreement, which may result in that page and its content being removed from Facebook.

To view the complete Facebook TOS, visit `www.facebook.com/legal/terms`.

Providing Profile information

Although you (or your child) can edit personal information on a Facebook account at any time, most information is collected while you're creating the account. After a Facebook account has been created, this information becomes that user's "Profile." Discuss with your children which personal information should and should not be shared via a Facebook Profile prior to creating their accounts.

You must have an e-mail address in order to create a Facebook account. Here's how to create a Profile on Facebook:

1. **Visit `www.facebook.com`, provide the following basic information (which can be hidden from public view later), and select a password (see Figure 12-1):**

   - First name

   - Last name

   - E-mail address

   - Gender

   - Birthday

2. **(Optional) Allow Facebook to access the account holder's e-mail accounts to find friends who are already on Facebook.**

   You don't have to allow Facebook access to e-mail address books. Allowing access can help you start locating other Friends on Facebook, but there are other ways to find people you know if you'd prefer to skip this step.

3. **(Optional) Provide the following optional information to connect with past/current classmates and co-workers:**

   - High School

   - College/University

   - Employer

4. **Upload a profile picture, which I discuss in Chapter 4.**

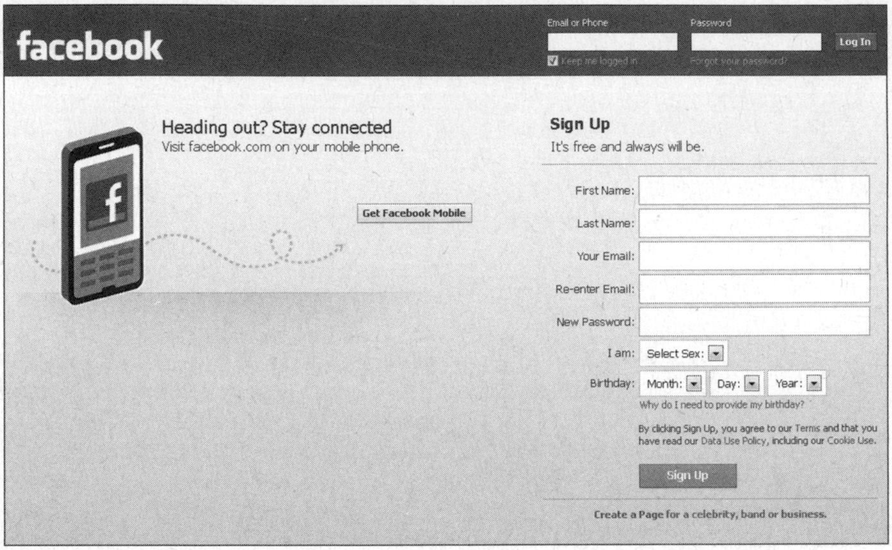

Figure 12-1:
Facebook
Sign Up
page.

After you complete these steps (see Figure 12-2), you will be prompted to edit the general account settings: username, e-mail address, password, school or work networks, and language settings. You can also set security settings, choose how to receive notifications for each Facebook feature, and decide whether to allow subscribers to your page.

Figure 12-2:
Facebook
general
account
information.

TIP

Allowing subscribers permits non-Friends to receive your child's public posts in their News Feed without adding your child as a Friend. For safety's sake, I would strongly recommend that your child's account not allow subscribers.

On the About page of your account, you also have the option to add a contact phone number under the Contact Information heading. This isn't required, though, and not all users opt to provide this. I recommend not including a phone number in the contact information of a teen's account.

Sharing personal information

To select the information to share on a Facebook Profile, you edit the About page by clicking the About heading on your Profile page (see Figure 12-3). On this page, you can add your education, work history, hometown, current town, relationship status, and a paragraph telling other users a bit about you.

To select other personal information to display on your Profile, click the Basic Info section's Edit button (refer to Figure 12-3). Here, you can choose whether your gender and birthday are shown on the Profile. You can also indicate such preferences as religion and political affiliations.

From the About page's Contact Info section, you can edit your contact information, including your phone number, address, and instant messaging (IM) screen names.

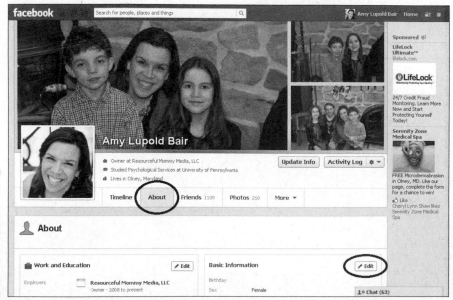

Figure 12-3:
Use the About page to select what information to share.

Selecting your audience

The fastest and easiest way to control what users see of you in their News Feed is the Audience Selector button (shown in Figure 12-4). Using this button lets you choose who can see each one of your actions, such as a status update or the posting of a photo, while you're performing the action.

For example, your children can choose who can view a particular photo album. They might also choose to allow content on their Timeline to be seen only by specifically created Groups (think distribution lists), such as close friends or family members. I discuss Groups in the upcoming "Participating in Facebook Groups" section.

Encourage your children to use the audience selector for each of their Facebook actions to ensure increased privacy for some photos and updates while still allowing less private options for basic updates.

If your children change the audience for an individual action, they may need to use the audience selector in their next update to restore settings to what was initially selected.

Audience selector

Figure 12-4:
The Audience Selector button offers an individualized privacy control.

Customizing privacy settings

Facebook privacy settings provide a way to manage what information you share via your Facebook account. You use the Privacy Settings page to select preferences for your entire account. Simply click the Edit Account drop-down arrow in the upper-right corner of any Facebook page and choose Privacy Settings, as shown in Figure 12-5.

The Privacy Settings and Tools page shows all the general privacy settings for your Facebook account. Your Profile's default privacy setting applies to status updates and photos posted to your Timeline.

You have five options for your account's general privacy setting (affecting all future posts), as shown in Figure 12-6:

✔ **Public**

✔ **Friends**

✔ **Friends except Acquaintances**

✔ **Only Me**

✔ **Custom**

  Use this setting to create a customized list, excluding specific friends.

You can also choose to only share future posts with lists you have created, such as Close Friends and Family.

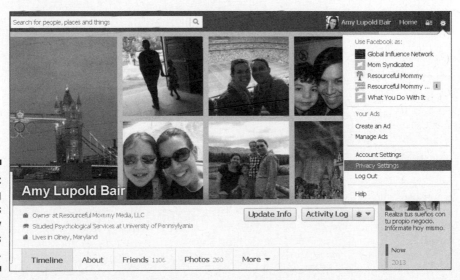

Figure 12-5: Finding Facebook's Privacy Settings page.

Figure 12-6:
Use the
Privacy
Settings and
Tools page
to decide
who can see
your future
Facebook
posts.

If you select Custom, the Custom Privacy dialog box appears, allowing you to choose more specific privacy settings, as shown in Figure 12-7. Use this feature to keep certain groups, networks, and Friends from viewing the status updates and photos that you upload to your account.

Figure 12-7:
Custom
Privacy
dialog box.

Encourage your children to use the Custom privacy setting to create a thoroughly protected account and actively make decisions about the privacy of each area of their account.

Limiting the audience for past posts

If you have a Facebook account and want to change the privacy settings for past posts, click the Limit Past Posts link next to Limit the Audience for Posts You've Shared with Friends of Friends or Public? on your Privacy Settings and Tools page. By clicking the Limit Old Posts button in the dialog box that appears (see Figure 12-8), your past content on your Timeline that is available to Friends of Friends, public, or a specific set of restricted Friends changes to Friends only.

Figure 12-8:
Limiting the
audience for
past posts
privacy
setting.

Selecting this option cannot be undone with a single click after you confirm this action. Should you choose to undo this setting, you will need to change the audience for each past post one at a time.

Choosing contact options

To select how people can locate you on Facebook, click the Edit links in the Who Can Look Me Up? section of your Privacy Settings and Tools page.

The default setting for who can look you up using the e-mail address or phone number you provided is Everyone. Click Edit to choose from the two additional options (as shown in Figure 12-9):

✔ Only Friends of Friends

✔ Only Friends

Figure 12-9:
Who can
look you
up privacy
setting.

You may also edit whether search engines can link to your Timeline. Keeping this feature on allows people to search for your Facebook profile via non-Facebook search engines (such as Bing and Google). The version of your Facebook Timeline that will appear in search results includes only the parts of your Profile that you have made public. Some people prefer to keep this setting on so that it is easier for friends to locate their Facebook profiles.

Selecting Timeline and tagging settings

To select what happens when Friends tag you or your content, or post on your Timeline, you click Timeline and Tagging on the left sidebar of your Privacy Settings page. The Timeline and Tagging page (see Figure 12-10) appears, and you can customize the following settings:

- ✔ Who can post on your Timeline
- ✔ Whether you require the ability to review posts from Friends that tag you before they can appear on your Timeline
- ✔ Who can see what others post on your Timeline
- ✔ Who can see posts you've been tagged in on your Timeline
- ✔ Whether to review tags Friends add to your own posts on Facebook
- ✔ Who is added to the audience of posts you've been tagged in (such as your Friends if they are not already part of that post's audience)
- ✔ Who sees tag suggestions when photos that look like you are uploaded

You can also use this page to preview what your Timeline looks like to people who are not your Friends.

Even if your children do not choose to review photo tags on photos in which they appear, they may still choose to remove tags from those photos after they have been tagged.

The name, profile picture, gender, networks, username and user ID of all Facebook account holders are always publicly available. This also means that this information is available to applications; therefore, any information you have chosen to make public is available to apps.

Figure 12-10:
Timeline
and Tagging
Settings
page.

Timeline and Tagging Settings

Who can add things to my timeline?	Who can post on your timeline?	Friends	Edit
	Review posts friends tag you in before they appear on your timeline?	Off	Edit
Who can see things on my timeline?	Review what other people see on your timeline		View As
	Who can see posts you've been tagged in on your timeline?	Friends	Edit
	Who can see what others post on your timeline?	Custom	Edit
How can I manage tags people add and tagging suggestions?	Review tags people add to your own posts before the tags appear on Facebook?	Off	Edit
	When you're tagged in a post, who do you want to add to the audience if they aren't already in it?	Friends	Edit
	Who sees tag suggestions when photos that look like you are uploaded?	Friends	Edit

facebook — Search for people, places and things — Amy Lupold Bair — Home

General
Security
Privacy
Timeline and Tagging
Blocking
Notifications
Mobile
Followers
Apps
Ads
Payments
Gifts
Support Dashboard

Choosing ad and app settings

To remove unwanted applications' default access to your account information, you click Apps on the left sidebar of your Privacy Settings page to go to your App Settings page. On the App Settings page (shown in Figure 12-11), you can delete individual apps from your account and also

✔ Select how your Friends can take your information with them to the apps they use, such as your e-mail address, which they might share with the apps they've selected.

✔ Enable instant personalization on partner sites, such as the search engine Bing, which allows you to see search results associated with Facebook Friends' interests.

✔ Edit the privacy settings of items you post on old versions of Facebook mobile that do not have the inline audience selector.

To change the way Facebook uses the actions you take on Facebook in ads, click Ads in the left sidebar of the Privacy Settings page. The Facebook ads page allows you to do the following:

✔ Restrict Facebook from sharing your information with social plugins, such as tools that allow your Friends to see what Facebook-related actions you have taken elsewhere around the Internet (such as liking a brand).

✔ Restrict Facebook from using your profile image and actions you have taken on Facebook in ads.

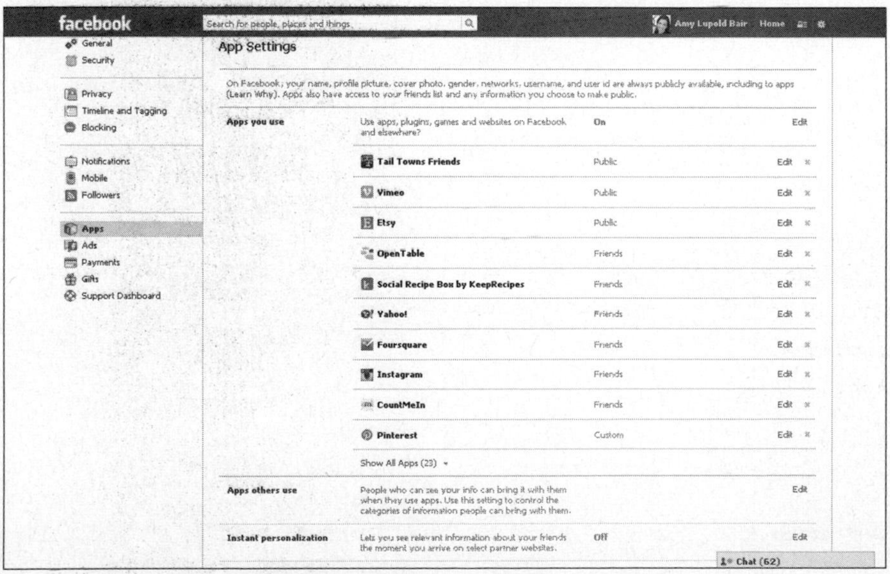

Figure 12-11:
Privacy settings for apps.

Blocking people and apps

To manage people and apps by blocking them, you click Blocking in the left sidebar of your Privacy Settings page. On the Manage Blocking page that appears (shown in Figure 12-12), you can

- ✔ **Add Friends to your Restricted list.** This allows you to restrict specific Friends from seeing your content. Friends will not receive notification that they have been blocked.

- ✔ **Block users.** This allows you to block users from being your Friend on Facebook or interacting with you as part of games, groups, or apps on Facebook. You may select which users to block based on their name or e-mail address.

- ✔ **Block app invites.** Type the name of a Friend to prohibit them from sending you app invites.

- ✔ **Block event invites.** Type the name of a Friend to prohibit them from sending you an event invitation. Facebook account holders are able to create event listings for both online and offline events.

- ✔ **Block apps.** Type the name of a specific app to keep that app from contacting you or receiving nonpublic information about you through Facebook.

Facebook privacy options are subject to change, so be sure to visit this setting from time to time to check for updates.

Figure 12-12:
Privacy settings for blocking people, events, and apps.

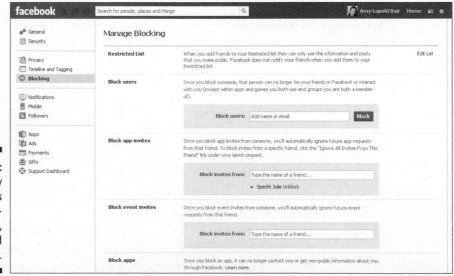

Considering creating a family page

A great option for families interested in using the social networking platform that Facebook offers is creating a family page. Many users creatively use the name fields on the account sign-up page to indicate that this account represents every member of the family. For example, were I to create a family page, I might insert "TheBair" as the first name and "Family" as the last name for the account.

There are a variety of things to consider should you choose to take this route when engaging as a family on Facebook. Your family will need to create rules regarding the following:

- ✔ **Who is allowed to post mobile photos and when**
- ✔ **Who is able to create photo albums**
- ✔ **Privacy settings**
- ✔ **Selection of Friends**

    Will you allow friends of each parent, friends of each child, or just people that the entire family knows?

- ✔ **Participation in groups**
- ✔ **Apps and games**
- ✔ **Who can update the account status**
- ✔ **What can be posted on the Wall and by whom**

All these rules and decisions should be discussed prior to the creation of the account and presented in the Digital Family Policy.

Use the permalink displayed at the bottom of Facebook photo albums to share your family photo albums with non-Facebook users and Facebook account holders who are not Friends with your account.

Engaging with companies and brands

Many brands and companies use Facebook to connect with their online consumer audience. This includes many of the brands and companies your children recognize and enjoy. One way that Facebook account holders show appreciation for a favorite brand is by clicking the Like button on that brand's page (see Figure 12-13).

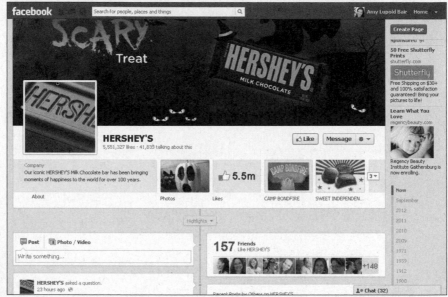

Figure 12-13:
Facebook
brand page
Like button.

After a Facebook user clicks the Like button on a page, the following happens:

- ✔ A story about your Like will appear in your Timeline and may, therefore, also appear in your News Feed.

- ✔ Your name and profile photo may be displayed on that page.

- ✔ Your name and profile photo may appear in advertisements about that page.

- ✔ You have granted permission for that page's updates to appear in your News Feed and for that page to send you messages.

While clicking Like on a Friend's content simply shows others your approval or enjoyment of that content, clicking Like on a brand page creates a connection between your account and that page. However, "liking" a page does not provide that page with access to your Timeline, only your profile picture and name.

Although you can view Facebook brand pages without first liking the page, many brands use the Like button as a gateway to participate in contests, receive special offers, and learn about company announcements before that information is made available to the general public.

It is natural for kids to want to connect with their favorite brands and celebrities through their Facebook accounts, but at the same time, it's important for them to understand how clicking the Like button affects their account. Discuss with your children the ramifications of choosing to Like a brand or celebrity on Facebook, including any concerns regarding privacy. Be sure to include rules regarding the Liking of brand pages when creating your Digital Family Policy.

Participating in Facebook Groups

The Groups feature on Facebook allows users to create a private space in which members can share updates, images, documents, and more. After a user has created a Group, they may add Friends to that Group without their permission or request. Many organizations, clubs, sports teams, families, and professional organizations use Facebook Groups as a way to stay connected and share information related to the Group.

Facebook Groups can be a wonderful place for you and your family to interact with local groups, clubs, and even class groups. They can be a way for fellow students to share class information and for sports teams to share practice schedules, but they can also make your child's account more public than you initially chose when creating the account.

Groups provide your child with a platform to interact on Facebook with non-Friends. However, non-Friends who are in the same group as your children can't see information on your child's Timeline that her privacy settings prohibits from being seen by non-Friends. Also, blocked members who are in the same Group as your children will not be seen in the Group member's list, nor will the content generated by that person be seen.

Creating a Facebook Group? Consider reaching out to potential members to ask their permission before adding them to your Group. It's a great way to start your Group off on a respectful foot.

Group creators select one of the following privacy settings:

- ✔ **Secret:** Facebook Groups categorized as secret are visible only to members of the Group. Other users may not see the Group name, the Group members, or the Group content. This type of Group protects the privacy of Group members the most. If your teens are part of Secret Facebook Groups associated with teams and after-school activities, ask to be added as a Group member as well in order to see the Group's activity.

- ✔ **Closed:** Closed Facebook Groups are visible to the public as is the list of Group members. Group content, however, is only viewable by the members of the Group.

- ✔ **Open:** These Groups are visible by anyone. This means that the Group, the member list, and the content posted within the Group is all visible to nonmembers as well as members.

Facebook Group administrators who are Friends with you on Facebook may add you to a Group without first requesting your permission or approval. If a Friend adds you to a Facebook Group, you will receive a notification. This will also cause stories from the group to appear in your news feed.

Consider including a rule in your Digital Family Policy regarding participation in Groups. Facebook Groups connect users with a range of people beyond their Facebook "Friends," which may concern some parents. If your teens want to join Groups for clubs or other activities, joining the Group from your own account as well allows you to monitor the activity within that Group.

Because users may add Friends to a Facebook Group without their permission, your teens may find the need to remove themselves from Groups in which they do not wish to belong. To leave a Facebook Group, go to the Group page and click Leave Group in the upper-right corner. (See Figure 12-14.) If you choose to leave a Group, no one within that Group can re-add you unless you request to be re-added.

Figure 12-14:
How to
leave a
Facebook
Group.

You can't prevent your children's friends from adding your child to a Facebook Group, but they cannot re-add your children without their request after your child has left the Group.

Allowing applications to access your information

When creating the Facebook portion of your Digital Family Policy, consider the effect that the use of Facebook applications will have on the privacy of your account information. Apps include popular games (such as FarmVille) as well as popular quiz-taking and cause-sharing apps, for example. The use of applications is a favorite feature of many Facebook users, including teens, but will affect who has access to the information on your child's Facebook account. Also stipulate in your family's policy whether children need to request parental permission for each individual app before granting that application access to the account.

Applications are used by Facebook account holders for anything from gaming to reading the news via your Profile page. When you install an app, you're granting it permission to access your public information. Earlier in this chapter, I walk you through selecting what information to make public and keep private. This request for information is shown in Figure 12-15 and may include such information as your name, profile picture, e-mail address, and birthday.

Figure 12-15:
Application
permission
request
screen.

You may also be allowing the application access to additional information so that it may post updates on your behalf and allow other users of the app to see your notifications. The additional information requested generally appears during the application's install. (See Figure 12-16.)

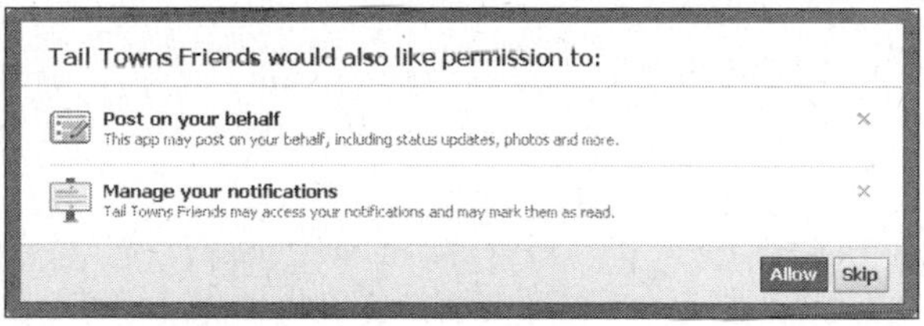

Figure 12-16:
Application
dialog box
showing
additional
information
it wants to
access.

Account holders may choose to remove permission for an application to access their account information even after they have granted the app permission. If you're helping your teen update their account settings to create a more private account, you may want to encourage them to change these permission settings. To restrict an application from accessing your information after you chose to allow access, click the Edit Account drop-down arrow in the upper-right corner of any Facebook page and choose Account Settings. Then click Apps in the left sidebar to visit the App Settings page (shown in Figure 12-17), where you can edit an application's settings or delete an application.

Figure 12-17:
Use the App Settings page to restrict access to your account.

By clicking Edit next to an application on the App Settings page, you discover the following:

✔ Last date logged in to the app

✔ Information the app needs to access

✔ Last data accessed

✔ Who can see posts the app makes on your Facebook Timeline

✔ When the app is permitted to send you a notification

You may wish to change some permission settings as a matter of convenience. Many Facebook users simply don't want to receive frequent notifications from the apps that they use. Other permission settings are a matter of privacy, such as having access to your e-mail address and Friends list.

When covering Facebook rules in your Digital Family Policy, include whether you will have access to your children's Facebook accounts. At the very least, I strongly suggest that you require your teens to "Friend" your Facebook account. You may also require your children to provide you with their Facebook username and password in order to monitor their activity and protect their safety. The actions that teens take on Facebook today will affect them for years into the future (including college admission and employment) because of their digital footprints (as discussed in Chapter 3).

If you or your teen are experiencing abusive behavior on Facebook — such as hateful or slanderous speech — you can report this behavior:

1. **Click the gear menu next to the item you wish to report to Facebook.**
2. **Select the Report option.**

If your child is under age 13 and has created a Facebook account, you can report this by filling out the form here:

```
http://www.facebook.com/help/contact/?id=210036389087590
```

If Facebook can verify that the child is younger than 13, Facebook will delete the account.

If you or your child would like to delete your Facebook account, you may do so here:

```
https://www.facebook.com/help/delete_account
```

Understanding Twitter

With more than 100 million active accounts, Twitter is the second largest social media platform today. Considered a micro-blogging platform, Twitter users post updates limited to only 140 characters. These updates can include links, photographs, and even video. Used by businesses to connect with consumers, celebrities to chat with their fans, and the average American to share everything from what they're eating for lunch to their most personal hopes and dreams, Twitter is a social media powerhouse with nothing but growth on the horizon.

Although Twitter doesn't currently require users to meet an age restriction, the platform isn't appropriate for children. Many teens, however, use the account daily, and for parents with social media–savvy teens, Twitter can also feel like a strange new world where users speak in hashtags and snippets of thought only 140 characters long. Many teens use Twitter to share anything from how they feel about the football game they're watching to what they're eating for lunch. For some users, Twitter can be terribly addicting, and for many teens, Twitter offers the potential for oversharing. This section will walk you through the Twitter basics for when your teen begins to tweet or when you decide to join Twitter yourself.

Selecting a protected or a public account

All you need to create a Twitter account is an e-mail address and an account name not currently in use. To create a new account, simply visit `https://twitter.com` and follow these steps:

1. **Provide your e-mail address and preferred username.**

2. **Agree to the Terms of Service (TOS).**

3. **Read through a brief Twitter tutorial covering the basics of creating Twitter status updates — "tweeting."**

4. **(Optional) Select accounts to "follow."**

    Following an account on Twitter means that the updates generated by those accounts will appear in your Twitter timeline. (See Figure 12-18.)

5. **Select a profile image and account description.**

You can now tweet from your account although you can choose additional settings. One option is Tweet Privacy, and this selection allows you to protect your tweets. (See Figure 12-19.)

TIP

If you change a Twitter account from public to protected, all tweets sent prior to the change will still be public and searchable.

Figure 12-18: Click the Twitter Follow button to follow an account on Twitter.

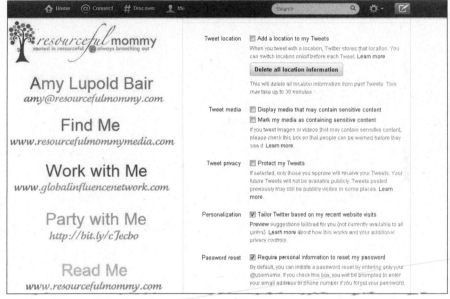

Figure 12-19:
Tweet
privacy
selection
option.

Choosing to protect your account's tweets also affects your account in the following ways:

- Other account holders won't be able to resend your tweets through their account via a tool called a "retweet."

- Permanent links to your tweets will be viewable only to account holders who you have approved to follow your tweets.

- Your tweets won't appear in either a Google search or a Twitter search.

- You won't be able to tweet to people who haven't chosen to follow you because your tweets aren't visible to them.

The option to create a Twitter account with protected tweets is useful for families who want to allow family members to tweet with a selected group of friends or family without those tweets being viewed by the public. Be sure to consider this option when referencing the use of Twitter in your Digital Family Policy. Also discuss the selection of accounts to follow because the content tweeted by some accounts may not be suitable for all ages.

Public tweets versus private direct messages

When you send an update — a *tweet* — from an unprotected account, that message is visible to anyone who chooses to see it. There is a way, however, for public accounts to send messages on Twitter that are visible to only one other person. (See Figure 12-20.) These private messages between two individuals are *direct messages.* Like public tweets, direct messages are limited to 140 characters per message. To send a direct message to a user, that user must be following your account. Likewise, to receive a direct message from another user, you must be following that user's account. Twitter users may opt for direct message notifications to be sent to them via e-mail or have direct messages delivered to your mobile phone via text. Keep in mind that text message rates will apply!

On the plus side, direct messages allow your teen to communicate with friends via Twitter without sharing information publicly. During the creation of your Digital Family Policy, discuss what types of information might be better suited for a direct message than a public tweet.

Follow these steps to send a direct message to another user:

1. **Click the person icon on the Twitter.com navigation bar.**

2. **Select Direct Messages.**

3. **Click New Message.**

4. **Next to the egg image, type the name of the account you would like to message.**

5. **Type your message of 140 characters or less into the message field.**

6. **Choose Send Message.**

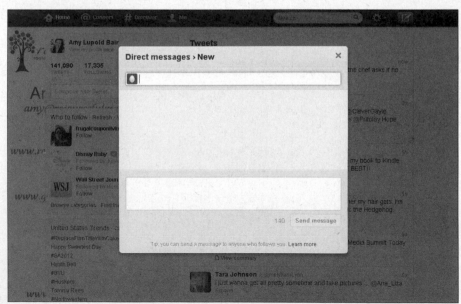

Figure 12-20:
Sending
a direct
message.

REMEMBER

To "follow" another Twitter account, go to that account profile and click the Follow button.

Navigating hashtagged conversations

Twitter began as a micro-blogging platform where users answered the question, "What are you doing?" but quickly developed into a social media site where users hold conversations. One way that these conversations are organized is with a hashtag.

By tweeting with the same hashtag — a # sign followed by a keyword — all tweets following the same topic are searchable (as shown in Figure 12-21). For example, a user might tweet, `I can't believe that call from the officials! #SuperBowl` for their tweet to appear in searches of the #SuperBowl hashtag during the big game.

These tweets can then be located via hashtag conversation tools and other third-party applications. Typically, these platforms format all tweets that contain the same hashtag in a scrolling conversation very much like an IM or chat room tool.

To participate in hashtagged conversations, simply add this tag to each of your tweets. You may wish to use a party platform, such as Tweetchat.com or Tweetgrid.com, to view all the other tweets associated with the chat. These events usually are facilitated by a host who may be asking conversational questions to drive the chat. Often, other participants will retweet the questions after the host has posted them.

Figure 12-21: One example of searching Twitter using a hashtag.

A *retweet* is the reposting of someone else's tweet so that it appears on your Twitter timeline.

During these topical conversations, participants are sometimes asked to answer trivia or view additional content on other platforms. Many hashtagged conversations are sponsored by a brand or company hoping to gain exposure for a new product or service. These chats also often include prize giveaways facilitated by the event host.

Although many events include an RSVP page on a blog or event landing page, they are typically open to anyone wishing to participate, and an advance RSVP is rarely required.

Participating in hashtagged conversations allows your teen to engage in conversations with account holders who do not follow that account and whose account your teen does not follow. Because of the effect that hashtagged conversations may have on your teen's privacy, be sure to discuss your family's policy regarding participation in these events.

Allowing access to third-party applications

Using Twitter.com is the main way to tweet, send direct messages, and search Twitter content, but many Twitter users choose instead to use Twitter via a variety of third-party applications, created and run by developers not associated with Twitter.com. These applications allow Twitter account holders to perform a variety of tasks not available on Twitter.com, such as scheduling tweets to be shared at a future date and time. They also allow users to organize how they receive tweets from the accounts they follow according to criteria not available on the actual Twitter platform.

Such third-party applications have been developed apart from Twitter.com and are not official Twitter.com apps. You must contact that app directly with any questions or concerns.

To use these third-party applications, you will grant each application permission to access your Twitter account. Typically, you allow the application to access your account by clicking a button asking to connect to Twitter, and then you're redirected to a Twitter website asking you to log in to your account and approve the application. Just like the Facebook applications that I discuss earlier, this permission screen asks the exact permissions you're granting to this application. (See Figure 12-22.) The items listed in green are the permissions you are allowing. Items listed in red are the permissions you are not allowing. To connect to the app, click Authorize App.

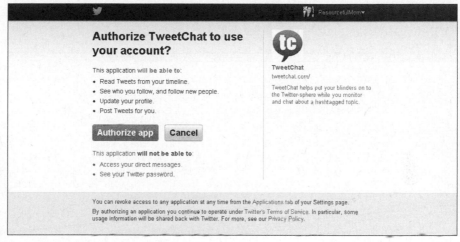

Figure 12-22:
Third-party application authorization screen.

To review the applications that you connected to your Twitter account, visit the Apps tab of your account settings. (See Figure 12-23.) You may remove permissions granted to an application at any time by clicking the Revoke Access button next to the application.

Using third-party applications to access Twitter is very common. Discuss as a family what it means to allow a third-party application access to your Twitter account, and consider creating a list of most trusted third-party apps to keep in your Digital Family Policy's social media section.

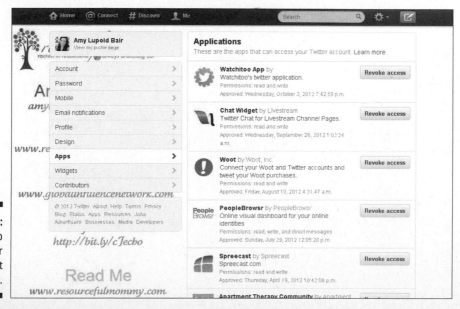

Figure 12-23:
Apps tab in Twitter account settings.

Discussing giveaways and contests

Many brands, bloggers, and other organizations use the Twitter platform as a place to hold giveaways and contests. There is currently no minimum age for Twitter account holders, but that does not mean that every giveaway hosted on Twitter is open to all ages or even residents of every state or country. To avoid wasted time, disappointment, and even legal hassles, parents of teens who tweet may wish to set ground rules for participation in sweepstakes on Twitter.

The majority of the contests held on Twitter have no actual affiliation to Twitter.com. Although the Facebook platform is highly regulated by Facebook with very strict guidelines for sweepstakes, Twitter has taken a much more *laissez-faire* approach to this issue. Contests on Twitter are regulated at the discretion and the supervision of the giveaway sponsor only.

To determine the rules of the sweepstakes, visit the Twitter account being used to implement the giveaway. Look for links to contest rules or posts advertising the contest to determine the following:

- ✔ Giveaway sponsor
- ✔ Complete list and value of prizes
- ✔ Age requirements
- ✔ Residency requirements
- ✔ Steps required to enter to win
- ✔ Any costs associated with receiving the prize

Most giveaways are available to users who are 18 years of age or older, and many are open to U.S. residents only. Beware of contests that require you to provide personal information prior to winning or that ask you to pay sales tax and shipping on the prizes.

Chapter 13

Searching and Sharing Safely on YouTube

. . . .

In This Chapter

▶ Creating a Google account

▶ Getting into YouTube

▶ Making your YouTube experience safer

▶ Using video filters

▶ Activating YouTube privacy settings

. . . .

Accoording to YouTube, an hour of video is uploaded to YouTube each second of the day, and more than 800 million unique users visit YouTube monthly. Additionally, more than 21 million teens are on YouTube. Users at this video-sharing website can find everything from their favorite song to how-to videos. With the ability to share and view YouTube videos via Facebook and Twitter, many families also use YouTube to share memorable moments with friends and family.

Subsequently, YouTube posts millions of videos with content that may be enjoyable to children, from videos of favorite theme park rides to kid-friendly events to class science projects. Just as children turn to search engines to find information, many also turn to YouTube to learn about a topic or to check out the latest viral videos.

Additionally, anyone with a YouTube account in good standing can upload video content to their account. Therefore, YouTube can be a fantastic creative outlet for budding filmmakers, musicians, and video bloggers.

Taking the time to understand the benefits and potential pitfalls of YouTube will help you guide your children as viewers and content creators. Understanding YouTube's filters and privacy settings can help you minimize encountering content that, by many parents' standards, isn't very suitable for children. For example, videos with violent content and inappropriate language are common. Despite YouTube regulations, videos with highly sexual content are also commonplace and can be difficult to avoid.

Starting with a Google Account

You don't need a YouTube account to search and view videos. But, because YouTube is owned by Google, you need a (free) Google account before you can create a YouTube account. Benefits of creating a YouTube account include being able to create a personalized channel guide as well as being able to upload video content and access search filters.

If you already have a Google account, simply go to www.youtube.com to sign in and begin customizing your experience.

According to Google Terms of Service, account holders in the United States must be at least 13 years old.

To grab a Google account

1. **Go to https://accounts.google.com/SignUp (see Figure 13-1).**

2. **Provide Google with the following information:**

    • First and last name

    • Selected username

    • Created password

    • Birthday

    • Gender

    • Current e-mail address

    • Country location

3. **Complete a verification password.**

4. **Agree to the Google Terms of Service and Privacy Policy.**

Google will ask you for a mobile phone number, but feel free to skip this field. You do need an e-mail account, though.

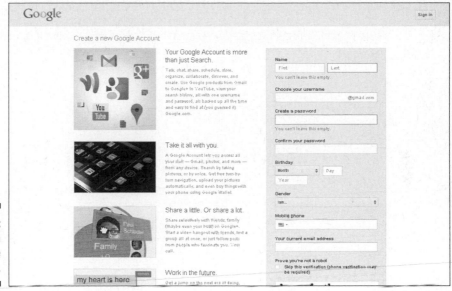

You can also personalize your public profile with a profile photo.

Signing In to YouTube

After creating your Google account, access YouTube by selecting YouTube from the Google navigation bar at the top of your screen. (See Figure 13-2.)

Click the upper-right Sign-In button (see Figure 13-3), provide your Google e-mail address and password on the page that appears, and click Sign In.

After you sign in to your YouTube account, you can subscribe to favorite channels, personalize your search settings, and upload content. A YouTube *channel* is simply a page containing all the videos uploaded by one YouTube account holder. YouTube will also suggest content based on past searches as well as the channels to which you subscribe. You can also opt to connect other social accounts to your YouTube account. Connecting social media accounts (such as Facebook) allows you to share your YouTube activity with Friends and followers.

YouTube tab

Figure 13-2:
Select
YouTube
from the
Google
menu.

Sign In button

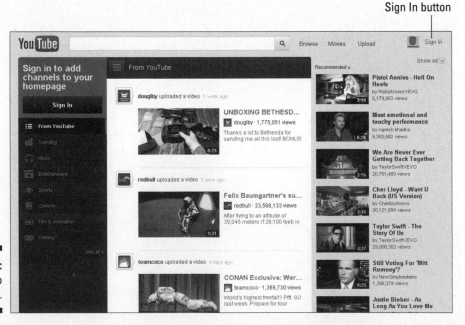

Figure 13-3:
Signing in to
YouTube.

Now is also a good time to sit down with your teens and read the YouTube Community Guidelines found at

```
www.youtube.com/t/community_guidelines
```

Your teens have to agree to follow these content guidelines to upload content to YouTube. Copyright violations are prohibited on YouTube, so be sure to explain copyright basics.

YouTube users are not allowed to upload content that they have not created or been given express permission to upload. This also means that teens may not use music in their videos that they did not create themselves or pay for permission to use. More information on YouTube copyright rules can be found at

```
www.youtube.com/t/howto_copyright
```

Customizing Your YouTube Settings for Safety

One of the main reasons to create a YouTube channel is to gain access to customized settings, which determine the privacy level of your profile information and your YouTube channel's content. These settings not only affect any videos uploaded by you or your teen to the account, but also affect the video searches conducted via that account. This provides you with the opportunity to filter what your children see when watching content on YouTube.

YouTube settings should be a critical piece of your Digital Family Policy regarding video sharing.

Editing your profile

You can change your YouTube channel settings to edit what personal information about the channel's content provider appears to the public when videos uploaded by that account are viewed. You can use this setting to keep the public from knowing that a channel is owned by a teenager, for example. By default, the age of the account holder appears on the channel while video posted on that channel is viewed. In fact, other YouTube users can see the age of an account holder even before that account holder has uploaded content.

To edit these settings

1. **Click the down arrow next to your account name (upper right) and then click the My Channel link below the YouTube heading. (See Figure 13-4.)**

2. **On the profile page that appears, click the Edit button to the right of your username. (See Figure 13-5.)**

3. **Under the Created By section, you can hide specific account holder information by clicking the Hide link next to that information (see Figure 13-6).**

4. **After you update your channel's profile information, click Apply to accept the changes (or click Cancel if you change your mind).**

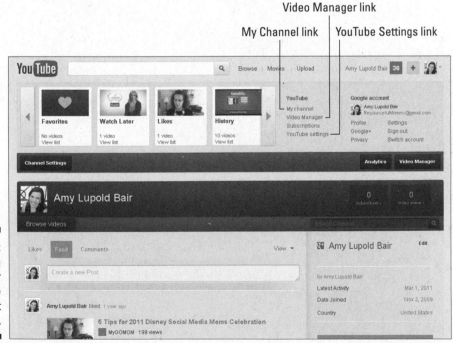

Video Manager link

My Channel link   YouTube Settings link

Figure 13-4: Changing your YouTube account settings.

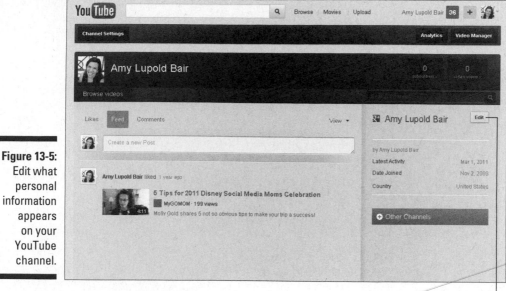

Figure 13-5:
Edit what
personal
information
appears
on your
YouTube
channel.

Edit your channel's profile

Figure 13-6:
You can
hide
personal
information
on your
YouTube
account.

Selecting what actions to share

YouTube account holders can connect their YouTube account to their Orkut,
Facebook, and Twitter social media accounts. If you choose to connect your
YouTube account to a social media site, updates regarding your YouTube
activity are sent automatically to the social network. You will likely want to

customize these settings to maintain privacy. If, on the other hand, you want to share your YouTube activity with social media contacts, these settings may provide useful to you.

To connect your YouTube account and select the Sharing settings

1. **Click the down arrow next to your account name (upper right) and then click the YouTube Settings link below the YouTube heading. (Refer to Figure 13-4.)**

2. **On the Account Settings page that appears, select Sharing in the left sidebar, as shown in Figure 13-7.**

3. **Click the Connect button next to the social media account you want linked to your YouTube account.**

4. **In the Share Your Activity section, select how YouTube shares your YouTube actions on YouTube and your connected accounts (such as Orkut, Twitter, and Facebook).**

   Select the check boxes for the actions you want to share. Such actions include uploading a video, adding a video to a playlist, marking a video as a favorite, liking a video, commenting on a video, and subscribing to a channel.

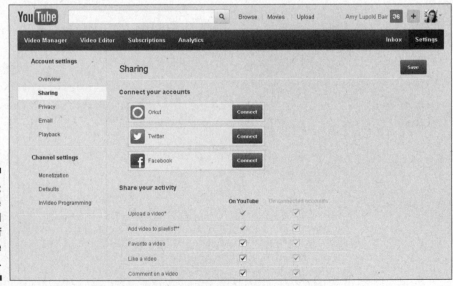

Figure 13-7: Customize social sharing of YouTube actions.

Some actions are selected by default already; deselect those actions that you don't want to share via YouTube or a connected social media site.

5. After you finish your selections, click Save.

When helping your teens select these settings, discuss factors such as how frequently they take each action on their YouTube account and how they use the other social media platforms. Will they be sharing YouTube actions with an audience of friends and family who may feel inundated by frequent updates? Is the YouTube account your child's account, but the Facebook account is for the entire family? Answering these questions might help you form your Digital Family Policy.

Protecting yourself with privacy settings

Like other social networking sites, YouTube allows users to connect to other users through features such as comments and private messages. You may wish to create a YouTube account for your family or children to access personalization settings. You may not, however, wish to be contacted by the public through your YouTube account. YouTube privacy settings allow you to decide not only how the public interacts with your account, but also how YouTube itself accesses and shares your account information.

Here's how to change the privacy settings on your YouTube account:

1. Click the down arrow next to your account name (upper right) and then click the YouTube Settings link below the YouTube heading. (Refer to Figure 13-4.)

2. On the Account Settings page that appears, select Privacy in the left sidebar, as shown in Figure 13-8.

Here you can set the following privacy settings for your account:

- *Search and Contacts:* Set whether contacts can send you messages and share videos and whether people can find your channel if they have your e-mail address.

- *Ads Based on My Interest:* Elect whether YouTube can use your information to send you ads that Google believes relevant to your interests.

- *Statistics and Data:* Decide whether YouTube can share statistics and data about your videos publicly. For example, do you want the public to be able to see how many people have viewed your videos? Do you want the public to see the comments on your videos?

3. **After you finish your selections, click Save.**

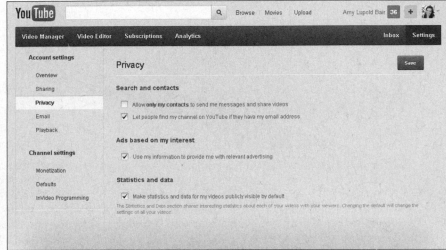

Figure 13-8:
Select privacy settings for your YouTube account.

Using Content Filters

Because YouTube hosts a seemingly unlimited variety of video content, take advantage of the parental control option, which sports multiple features parents can use to protect their children from inappropriate content.

After a video is viewed on YouTube, a screen appears with recommended and related content that YouTube suggests you may want to view next. Parents should discuss with their kids that these images will appear without prompting.

The YouTube Safety Mode provides the following features:

✔ Hides videos with potentially objectionable material

✔ Hides comments on videos unless you elect to show comments

✔ Replaces most inappropriate language in comments with stars

To implement Safety Mode, take the following steps:

1. **Go to** www.youtube.com, **scroll to the bottom of the page, and click the Safety drop-down arrow (see Figure 13-9).**

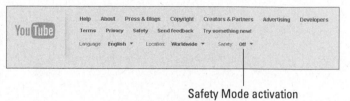

Safety Mode activation

2. **In the Choose Your Safety Mode drop-down window that appears, select the On radio button.**

   The Safety Mode Lock check box appears.

3. **Select the Lock Safety Mode on This Browser check box (see Figure 13-10).**

   With Safety Mode enabled, you can also lock Safety Mode for the browser you're currently in. Locking Safety Mode on a browser means that even if you sign out of your Google account, YouTube will remain in Safety Mode when accessed through that browser.

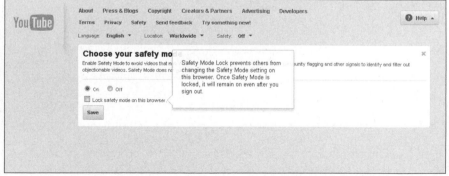

Figure 13-10:
Set Safety
Mode to
On and
lock Safety
Mode
for every
browser
you use.

4. **Click the Save button.**

   If your family uses multiple web browsers, be sure to repeat the locking process on each one.

If you've set YouTube content filters but still don't feel comfortable allowing your children and teens to search for YouTube content without parental supervision, consider screening content prior to showing it to your children. After you deem the content appropriate, allow your children to view the video with supervision. Be prepared that at the end of the video, though, suggested content thumbnails will appear.

If your children are permitted to view only prescreened YouTube content, with adult supervision, be sure to include this stipulation in your Digital Family Policy.

Public versus Private Videos on YouTube

When you upload a video to YouTube, you have the option to make the video private or public. *Public* videos can be viewed by anyone searching for content on YouTube. Electing to make a video private does not mean that the video cannot be shared, though. When a video is private, it

- ✔ Does not appear on your YouTube channel
- ✔ Is not listed in search results
- ✔ Can be shared with up to 50 invited viewers
- ✔ Does not appear in playlists

YouTube users may share private videos only with other YouTube account holders.

To share a private video, take the following steps:

1. **Sign in to your YouTube account (www.youtube.com).**

2. **Click the down arrow next to your account name (upper right).**

3. **Click the Video Manager link (refer to Figure 13-4).**

4. **Select Uploads in the left sidebar.**

5. **Choose the video you want to share and then click the Edit button (see Figure 13-11).**

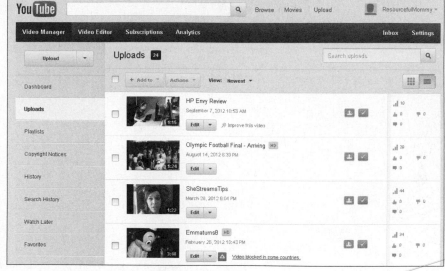

Figure 13-11:
Select a
YouTube
video to
share
privately.

6. **On the Basic Info tab, enter up to 50 YouTube usernames to whom you grant access to your video, as shown in Figure 13-12.**

7. **Click Save Changes.**

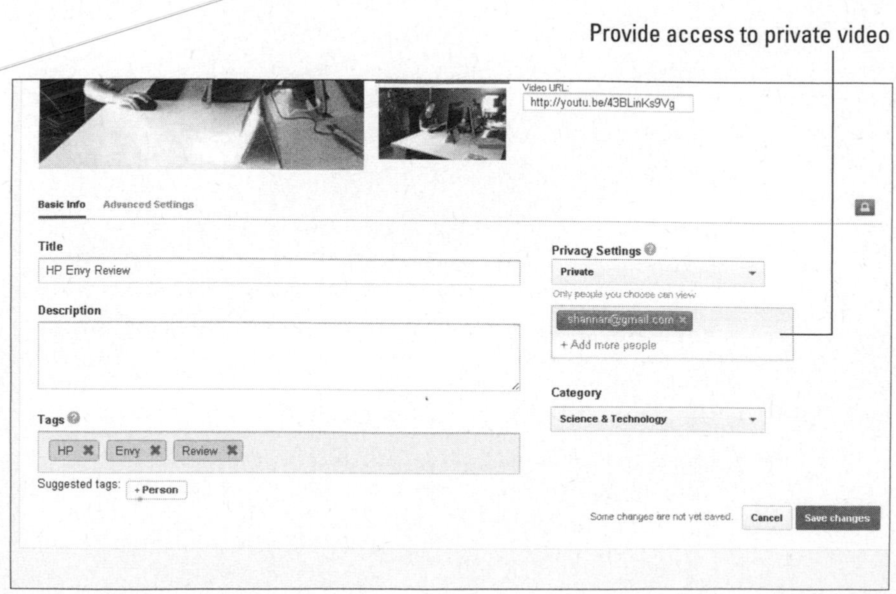

Provide access to private video

Figure 13-12:
Choose
who can
view your
YouTube
video.

Another privacy option for YouTube content is the Unlisted setting. Unlisted is different from Private in the following ways:

✔ Users don't need a YouTube account to watch the video.

✔ You can share the video with more than 50 people.

To change the privacy setting of your YouTube video to Unlisted, follow the preceding steps — but, on the Basic Info tab for your video, select the Unlisted privacy setting. (See Figure 13-13.)

Figure 13-13:
Change a
YouTube
video
setting to
Unlisted.

You can now share this video with anyone via a link. Unlisted videos

✔ Do not appear on your YouTube channel

✔ Are not listed in search results

✔ Can be shared with anyone via a link

✔ Do not appear in playlists

In addition to selecting privacy settings for individual videos, you can also change your YouTube account's default privacy setting for uploaded videos.

1. **Go to** www.youtube.com **and sign in to your account.**

2. **Click the down arrow next to your account name (upper right) and then click the YouTube Settings link below the YouTube heading. (Refer to Figure 13-4.)**

3. Under Channel Settings in the left sidebar, choose Defaults.

4. On the Upload Defaults page, you may choose to make future uploads Public, Unlisted, or Private (see Figure 13-14).

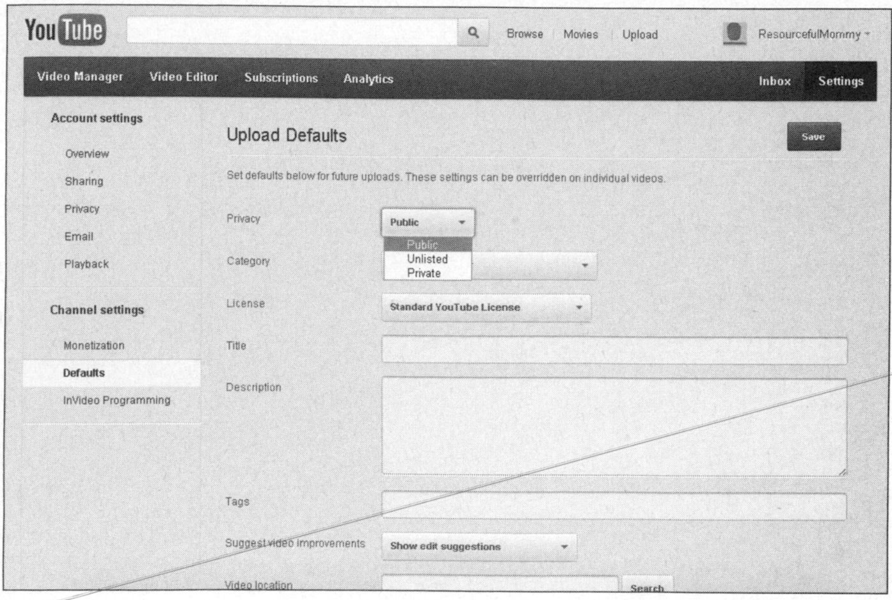

Figure 13-14: Set the default status of YouTube uploads.

Chapter 14

Blogging, Creating, and Conducting Business Online for Kids

Thanks to technology, one of the most amazing aspects of raising children in this digital age is the vast number of opportunities for kids. Kids looking for a creative outlet online may develop an interest in blogging, which could open doors for them to become web publishers, creating original content and sharing it with the world. If you decide this path could be a positive and fruitful outlet for your child, take care to protect their safety while they venture into the world of online publishing. This chapter shows you how to manage both.

Helping Your Kids Decide Whether to Blog

Before your child decides whether to launch a blog, consider the following:

Pros

- Blogging can be fun.
- Blogging provides a creative outlet.
- Blogs can be created for little to no cost.
- Blogging can help your child create a positive digital footprint.

Cons

- Blogging can become incredibly time-consuming.
- Blogging places your child in the public eye.
- Blogs can become very expensive.

Help guide your children through this decision process so that should they decide to blog, that decision will have been thoughtfully made.

Talking about their motivation

Understanding your child's motivation for launching a blog may help you decide whether to encourage their blogging. Regardless of what their motivation reason(s), help them clarify why they believe they should blog.

Here are some of the main reasons why kids elect to launch a blog:

- ✔ **Extension of their online profiles:** Most teenagers and many younger children have online profiles through some social media venue. Kids age 13 and older may participate in popular social media platforms (Facebook and Twitter), and many children also hold accounts on various social media sites created for children, such as those I discuss in Chapters 11 and 21. For these digitally savvy kids, a blog may feel like the natural next step in developing the online profile that they share with friends and followers.

- ✔ **Writing portfolio:** For the child who enjoys writing, a blog is a way to create an online writing portfolio, which they can share with anyone with just a click of the mouse.

- ✔ **Creative outlet:** Children typically enjoy creating and telling original stories, and many kids also enjoy journaling in a diary. Blogging allows the digitally connected child to create these stories and journal entries online in posts rather than simply in a notebook at home.

As I discuss in Chapter 3, kids need to be aware of the potential dangers of oversharing online.

- ✔ **Class assignment:** Today's students in a digitally connected education system often receive blog post–creation assignments in addition to standard writing assignments. These projects often involve contributing to a classroom blog (not creating individual blogs) although some schools teach, facilitate, and monitor the creation of individual student blogs. In Chapter 18, I talk about digitally connected schools in more depth.

- ✔ **Group blogging:** Just as adult bloggers now often write as part of a larger collective site — a multi-author blog (MAB) — group blogs with teen authors are appearing. Read more about blogging communities later in this chapter.

✔ **Creating of a fan site:** For some kids, blogs are an outlet to show their support of a particular sports star or celebrity. Acting like virtual walls covered in celebrity posters, fan blogs often include updates from concerts, snippets of news taken from celebrity gossip magazines, and images from around the web.

✔ **Creating a positive digital footprint:** As I discuss in Chapter 3, many colleges and employers now include a search of a teen's digital footprint in the decision-making process before offering a job or admission. Creating a blog with a place to show not only writing skills but also work and volunteer experience is one way kids can take control of their digital footprint and showcase positive aspects of their lives.

Looking at time commitments

A blog can require fairly little time beyond the initial creation period, but blogs can also become incredibly time consuming with options for customization, frequent posting, and community participation. When helping your child determine whether to blog, consider the following basic aspects of blogging and how they affect the time commitment required of bloggers.

Blog creation

Blog creation can be as simple as selecting a name and opening a free blog account by using a standard, provided blog template.

However, if your teen child wants to own her own URL (Uniform Resource Locator), or website address, rather than simply having a blog on a free platform, that means more time to purchase that URL, subscribe to a web-hosting service, and then create their blog. The first route can easily be done in a weekend, but going for a URL can take weeks, depending on the skill and knowledge level of the child.

Blog customization

Simple templates can make blogging an activity that requires little time. If your child begins to customize both the look and functionality of his blog, though, that time commitment may increase dramatically. Show your child the visual differences between a blog with little to no customization (see Figure 14-1) and one that has been personalized (see Figure 14-2). Your child might not want to really invest in time commitment and cost for the customized version.

Post creation

Some bloggers take hours to create a single post. Others write and publish posts in 20 minutes or less. Ask your child to think critically about the types of posts she would like to publish and how long it typically takes her to write those types of pieces. Then have your child consider how often she would like to post. Some bloggers post daily; others publish content only periodically.

Figure 14-1:
A basic blog with little to no customization might look like this.

Figure 14-2:
A highly customized blog can look like this.

Post promotion

Although not a required component of blogging, post promotion is the best way to get readers to visit a blog and view the content. This may include sharing the link on social media (as shown in Figure 14-3), commenting and linking on other blogs, and sharing the post link within blog communities. Young authors looking to build their audience will want to include some time for post promotion.

Responding to comments

One of the most fulfilling aspects of publishing your writing online is receiving a response from your readers. Teen publishers who have engaged an audience and allowed this audience to comment on their writing will want to set aside some time periodically to respond to those comments, as shown in Figure 14-4.

Determining costs

Blogging — like most hobbies — can be expensive to begin and maintain. However, digitally savvy kids can enjoy online creativity entirely for free. To help determine (or avoid) blogging costs before supporting your budding digital author, look at some blogging basics: everything from creating a blog name to customizing your blog platform. When discussing your child's motivation to begin blogging, also be sure to understand their expectations in order to help determine the costs associated with their blog:

✔ **Subscribing to a hosting service:** If your child chooses to blog on a free platform, the need to pay for a hosting service is eliminated. Some free platforms are Blogger and WordPress, which you can read about later in the section, "Understanding basics: From publishing to plug-ins."

For those blogging on their own platform with a unique domain name, a website hosting service is required. Hosting services are a recurring fee and typically cost between $3 and $5 per month. Read more about such services in the upcoming section, "Selecting a platform."

✔ **Purchasing a domain name:** As I mention earlier in this chapter, if your child wants to obtain and own a unique website address, or URL (mine, for example, is www.resourcefulmommy.com), she needs to buy and register that domain name through a service. Domain names are a recurring cost; they need to be renewed periodically. Read more about domain names in "Understanding basics: From publishing to plug-ins."

✔ **Procuring a site theme:** After choosing a web host and optionally securing a domain name, your child needs to download a template, or theme, on which to create their blog. Thousands of free themes are available online, but paid themes typically range from $30 to $100. This is generally a one-time cost, though.

✔ **Paying for images/graphics:** Many bloggers use their own images (uploading photos they've taken) for their blog posts. You can purchase stock photography for a blog, though, and those photos range from a few dollars to several hundred dollars per image. You can even go as far as hiring a graphic artist to create an original blog logo or image, as shown in Figure 14-5.

Custom logo

Figure 14-5:
A custom blog logo created by a graphic artist.

✔ **Hiring a site designer:** A creative teen — who even isn't particularly technically savvy — can create a basic blog. For a more complicated, self-hosted blog, you probably need the help of a site designer. The one-time cost for the creation of a website can cost anywhere from a few hundred to a few thousand dollars, depending on the requirements and characteristics of the site.

✔ **Purchasing additional blogging tools:** As I discuss later in this chapter, blogs may contain an endless list of features, from virtual bookshelves to e-commerce store fronts. A young blogger who has made the decision to devote a great deal of time and effort to the craft may eventually wish to purchase additional tools for their site.

Facilitating Your Kids' Blogging

Parents supporting their kids' blogging goals should gain a basic understanding of blogging to both guide their budding authors and also help protect their safety online. The following fundamentals provide everything you need to know to help your child get started in the blogging world.

Understanding basics: From publishing to plug-ins

The first step in creating a blog is choosing a blogging platform. You can find more detailed information about selecting a blogging platform later in this chapter. All free blog platform sites require users to be at least 13 years of age. These standards are in place partly for the safety of your children; like age restrictions on social media sites, you should not ignore the age requirements. You can also choose to pay for a self-hosted site by purchasing a domain name and registering with a hosting service. These options are explored further in the upcoming section "Selecting a platform."

Here are some main players for free blogging platforms:

✔ **WordPress.com:** `http://wordpress.com`

✔ **Blogger (owned by Google):** `www.blogger.com`

✔ **Tumblr:** `https://www.tumblr.com`

If your child would like to blog but is younger than age 13, consider creating a family blog together.

After your teen selects a blogging platform (with your guidance), it's time to choose a site name. At this point, you should consider purchasing the related domain name or URL to not only protect your teen's site name from being taken by someone else but also make sure that the name isn't already in use.

A variety of services allow you to register a domain name:

✔ **GoDaddy:** www.godaddy.com

✔ **NameCheap:** www.namecheap.com

✔ **1&1:** www.1and1.com

✔ **Network Solutions:** www.networksolutions.com

✔ **eNom:** www.enom.com

If you choose to self-host your teen's website, you likely will also be able to register the site domain through your hosting service.

Ask your teen to consider the following when selecting a domain name.

✔ What will be the focus of the blog?

✔ Will the site name make it easy for readers to find?

✔ Does the name allow the blog to grow and change with your teen?

✔ Is the name appropriate for a site owned by a teen?

✔ Would they be okay with future employers and universities locating this site?

✔ Is the name unique and not too similar to existing blogs?

If your child will be blogging on a self-hosted server (rather than a free blog platform), you will likely need to install WordPress, which is a free blogging tool and is the most popular blogging system (http://wordpress.org). (See Figure 14-6.)

The next step in creating a blog is to select a blog *theme,* which is a template that determines the appearance of the blog as well as some blog features. All blogging platforms provide users with a selection of free themes from which to choose. Users may also elect to upload and use additional blog themes, some of which are free, and some are for purchase.

Every blog theme requires users to select certain settings, including options such as allowing comments from readers. WordPress themes also allow for the installation of *plug-ins,* which are software that allows the site to perform specific abilities (such as automatically sharing new posts on Facebook and allowing readers to pin post images on Pinterest). Later in this chapter, I talk more about blog customization with themes and plug-ins.

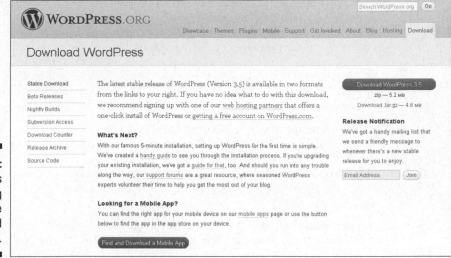

Figure 14-6:
WordPress
blogging
software
download
page.

If your teen is blogging using WordPress software, consider asking your teen to create a user account for you, complete with username and login. This will allow you to help with technical issues as well as monitor comments and content.

After your teen sets up a basic blogging platform with a name and a theme, it's time to create both pages and posts. A blog page is just a static location that typically contains information such as author biography, site purpose, and contact information. A blog post is a singular blog entry, much like a daily diary entry. Most blogs display blog posts chronologically, with most recent on top.

Selecting a platform

As I mention earlier, a variety of free blogging platforms are available. Three of the most popular are WordPress.com, Blogger, and Tumblr (see Chapter 22). If you and your teen opt for one of these free hosting services, your teen will not technically own the blog *nor the content they have written*.

Your teen can, however, start blogging on a free platform and then migrate that content to a self-hosted website should your teen choose to invest more time and money into blogging.

Another option is to select a fee-based platform that's not self-hosted. The most popular blog platform of this kind is Typepad (www.typepad.com), where you can select a plan ranging from about $9 to $30 per month. Typepad is very user friendly and provides a simple solution for bloggers just getting started who want to own their own content. However, more developers are creating tools for use with WordPress blogs than Typepad, making Typepad a somewhat more limited tool.

The third option is to purchase a URL and a hosting plan from a third party, which you pay to host your site.

Consider the following when selecting a blogging platform:

✔ **Cost:** Costs can range from completely free blogging platforms to completely self-hosted sites that require the purchase of everything from the URL to the hosting server.

✔ **Features:** Self-hosted sites provide the flexibility for users to install a full range of features through plug-ins and widgets. Widgets allow bloggers to add images and features to their sites without requiring an in-depth knowledge of blog code. Free blogging platforms provide fewer features to add. Read more about plug-ins in the upcoming section, "Considering customization."

✔ **Customization options:** Although you can modify the design of a blog hosted on any platform, it is much more difficult to do so on a site such as Blogger, which offers limited flexibility and requires the user to either have knowledge of coding — or hiring someone who does.

✔ **Ease of use:** Some bloggers prefer to have the option to highly customize their site, but with additional options comes additional complexity of use. Teens looking for most simple ease of use should consider a ready-made, free blogging platform with a limited selection of options.

Know your child's level of technical ability before selecting a blogging platform.

If your teen chooses to self-host their blog, there are many website hosts from which to choose. Some of the most popular with bloggers include the following. *Note:* Pricing changes rapidly; these prices are current as of this writing.

✔ **HostGator:** HostGator web-hosting plans begin at $3.96 per month and can be purchased at www.hostgator.com.

✔ **DreamHost:** DreamHost offers monthly plans beginning at $8.95. Visit http://dreamhost.com for more information.

✔ **Bluehost:** Bluehost plans begin at $3.95 per month and can be found at www.bluehost.com.

✔ **GoDaddy:** GoDaddy web-hosting pricing starts at $1 per month and is located at www.godaddy.com.

✔ **1&1:** 1&1 web-hosting plans begin at $0.99 per month for the first 12 months. This service can be found at www.1and1.com.

Considering customization

For many bloggers, one of the most enjoyable aspects of blogging is personalizing and customizing your blog. Sure, you can host and even customize a free blog, but there are many more options for customization on self-hosted blogs:

- ✔ **Theme:** A blog's theme acts as the template for a blog, setting visual aspects, such as number of columns, font style and size, and color schemes. With thousands of blog themes available, downloading and installing a theme is a fairly easy way to customize a blog.

- ✔ **Graphics:** All blog themes allow users to install graphics in such locations as the blog headers, as shown in Figure 14-7, as well as the blog background. Bloggers may upload photographs or other graphics through the image widgets in their blog theme to help give their site a customized look.

- ✔ **Plug-ins and widgets:** Plug-ins and widgets allow bloggers to add a variety of customized features to their sites including elements, such as search engine optimization, contact forms, spam filter, social media sharing icons, comment forms, and more. Figure 14-8 shows an example of social media sharing icons installed on a blog via a WordPress plug-in.

- ✔ **Coding:** Coding in the form of HTML (as shown in Figure 14-9) or a theme stylesheet is the language that determines the look and features of a blog. Many bloggers enjoy learning about how coding works and customizing their blogs by manipulating their blogs' coding. This can be complicated and time-consuming but is often a self-taught skill. Some bloggers hire others to customize their sites through changes to their blogs' coding.

Figure 14-7:
Example of a blog header image.

Figure 14-8:
Social media sharing icons installed on a blog via a plug-in.

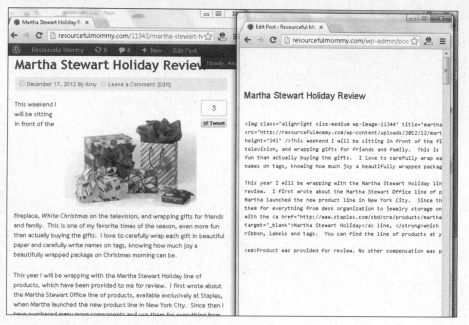

Figure 14-9:
Some teens
like to cus-
tomize a
blog by edit-
ing its HTML
underpin-
nings.

Discussing Safety Concerns

As I discuss at length in Chapter 3, the life of a digitally connected child
can be both incredibly rewarding but also risky due to the safety issues
that stem from a child creating a public profile and interacting via that
profile with strangers. Like social media accounts, blogging may place
your child in the public eye and may allow people that your child doesn't
know to both learn personal information about them as well as contact
them.

Public versus private blogging

Even if your child wants to create a blog and you're okay with that, this
doesn't mean that the blog needs to be available for anyone to see and read.
If you're not okay with "going all public," you can indeed create a blog visible
only to the author or only through invitation and approval.

Your child's motivation for blogging may help you decide whether the blog should be public or private. For example, if your child wants to blog as a way to maintain an online journal, it may make more sense for her to keep this blog private just like a child would protect entries in a diary. This still allows the child to make use of technology in her journal keeping without the dangers associated with oversharing (as outlined in Chapter 3). Your child may also consider creating a daily journal blog visible only to family members or even close friends.

For bloggers writing on the free Blogger platform, here's how to make their blog private:

1. **Sign in to your Blogger account and click the Dashboard.**
2. **Select the Settings link on the left sidebar. (See Figure 14-10.)**
3. **Click the Permissions heading and then click Edit in the Blog Readers section. (See Figure 14-11.)**
4. **Change the default Blog Readers setting (it's a radio button) from Anybody to Only These Readers. (See Figure 14-12.)**
5. **Click Save Changes.**

Figure 14-10: Managing your blog settings on the Blogger platform.

After you set your Blogger site as private, you can then share the blog with friends and family by adding their e-mail addresses to the Invite field just below the Only These Readers selection. You can also choose to keep a Blogger blog completely private. At the time of this writing, you can't share only individual posts via Blogger.

For bloggers posting using WordPress, either at WordPress.org or on a web host using a unique domain name, you can make an individual blog post public or private. For example, WordPress users can opt to do the following, as shown in Figure 14-13:

✔ Make a blog post public.

✔ Protect a blog post with a password.

✔ Make a blog post completely private.

Bloggers writing on WordPress can also install plug-ins that allow them to do the following:

✔ Make your blog completely private and visible only through a password.

✔ Keep people from accessing your blog through an RSS (really simple syndication) feed.

✔ Block search engines from indexing your blog. Allowing search engines to index your blog makes it easier for readers to find your site.

Although most blogs are public by default and provide options for users to make either a post or the blog itself private, some platforms are private by default and provide authors with the option to share individual online journal entries. One platform to create a completely private online journal is Penzu (www.penzu.com). Each individual Penzu post may be shared via e-mail or by providing a friend or family member with a unique sharing link for that post.

Figure 14-13:
Set
WordPress
post permis-
sion options.

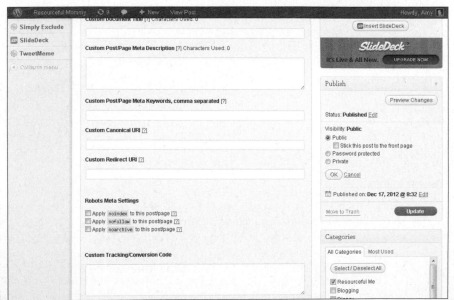

Remind your kids that anything they share online can be seen and reshared by anyone. There is no taking it back!

Creating a safe blogging profile

Bloggers typically include information about themselves somewhere on their blogs on either an About page (see Figure 14-14) or in the blog sidebar or bottom (see Figure 14-15). As I discuss in Chapter 3, help guide your kids to carefully select both the amount and type of information they share about themselves online. Kids creating a public blogger profile should avoid sharing any of the following information on their profile page:

- ✔ Full name
- ✔ Birthdate
- ✔ Home address
- ✔ School name and address
- ✔ E-mail address
- ✔ Cellphone number

Many blogger profile pages include a photograph of the blogger. Discuss with your kids what image of themselves they are promoting with the selection of their profile image. Young bloggers should avoid using profile images that make them look older or are sexual in any way. They should also be aware of any identifying information appearing in the background such as street signs or house numbers. Your kids may wish to use a photograph that does not show their face clearly or even include an image of them at all. For example, they may want to use a photo of a favorite vacation location or family pet. For more information about creating an appropriate online profile, see Chapter 4.

There is no way to keep your profile picture from being downloaded and used by anyone who can view it.

Using contact forms

Bloggers who share their writing publicly may have readers who wish to contact them outside of blog comments. They may even hear from companies hoping to purchase advertising space on the website. However, I do not advise that young bloggers share their contact information publicly on their sites.

As a workaround, choose from a variety of free tools that can be used to create a contact form on a website. A contact form, as shown in Figure 14-16, allows a blogger to receive correspondence from anyone using their site without sharing any of their personal contact information. The form collects the data from the correspondent and then e-mails it to the blogger. Most contact forms also include filters to keep spam messages from being sent to the blogger. Parents wishing to monitor any correspondence to their child can opt to have the contact form message copied to their email address or even sent only to the parent e-mail address.

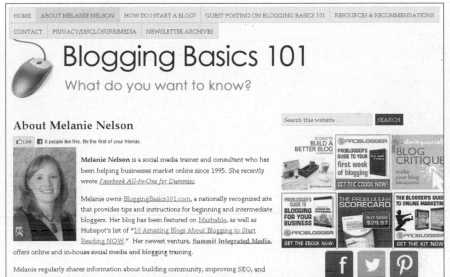

Figure 14-14: The About page on the blog hosts biographical information about the author.

Figure 14-15: Sometimes the About paragraph is located in a sidebar on the blog.

Figure 14-16:
Use contact forms on a website to help maintain privacy.

Joining Blogging Communities

At first glance, it may seem that blogging is a very isolating hobby, with teens spending hours blogging alone at their computer. However, many bloggers enjoy joining online communities where they can connect with other online authors. Not all that many active, well-maintained online communities exist specifically for teen bloggers, but here are some reasons why teens may choose to join existing blog communities:

- **Connecting with other affinity groups:** Many bloggers write about a specific topic, such as sports, photography, pets, or music. Blogging communities are a great way to connect with like-minded online writers who also cover similar topics.

- **Participating in class blogs:** Many teachers have created websites for use by their students, some including student blogs. Participation in these student blogging projects is often optional, but teens may find these classroom communities to be a safe place to practice writing skills and learn more about blogging in general.

- **Asking blogging questions:** For most bloggers, creating and maintaining a blog is a self-taught skill. Participation in blogging communities provides teens with a place to ask questions and find information on everything from the best plug-ins to install to how to change a site's coding.

- **Promoting their blog:** A common activity in most blogging communities is promotion of blog posts. Members often support one another by visiting, commenting on, and sharing blog posts of fellow members.

Blogging communities are not necessarily kid-friendly, and your teen's participation in such online communities should be monitored.

Kids as Online Entrepreneurs

Just as blogging allows kids to be self-published authors online, living in a digital world also allows kids unlimited possibilities in terms of entrepreneurship. This digital age provides kids with a unique skill set with the opportunity to share that skill with others, adding "online business owner" to the list of possible after-school and summer jobs available to kids today.

Game creation

One area where digitally savvy teens with an entrepreneurial spirit excel is in video game creation. There are a variety of online and offline courses for teens looking to learn about game creation, programming, and game development as well as summer camps for those looking for a concentrated curriculum to learn the skills needed to create video games. These camps and courses allow teens to interact with professionals in the field and develop skills that can immediately be put to use in game creation. Examples of such camps include

- ✔ Video Game Design Camp at Michigan State University

    `www.spartanyouth.msu.edu`

- ✔ New York Film Academy Game Design Camp

    `www.nyfa.edu`

- ✔ iD Gaming Academy

    `www.internaldrive.com/idga`

- ✔ Emagination Game Design Camp

    `www.computercamps.com/video/game/design_for_teens.html`

- ✔ Digital Media Academy

    `www.digitalmediaacademy.org`

If you would like to support your child or teen in exploring video game creation, you may want to download or purchase video game creation software. The following free tools are available for those interested in learning more about game development:

- ✔ **Game Maker 8:** This free development software allows users to create games with the help of tutorials and a drag-and-drop interface. Users with more experience and understanding of programming language are able to create more customization within their games. Learn more at `www.yoyogames.com/gamemaker`.

✔ **Phrogram:** Phrogram is free development software best suited for folks with some computer programming experience who like to turn those skills into game development knowledge. Phrogram also introduces computer programming newbies to the world of game creation. Phrogram isn't entirely free but does offer a 30-day free trial option. Learn more at `www.phrogram.com`.

✔ **Sploder:** `www.sploder.com` is a website allowing game creation beginners to make their own game for free. This service allows users to save games and share them with other users on Sploder. Users can also share the games they've created on their own website so that anyone can play the games.

✔ **RPG Maker XP:** This software focuses on role-playing games (RPGs). After a user has created a game with RPG Maker XP, he can share that game with any Windows PC user. Members of a highly active user community share fan sites they have created along with game creation tutorials. RPG Maker XP can be found at `www.rpgmakerweb.com`.

✔ **Pygame:** This free online tool uses a specific game creation language — Python — which is one of the easier computer programming languages to learn. To learn more, visit `www.pygame.org`.

Computer animation and graphic design

Like video game creation, the fields of computer animation and graphic design are areas where technologically savvy teens can explore career options from the comfort of their home computer. In fact, according to Fast Company (`www.fastcompany.com`), one teenage girl became a young millionaire after creating a MySpace customization service and launching her business online.

Like game creation, many programs and camps exist to support kids interested in learning more about computer animation and graphic design. Here are just a few resources available:

✔ New York Film Academy 3D Animation Camp

    `www.nyfa.edu`

✔ North Carolina State University College of Design, Design Camp

    `www.camraleigh.org/programs-education/high-school/design-camp`

✔ iD Tech Camps Game Design & Graphic Arts Hybrid

    `www.internaldrive.com/courses-programs`

- ✔ Auburn University Design Workshop

  `www.auburn.edu`

- ✔ Rocky Mountain College of Art and Design, High School Programs

  `www.rmcad.edu/nowatrmcad/programs-and-workshops`

- ✔ Digital Media Academy

  `www.digitalmediaacademy.org`

- ✔ Michigan State University 3D Graphics & Animation Camp

  `www.tc.msu.edu/3d-graphics-animation-camp`

Business owners

Just as kids can create their own blogs with just a little help from a parent, they can also create easy-to-navigate websites to showcase their skills and run an online business. A variety of sites exist for teens hoping to sell a product or service online who do want to create their own website:

Bizinate

Bizinate (formerly, Kidworth) helps young entrepreneurs start their own businesses, guiding them through everything from the financial aspects of owning a business to the logistics of setting up an online storefront. The site claims that through their site, an ambitious teen can launch a business in three minutes with no knowledge of coding, need to own a credit card, or filing of legal paperwork. With tens of thousands of users already, the Bizinate goal is to empower a new generation of entrepreneurs, starting with digitally savvy teens.

Parents of Bizinate users can create a master account for their kids, which they can run on their own, delegating aspects of the business to their child. Teens can create and manage their accounts on Bizinate. For more information, visit `www.bizinate.com`.

Etsy

Etsy is an online marketplace where users can create virtual storefronts in order to sell the crafts and items they have created. Etsy account holders must be at least 18 years of age. However, Etsy is a great way for parents to facilitate their child's budding business skills and creativity by working with them to create a family online store. Learn more at `www.etsy.com`.

eBay

Like Etsy, eBay also requires sellers to be at least 18 years old. However, this online auction site allows families to support children in selling gently used items in what amounts to a digital yard sale, giving kids the opportunity to use technology to earn money and gain basic marketing skills. Start at `www.ebay.com`.

Part IV
Left to Their Own Devices

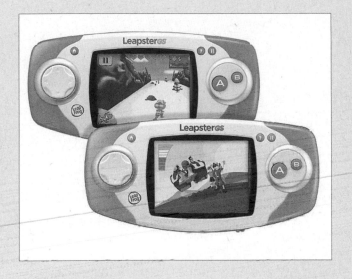

In this part . . .

✔ Meet some of the most popular handheld gaming devices created for children and learn about their features and settings.

✔ Explore tablets created specifically for children while learning how your tablet device might be suitable for the entire family.

✔ Decide when the time is right for your children to receive their first cell phone and learn how to talk to them about issues ranging from safety to sexting.

Chapter 15

Handheld Gaming

The digital world has come a long way since Game Boys and listening to cassettes on a Walkman. There are now a variety of handheld gaming consoles for children as young as four years old. Like most technology, not all handheld gaming systems are the same, each with unique features and a varied assortment of game cartridges and applications. This chapter will guide you through what you need to know when purchasing a handheld game device for your kids as well as introduce you to some of the top handheld game consoles available.

Previewing Games for Content

Regardless of the brand of any handheld game device, preview each game for content. All current devices come with a suggested age range, but that doesn't mean that every game available for the platform is also suitable for the youngest kids within that age group.

Some systems, such as the LeapFrog LeapsterGS (see Figure 15-1), come with preloaded games. Before turning the device over to your little one, though, take some time to go through each game on the device to ensure that you feel comfortable with the graphics and the language used throughout the game. Some games with age-appropriate educational points, graphics, and activities may have dialog that you don't deem appropriate for your child.

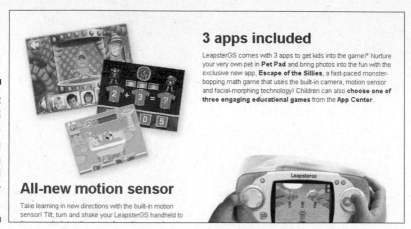

Figure 15-1:
LeapsterGS
is a hand-
held gaming
device with
preloaded
games for
children.

When purchasing additional games for the handheld devices in your home, look at the front of the packaging (or a product website) to determine the recommended age for that game. Games for VTech, LeapFrog, and Fisher-Price devices don't contain Entertainment Software Rating Board (ESRB) ratings. However, they do display the age range and learning goals for which the game was created, as shown in Figure 15-2. Consider previewing the content before sharing it with your child, just as for preloaded games.

Figure 15-2:
Look for
suggested
age ranges
and learning
goals
on game
packages.

Games created for Nintendo handheld gaming devices and Sony handheld game consoles are rated by the ESRB. Look on the front of the game packaging to locate the ESRB rating for those games.

For more information on ESRB ratings, see Chapter 6. These ratings not only tell you the suggested age group for the game, but also give you specific information about content, such as violence and sexual material.

Comparing Educational and Entertainment Games

Many handheld gaming devices are popular with children and parents because of their educational content. However, not all content created for educational handheld devices is equally instructive. Likewise, you can find educational games for entertainment-based handheld devices. The following products are included in the learning system category of handheld devices:

✔ VTech MobiGo and MobiGo 2

✔ LeapFrog LeapsterGS

✔ LeapFrog Leapster Explorer

Even after selecting a specific game console as a learning device category, you still may wish to look closely at the game description to preview the content for appropriateness. Some manufacturers of learning devices offer a "just for fun" category to identify clearly games and apps not meant to provide educational benefits, but rather simply to entertain. See Figure 15-3 for an example of this category of products for the LeapFrog Leapster Explorer.

Figure 15-3: Just for Fun titles available for learning devices.

Most learning device game cartridge packages are clearly labeled with the educational content and goals of that app (refer to Figure 15-2). Look for keywords like these:

- ✔ Rhyming, letters
- ✔ Shapes, colors
- ✔ Matching, patterns
- ✔ Counting, numbers
- ✔ Vocabulary, foreign language

The best way to locate educational games for handheld game consoles not in the learning device category is to look at both the ESRB rating as well as the game title and description. Learning games are most likely to be rated E (Everyone) by the ESRB. They will also likely include the learning objectives directly in the title — for example, *Kids Learn Music,* for Nintendo DS — and game packaging typically doesn't list learning objectives the same way as games created specifically for learning devices.

Comparing Handheld Gaming Devices

Here is an overview of current handheld game devices, including price point and recommended age range for each device.

Nintendo 3DS and 3DS XL

The Nintendo 3DS and 3DS XL (the larger screen version) both come with a 3-D screen that allows users to view 3-D features without using 3-D glasses. (See Figure 15-4.) The 3-D capability can be turned off or adjusted via its 3D Depth Slider. Each device also features a Circle Pad, motion sensor, and gyro sensor as part of the gaming interface.

Nintendo 3DS devices come equipped with the SpotPass feature, which allows for wireless Internet access, as well as StreetPass, which allows your child's 3DS device to exchange data with other 3DS systems. You can turn off both features if you don't want your child's device to connect to Wi-Fi or other devices. Each 3DS also includes a Nintendo 3DS Camera as well as access to Internet browsing.

Parental controls can be enabled on the 3DS to restrict game use by rating or Wi-Fi, 3D, and StreetPass. Prices for the 3DS and 3DS XL range from approximately $170 (US) to $200. Nintendo 3DS is recommended for kids age 6 and older.

Nintendo DS and Nintendo DS XL

Like the Nintendo 3DS, Nintendo DS handheld game consoles include a camera and Wi-Fi connectivity for Internet browsing. The Nintendo DS also allows for online and multiplayer games, which can be disabled via parental controls. The Nintendo DS is slightly smaller than the Nintendo 3DS and retails for about $100. The XL model has a bigger screen. Games for the Nintendo DS begin at a suggested age range of 4 years of age and older.

Online support for all Nintendo handheld gaming devices can be found at www.nintendo.com/consumer/index.jsp.

Sony PSPgo and PSP-3000

The Sony PSP handheld gaming devices all include built-in Wi-Fi that allows users to connect with their PS3 gaming console, read RSS feeds, browse the Internet, and make calls on the Skype platform. You can also listen to music and watch movies and television shows via the PSP game consoles. Each PSP device allows parents to set the following via parental controls:

- Game restriction according to ESRB rating
- Internet browser restrictions
- Video and TV show restrictions by rating

The PSPgo retails for about $200, and the PSP-3000 retails for about $130. Both are shown in Figure 15-5. Games for the PSPgo and PSP-3000 begin at a suggested age range of 7 years of age and older.

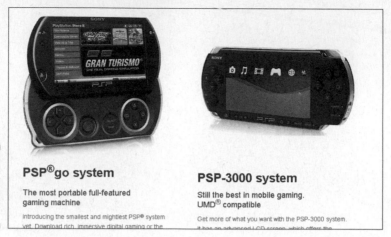

Figure 15-5:
The Sony
PSPgo and
PSP-3000.

Sony PS Vita

The Sony PS Vita is a handheld gaming system that comes in a Wi-Fi only option as well as a Wi-Fi plus 3G-connectivity option. Each handheld gaming console features a touch screen, motion sensor, cameras, GPS, and the ability to connect with the PS3 game console. The 3G connectivity unit is powered by the AT&T mobile broadband network. The PS Vita is sold at a suggested retail price of $250. Games for the PS Vita begin at a suggested age range of 8 years of age and older.

LeapFrog Leapster Explorer

The Leapster Explorer is recommended for ages 4 to 9 years and is touted to be a learning game system although it does include just-for-fun games. This device comes with preset games and videos, but also plays downloaded and cartridge-based games, videos, and e-books. The main goal of the Leapster Explorer is to provide kids with games that help them practice learning skills, such as reading, writing, math, and science.

Because the Leapster Explorer is a learning device, it includes access to an online application that allows parents to track their children's learning progress through the use of the games. Kids can also participate in a related online world, LeapWorld.

The Leapster Explorer, shown in Figure 15-6, retails for around $50.

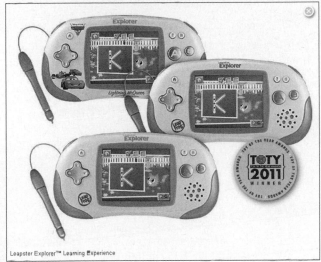

Figure 15-6:
The
LeapFrog
Leapster
Explorer.

LeapFrog LeapsterGS Explorer

The LeapsterGS Explorer (refer to Figure 15-1) includes a camera that takes pictures and videos as well as a touch screen and a motion sensor. Recommended for ages 4 to 9 years, this device comes with preloaded games and also plays downloaded and cartridge-based games and videos. Like the Leapster Explorer, the LeapsterGS focuses on learning skills, such as math, reading, and writing, and children's progress can be tracked online through the LeapFrog Learning Path.

The LeapsterGS Explorer retails for much less than its suggested price of $70.

VTech MobiGo

The VTech MobiGo handheld learning device, shown in Figure 15-7, is recommended for ages 3 to 8 years and retails for about $60. Each device comes with preloaded games and also uses downloaded and cartridge-based e-books, coloring books, an art studio, a photo album, games, and videos. The MobiGo also includes a slide-out keyboard as well as a microphone, touchscreen, and camera. Games focus on learning skills, such as math, vocabulary, spelling, reading, logic, and drawing.

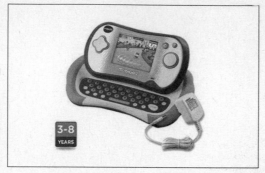

iPod touch

The iPod touch from Apple began primarily as a way to store and listen to music, but has evolved to include Wi-Fi capability, Internet browsing, camera and video capabilities, and a game center where users can download single and multi-player game apps from the App Store. There are parental restrictions available for the iPod touch that allow you to limit the types of apps and games your child may access. You can also use the parental controls to change settings, such as the ability to play multiplayer games and the use of location services. The iPod touch retails for a suggested starting price of $300.

Chapter 16

Exploring Tablets for Kids

In This Chapter

▶ Comparing kids' tablets

▶ Comparing adult tablets with kid-friendly functions

*E*very parent knows that the second you bring a digital device into your home, your kids want to check it out. (Hurray for Gorilla Glass!) Chances are that your kids are even savvier than you with everything from your smart phone to the family's home computer. Still, if you're not ready to turn your tablet over to your toddler, there are a few options for providing kids with their very own tablet device. And, there are some great applications and tablet features created primarily for adults that may keep your kids off your apps, even if they've got their hands on your tablet.

Knowing the Tablet Types

Here are four basic kinds of tablets to choose from when selecting a tablet for your children or entire family:

- **An Apple iPad:** The Apple iPad and iPad mini run on Apple's operating system (iOS) and feature games and applications downloaded from the Apple iTunes Store.

- **An Android tablet:** Barnes & Noble's NOOK and Amazon's Kindle Fire are examples of Android tablets. These tablets offer access to child-friendly e-books and downloads, but they're not created specifically for kids.

- **Android tablets for kids:** Some tablets created for children — such as the Nabi — run on an Android platform and use Android OS–based apps much like the NOOK and Kindle Fire.

- **Learning device tablets:** These tablets are created specifically for kids and use only the apps and cartridges developed specifically for them by the tablet's parent company.

The following are examples of Android tablets for kids or learning device tablets created specifically for children.

VTech InnoTab

The VTech InnoTab is a learning application tablet that features the following capabilities:

- ✔ Still camera
- ✔ Video camera
- ✔ MP3 player
- ✔ Photo view
- ✔ Video player
- ✔ "Friends" photo address book
- ✔ *Face Race* motion sensor game
- ✔ "Notes" notepad with onscreen keyboard
- ✔ Clock with stopwatch
- ✔ Calendar with stickers
- ✔ Calculator

The InnoTab also plays games purchased either in application or game cartridge form. The InnoTab includes 2GB of internal memory, but you can upgrade that to up to 32GB to store more photos, videos, and applications on the device. The tablet is designed with kids in mind, including protective silicone corners. Parents can change parental settings on this device, including using a content lock feature.

This device, shown in Figure 16-1, is designed for children between the ages of 3 and 9 years and retails at a suggested price of $80.

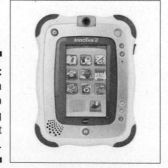

Figure 16-1:
The VTech
InnoTab
learning
tablet
for kids.

LeapFrog LeapPad

The LeapPad Learning Tablet is for children ages 4 to 9 years of age and retails for around $100. This device features the following capabilities:

- Built-in microphone
- Still camera
- Video camera
- Motion-based play
- 2GB of memory
- Story studio
- Art studio
- Animation studio
- Photo studio

Like the InnoTab, the LeapPad (see Figure 16-2) allows users to play games purchased in both downloads and on cartridges. Also, like the LeapFrog Leapster (which I mention in Chapter 15), parents of LeapPad users can track their progress on educational games by connecting their LeapPad to the online LeapFrog Learning Path.

Figure 16-2:
The LeapFrog LeapPad learning tablet.

LeapPad1
Shop Now
3-9 years

The #1 learning tablet* for kids.

*U.S. Source: #1 Learning Tablet based on the NPD Group/Consumer Tracking Service; PS Electronic Learning

Nabi

The Nabi is an Android tablet designed specifically for children. The Nabi features the following, all in a protective, easy-to-grip silicone casing:

- Microphone
- Still camera
- Video camera
- MP3 player
- Video viewer
- 8GB of expandable memory
- 2GB of free cloud storage
- Fooz Kids University (an integrated learning system)
- Nabi's Chore List
- Nabi's Treasure Box
- Spinlets+ (kid-friendly songs)
- Access to a filtered applications store
- Wi-Fi

The Nabi Android tablet, shown in Figure 16-3, retails for $200 and is suggested for kids age 7 years and older.

Figure 16-3:
The Nabi
Android
tablet
for kids.

Kurio

The Kurio is an Android tablet that allows up to eight profiles along with extensive parental control features, making it a tablet that the entire family can use. The Kurio include the following features:

- Extensive preloaded content
- Internet browsing with Wi-Fi
- Still camera
- Video recorder
- Educational apps at the Kurio Store
- An e-book reader
- MP3 player
- Touchscreen
- Microphone
- Compatibility with televisions
- 4GB storage

The Kurio Android tablet for families, shown in Figure 16-4, retails for $150.

Figure 16-4: Kurio Android tablet for families.

MEEP!

The MEEP! tablet for kids, from Oregon Scientific, is designed for kids age 6 and older. The MEEP! tablet runs on the Android platform and features the following capabilities:

- Protective silicone case
- Still camera
- Video camera

- Wi-Fi
- Internet access
- Access to applications that can be purchased with a virtual allowance provided by parents

The MEEP!, shown in Figure 16-5, is available for $150.

Figure 16-5:
MEEP! by
Oregon
Scientific.

Tabeo

The Tabeo tablet for kids runs on the Android platform and comes preloaded with more than 50 of the top applications enjoyed by kids — including Cut the Rope, Fruit Ninja, and Angry Birds — along with stories, puzzles, and more. Like other tablets on the market for kids, the available parental controls allow you to determine settings such as time limits and use times as well as create up to eight different accounts, each with different parental controls. This tablet also features the following:

- Still camera
- Video camera
- HDMI output
- Wi-Fi
- 4GB storage space
- Microphone

Although the Tabeo offers access to Android platform entertainment apps, it also comes preloaded with books and educational apps that allow kids to work on skills, such as learning the alphabet and math. The Tabeo, shown in Figure 16-6, is for kids age 5 and older and retails for $150.

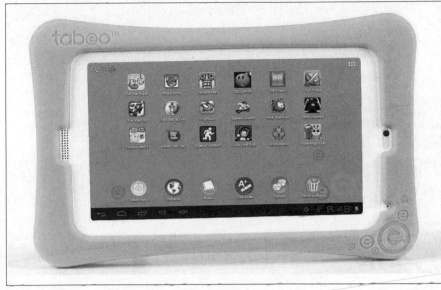

Figure 16-6:
The Tabeo
tablet
for kids.

Vinci

The Vinci tablet claims to be for children 1.5 to 9 years old and is labeled
by its owners as a "learning tablet." The games and programs on this tablet
are based on a scaffolding teaching method that encourages kids to build on
their learning in 43 learning subjects with three levels of assessment. Areas of
learning include the following:

- Thinking skills
- Emotional and social skills
- Language and literacy
- Math and logical reasoning
- General knowledge
- Science

The Vinci runs on the Android platform and includes the following technological characteristics:

- 8GB memory
- Wi-Fi
- Parental controls
- MP3 player
- Still camera

Shown in Figure 16-7, the Vinci sells for $200.

Figure 16-7:
The Vinci
tablet
for kids.

Choosing Apps and Features for Your Kids

There are tons of applications and features available for tablets. Here are some of the top applications available for children and teens on Android-based tablets, Android platform e-readers, and the Apple iPad.

Android and iPad tablets

With new apps being added to online marketplaces daily, it is nearly impossible to create a comprehensive list of family-friendly apps. However, if you're looking to turn your Android device or iPad into a family tablet, here are some applications to consider:

- ✔ **Madera & Figaro Save the Day:** This preschool-friendly story following a monkey and a frog allows kids to interact with the story as the heroes try to save the day and keep a festival from being cancelled.

- ✔ **Picasso – Mirror Draw!:** This drawing app allows kids to create symmetrical pictures and provides users with a series of both brush styles and paint colors.

- ✔ **Celeste SE:** This app allows users to capture images of the sky (with the tablet's camera) and learn more about the planets, moon, and sun.

- ✔ **Animal SnApp:** For iPad only, this application is a storybook for children that includes a slider game featuring favorite barnyard animals.

- ✔ **Star Chart:** Using your tablet's GPS, Star Chart guides your children to identify what they are seeing in the sky both in the daytime and at night.

- ✔ **UNO:** This app brings the classic card game to life on your tablet.

- **Doodle Jump:** This just-for-fun app requires users to tilt their tablets to help the Doodler jump higher and higher. This game has a multiplayer setting.

- **Toca Tailor:** This app allows your children to show off their design skills by selecting fabrics, uploading their own texture images, and creating outfits for four child models.

- **The Journals of Mama Mae & LeeLee:** This app with original music from Alicia Keys lets you explore a little girl's virtual room, write in a journal, and read interactive stories from her bookshelf.

- **Disney Creativity Studio:** This iPad-only app turns your tablet into a drawing board while teaching kids to draw some of their favorite Disney characters.

- **Spaghetti Marshmallows:** This app provides kids with physics lessons as they use marshmallows and raw spaghetti to build towers.

- **Me Books:** With one free book included, this e-book app allows you to buy books for kids, which they can read or listen to.

- **Doodle Joy:** This free Android application allows kids to draw, using more than 20 brushes with special features such as glowing neon and chalk.

- **Sweetapple:** Sweetapple applications for Android contain musical books with interactive animation.

Kindle Fire

If you own the Amazon Kindle Fire e-reader, you may be interested in a variety of applications and features that make this device incredibly kid-friendly, including

- Multiple user profiles to keep child and adult apps, movies, and books separate

- Immersion reading allows kids to listen to e-books as the words are highlighted on the page

- A wide selection of children's e-books, including many that are interactive, as shown in Figure 16-8

- Access to Amazon's library of instant videos and television shows, including many kid-friendly titles

- Access to kid-friendly Android apps, including educational games

- Capability to download graphic novels and comic books for tweens and teens

- Parental controls that allow you to change settings in areas, such as app purchasing and Internet browsing

Figure 16-8:
Interactive
e-books are
available for
the Kindle
Fire.

NOOK

Like the Kindle Fire, Barnes & Noble's NOOK series of e-readers allows children to interact with stories and more using these child-friendly features:

- ✔ NOOK Kids interactive picture books, which allow kids to read books, have books read to them, and interact with the images on the page
- ✔ Access to the NOOK Kids Store, shown in Figure 16-9, which allows you to shop for e-books and applications by age group
- ✔ Capability to download any Android application for kids
- ✔ Capability to create up to six profiles to keep books, videos, and applications separate for children and adults
- ✔ Use of parental controls to control purchases, access to content, and Internet use
- ✔ Capability to download learning tools and games for kids

Figure 16-9:
The NOOK
Kids Store
helps turn
the NOOK
e-reader
into a family
friendly
tablet
device.

Chapter 17

Being Smart with Mobile Phones

In This Chapter

▶ Deciding when to get your children a mobile phone

▶ Understanding service plan limit options

▶ Analyzing mobile phone safety concerns

Kids as young as elementary school age carry mobile phones and use technology ranging from texting to online chats. Providing your child with a mobile phone — whether a *smartphone* with advanced computing capability and connectivity or a *feature phone* with little more than voice call and text messaging functionality — may be a great way for your family to stay connected and stay safe when out with friends, at work, or attending after-school activities. The key to making mobile phones work for your family is to set clear guidelines by age group and location, focusing on each of the phone's capabilities when creating your Digital Family Policy (see Chapter 2). The following sections will help you create these guidelines, consider safety concerns, and monitor your family's mobile phones.

Determining the Right Age to Get a Phone

A study published by AT&T (www.att.com/familysafety) includes the following statistics about kids and phones:

✔ The average age for a child to receive their first mobile phone is 12.1 years.

✔ Nearly all (90 percent) of kids surveyed believe that it's okay for parents to set rules about phone usage.

✔ Nearly 40 percent of kids surveyed said that their parents have not discussed mobile phone safety with them.

And a 2012 Nielsen report claims that 58 percent of kids ages 13 to 17 years have their own smartphone.

```
www.blog.nielsen.com/online_mobile/young-adults-and-
             teens-lead-growth-among-smartphone-owners/
```

However, adding a data plan to your child's mobile phone requires an additional level of maturity beyond just call and text. Deciding on the right age to get your child their first phone will differ from child to child and family to family. You may choose to create rules based on specific situations and needs within your family rather than setting a family-wide rule by age.

To determine the right time to purchase your child's first mobile phone, consider the following questions:

- ✔ **Need to communicate:** Does your family's schedule require you to be in touch with your children regarding schedule changes such as activity pick up time and location or after school plans? Providing a child with a mobile phone allows convenient communication for busy families.

- ✔ **Safety concerns:** Do you feel like your children should have a mobile phone for safety reasons? Do they walk home from school or an activity alone? Is their bus stop out of view of your home?

- ✔ **Responsibility:** Is your child responsible enough to own a potentially expensive device, such as a smartphone? Will he lose it? Is he likely to break the phone and need it to be replaced often? Does he have a good track record of caring for other expensive devices such as handheld games or game consoles? Has he shown responsibility in other areas, such as caring for a family pet?

- ✔ **Tech-savvy:** Do you feel comfortable with your child having access to the technology that is included in a mobile phone's capabilities?

- ✔ **Rules:** Will your child follow the rules for phone use set in your Digital Family Policy (see Chapter 2)? Do you feel comfortable enforcing these rules, even if that means taking the phone away for a period of time?

- ✔ **True need:** Will your child actually use the phone? Do her friends also own phones (providing her with someone to text), or will a call-only plan suffice? Will there actually be times when your child is without adult supervision and need to contact you or be contacted by you directly?

- ✔ **Location-appropriate behavior:** Does your child understand that different settings require different behaviors and that mobile phone usage rules may differ throughout the day? For example, will your child follow a no-texting-in-school policy?

- ✔ **Alternatives:** Could your child borrow a parent's or sibling's phone during the rare occasion that he needs to have a phone?

- ✔ **Cost:** Will the family budget allow for the additional monthly cost?

During the creation of your Digital Family Policy, include a conversation about the potential need for a mobile phone.

When your child asks for his first mobile phone, find out more information about why he wants one to help you determine whether the time is right. Ask him to provide you with specifics including answers to the following questions:

- **Are you willing to sign a mobile phone use contract?** Be sure to include guidelines for phone use including time/text limits and phone etiquette in your family's contract.

- **Why do you need/want a phone?** Can your child justify asking for a mobile phone? Does she want one because her friends have them?

- **When would you like to be able to use your phone?** If your child wants a mobile phone for during the school day but your child's school has a policy that phones must be kept in lockers, perhaps there's not a justifiable reason to purchase a phone. If, however, he is asking because he would feel safer having a phone for after sporting events or after-school activities, you may want to consider honoring his request for a phone.

- **Do you want a smartphone or a feature phone?** If your child claims to only want a phone for the purpose of calling home while out with friends but then requests a smartphone, you may need to ask more questions about the intended use of the phone before making a decision.

Research the mobile phone policy at your child's school prior to making a family decision about when your child should have a mobile phone.

Choosing from call-only, kid-friendly, and prepaid phone options

If you decide that your child should have a mobile phone but he doesn't need smartphone functionality, you may want to purchase a feature phone with limited functions. Don't get "sold" that the only phones available are smartphones (like miniature, handheld computers). There are many options for parents wanting to provide their children with a bare-bones mobile phone without additional capabilities.

Many phone types are available as well as types of plans.

When selecting a phone with limited capabilities for your child, first determine whether you would like to purchase a standard phone contract or a prepaid phone plan, such as a phone with limited monthly minutes or one for which you can add minutes at a set rate per minute. Consider the following when making this decision:

- ✔ Will you save money with a prepaid plan over a contract based on the number of minutes your child will use the phone to make and receive calls?

- ✔ Will you be able to add additional features (such as text) without changing plans?

- ✔ Does your wireless provider allow you to add a child's phone for a minimal cost?

- ✔ Is it important to you to not be locked into a multiple year contract for your child's phone?

Your wireless phone service provider offers devices that don't include the data plans that come standard with a smartphone. While these phones typically include additional features (cameras and texting capability), you can indeed purchase a phone without being saddled with a texting or data plan.

Most major wireless service providers offer kid-friendly plans and parental controls.

You can also find phones and phone service plans created specifically with young children and tweens in mind. The following are examples of mobile phones and phone service plans available at the time of publishing:

- ✔ **Kajeet** (www.kajeet.com) is a pay-as-you-go mobile phone service created specifically for children. (See Figure 17-1.) You have the freedom to select a feature phone or a smartphone for your child and then link that phone to the Kajeet no-contract service. Kajeet's plan comes automatically linked to parental controls that allow you to limit the use of that phone to specific incoming calls, specific outgoing calls, and other limited functionality such as times of use. Kajeet phones also come with a GPS phone locator to help parents locate their child via their Kajeet phone. It costs as little as $4.99 per month for a child to use the Kajeet phone service.

- ✔ **Firefly** (www.fireflymobile.com), shown in Figure 17-2, sells mobile phones created specifically for children and tweens. Their phones allow kids to contact only pre-approved phone numbers and emergency numbers. Parents control what games and features their children have access to via a PIN-protected parental control. Like Kajeet, Firefly also provides mobile phone service that does not require an extended contract. At the time of this writing, Firefly provides the option to purchase either the Firefly glowPhone or the Nokia 100 for use with Firefly Mobile service.

Figure 17-1:
The Kajeet phone service for children comes equipped with extensive parental controls.

Figure 17-2:
Firefly Mobile allows children to have a mobile phone with strong parental controls and without a long-term service contract.

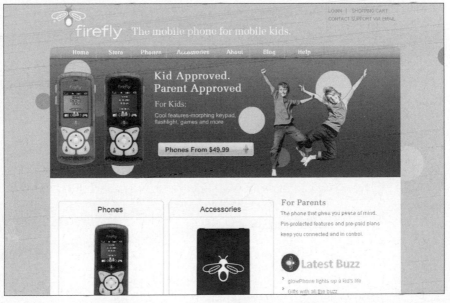

✔ **Jitterbug** (www.greatcall.com), shown in Figure 17-3, is a call-only phone from Samsung designed for users who may require a simple user experience with easy-to-understand functionality and large, easy-to-see, easy-to-press buttons. The Jitterbug service plan is provided by GreatCall, which does not require a long-term service plan. The GreatCall pay-as-you-go plan includes optional features, such as a personal calendar. This phone and plan were created with the elderly in mind, but may work well for parents who want to equip their children with a call-only, easy-to-use phone. Plans are $14.99 per month.

Figure 17-3:
The Jitterbug is a call-only phone option for parents who want to provide their children with an easy to use phone.

Deciding when to allow text, data, and applications

If you choose to purchase a phone for your child with texting and data capabilities, you need to decide the right time to allow access to these additional features. First, consider the additional cost of adding these features:

✔ Will you pay for the additional capabilities, or will your child be expected to pitch in to the cost?

✔ Will you need to pay for unlimited data? Overage charges on data plans can add up very quickly.

✔ Will your child text often enough to require an unlimited texting plan? Costs per text on most plans can also add up very quickly.

Beyond added expense, expanding the capabilities of your child's phone also brings with it added responsibility. For many tweens and teens, texting is their top form of communication, taking up a chunk of their day and requiring them to make mature decisions not only about proper use of the platform but also about boundaries. Texting can be a wonderful tool for friends and family to stay connected. It can also, however, become invasive and addictive for children who feel they must respond to friends' texts constantly, day and night. When evaluating whether your child is ready for texting, consider the following:

- ✔ Does your child need access to text messages or just want it?

- ✔ Will your child follow your family's guidelines regarding number of texts allowed and time periods when texting is permitted?

- ✔ Is your child mature enough to understand appropriate use of texting, such as what information is appropriate to share and what constitutes bullying?

Kids learn from watching their parents' behavior. Model the texting boundaries that you want your children to follow.

Remind your kids that the rules for appropriate mobile phone use extend beyond your family to include school and after school jobs and activities.

Unlike feature phones, it's difficult to make a case that a child requires a smartphone with a data plan. However, there is no denying the convenience of a smartphone with a data plan as well as the entertainment value of a smartphone with access to an endless assortment of games and applications. Many parents provide their children with access to apps through their own phones, but allowing your children to own their own smartphone is an additional level of access to the Internet and all that it has to offer, both good and bad.

Before deciding to add a data plan to your child's smartphone, consider the following questions:

- ✔ Will your child understand and follow limits for potentially expensive data usage?

- ✔ Will your child feel comfortable coming to you if she is accidentally exposed to inappropriate content or receives inappropriate contact?

- ✔ Is your child mature enough to understand how to use a smartphone safely?

- ✔ Are you ready for the added responsibility of monitoring your child's increased access to the Internet?

- ✔ Do you feel comfortable using parental controls to help protect your child from inappropriate content or overuse?

- ✔ Do the positives (such as a chance to learn responsibility and increased connectivity) outweigh the potential negatives (such as added cost and additional screen time)?

The average age when a child receives their first mobile phone is around the beginning of middle school.

Preparing your child for safe phone use

After (if) you determine that your child is old enough to have a mobile device of their own, here are some steps that you can take to help ensure safe use of the device:

✔ Include the device in your Digital Family Policy, discussed in Chapter 2. Each device's usage should be defined, such as appropriate usage, guidelines for when to share concerns with parents, and appropriate docking and charging locations.

✔ Set up parental controls prior to turning the device over to your children.

✔ Help your child select and set up a password for the device to protect your child's privacy as well as sensitive information. In Chapter 3, I talk about password protection in more depth.

✔ Add parents, other relatives, and emergency numbers to the device's contact list.

✔ Consider additional security and monitoring software, which I discuss in more detail later in this chapter.

✔ Create a mobile phone use contract with your children and include it in your Digital Family Policy. Consider including the following in your child's mobile phone contract:

- A phone curfew limiting the hours during which the phone can be used

- Guidelines concerning how phone time affects family screen time allowances

- Standards for texting etiquette, including strict guidelines regarding bullying or otherwise disrespectful or unkind behavior via the phone

- Specifics regarding answering calls from numbers your child doesn't recognize or placing calls to numbers not on an approved list of contacts

- Rules regarding downloading apps with parent permission only

- A strict "no texting while driving" and no-sexting policy (if age appropriate)

- Consequences for breaking any rule within the mobile phone contract

Smartphones and Parental Controls

Providing children with their first smartphone can be anxiety-causing for many parents, but you can find many tools available through service providers as well as additional available products to help parents protect not only their children, but also their wallets.

Comparing limit options through your service provider

Every mobile service provider offers products and services to help parents set limits and protect their children.

AT&T Mobile

AT&T Mobile offers the following options:

- **Content filter:** This free product allows users to block sites with mature content and turn off entry to mobile web searches.

- **Purchase blocker:** This free service allows you to block premium content purchases, such as games and applications.

- **AT&T DriveMode:** Available free of charge, this app sends a customizable auto-reply message to incoming texts letting them know that you are behind the wheel and can reply when it's safe.

- **AT&T FamilyMap:** This fee-based service allows parents to locate family members via your mobile device or PC. You can also set up a Schedule Check to have location information sent to you via text message or e-mail at set intervals or times.

- **AT&T Smart Limits for Wireless:** This fee-based service allows you to block specific numbers, limit purchases, set time restrictions on texting, set monthly text limits, and curb data usage.

For more information, visit www.att.net.

T-Mobile

T-Mobile offers the following safety and plan limit options:

- **FamilyWhere Locate:** This fee-based service allows you to locate any mobile device on your T-Mobile account.

- **DriveSmart:** This fee-based service detects that the mobile device is moving and directs incoming calls and texts to a messaging system.

- ✔ **Web Guard:** This free feature allows you to restrict mature web content.

- ✔ **Message blocking:** This free service allows you to block certain types of messages (such as messages from marketers or specific contacts) and avoid receiving unexpected message charges.

- ✔ **Family Allowances:** This tool allows you to set up front limits on the devices that are part of your family mobile plan.

To learn more, visit `http://family.t-mobile.com`.

Verizon Wireless

Verizon Wireless customers have access to the following tools:

- ✔ **Content Filters:** Verizon provides free filters allowing parents to only have access to content that falls within a certain ratings category.

- ✔ **Usage Controls:** This monthly fee-based service allows you to control how much data usage each member of your family is allowed to use each month. You can also use this tool to create time restrictions and set purchase limits.

- ✔ **Call & Message Blocking:** This free service allows you to block up to five phone numbers from sending texts or making calls to your child's phone.

- ✔ **Verizon Mobile Security:** This monthly fee-based service provides virus protection to your child's data-enabled mobile device.

- ✔ **Family Locator:** You can use this fee-based service to locate your children via their mobile devices using either your mobile device or your PC.

- ✔ **Network Programs & Permissions:** This free tool allows you to manage the applications on your child's phone that want to contact your child, access your child's personal information, or know your child's location.

- ✔ **Service Blocks:** This free service requires your children to receive your permission before adding apps to their mobile phone.

- ✔ **Usage Alerts:** This free service provides you with text messages and e-mail alerts when any device on your account is near to text, data, or voice limits.

Locate more information at `www.verizonwireless.com`.

Sprint

Sprint provides the following options to wireless users:

- ✓ **Sprint Guardian:** This fee-based service allows you to determine a family member's location and set mobile controls.

- ✓ **Sprint Family Locator:** Sprint Family Locator provides interactive maps to help you locate your children through their mobile devices. This is a fee-based service.

- ✓ **Sprint Mobile Controls:** This fee-based service provides you with a dashboard to monitor your child's phone usage and set limits by time of day and day of the week.

- ✓ **Account Controls:** This is a free service for Sprint customers that allows you to block or allow settings by device.

- ✓ **Sprint Drive First:** This fee-based app blocks phone usage if it detects motion more than 10 mph.

- ✓ **SMS and mobile ad controls:** This free service allows you to keep unsolicited text messages from being sent to your child's phone.

For more information, visit www.sprint.com.

Parental controls available by mobile device platform

Phones operating on both the Android operating system (OS) and Apple OS (iOS) have parental controls that can be activated prior to turning the phone over to your child.

To enable parental controls on your iOS device, take the following steps:

1. **Tap Settings.**

2. **Select General.**

3. **Select Restrictions and then tap Enable Restrictions.**

4. **Create a Restrictions Passcode.**

   You're asked to re-enter your passcode before accessing the Restrictions area.

After you enable parental controls and create a passcode (see Figure 17-4), you can control content, access to apps, privacy settings, and so on, including the following:

- ✔ Restrict access to applications and features on the phone including web browsing, installation of apps, and the phone's camera.

- ✔ Prevent specific content types including by rating.

- ✔ Block changes to the phone's privacy settings, including contacts, calendars, and location services.

- ✔ Prevent changes to account settings, such as contacts and volume limit.

- ✔ Restrict Game Center features, such as access to multiplayer games.

Figure 17-4:
Locating
parental
controls on
iOS phones.

Android devices aren't equipped with full system restrictions, but they do allow parents to set limits on app purchases. To enable these controls, take the following steps:

1. **Choose the Google Play Store icon, as shown in Figure 17-5.**

   The Play Store Settings page appears.

2. **Scroll down to User Controls.**

Figure 17-5:
Locating
the Google
Play appli-
cation on
the Android
menu.

3. **Select Set or Change PIN, and then create a PIN. (See Figure 17-6.)**

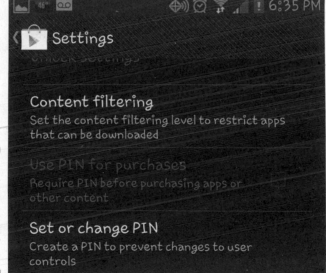

Figure 17-6:
The User
control
menu within
the Google
Play
application.

4. **Press OK.**

5. **Activate the PIN by selecting Use PIN for Purchases.**

Using monitors and restrictions for content and usage amounts

If you want more control or monitoring options for your child's mobile device consider purchasing parental control software or applications. You can find programs to monitor and control usage, block content, and locate your children through their phones.

None of the software that I mention here replaces having honest and frequent discussions with your kids about responsible and safe phone use. If used, these tools should be partnered with open communication with your children rather than replacing conversation. The best way to know what your kids are doing on their mobile devices is to talk with them.

These software tools can help you track or limit mobile phone use:

- ✔ **PhoneSheriff** allows parents to block functions according to time of day, track the mobile device via GPS, block communication with certain numbers, and record all text messages and phone calls. Learn more about this tool at www.phonesheriff.com.

- ✔ **Mobistealth** allows you to access your child's location in real-time as well as through a historical tracker, record calls, listen live to calls, access an activity log, view web history, and view contact details. Mobistealth is located at www.mobistealth.com.

- ✔ **My Mobile Watchdog** features location tracking, the ability to, via text messages, block any application (such as the phone's camera), block specific websites, and set time limits. Find this parental control app at www.mymobilewatchdog.com.

- ✔ **Mobile Spy** allows you to track location, record calls and texts, and restrict applications. Mobile Spy also allows you to record social media activity, such as Facebook messages. Mobile Spy software is located at www.mobile-spy.com.

- ✔ **Everstealth** records phone calls, tracks phone position, records web history, monitors contact lists, logs text and other messages, records images taken and received, and provides access to all social media communication on the device. More information regarding Everstealth software is located at www.everstealth.com.

- ✔ **eBlaster Mobile** allows parents to view transcripts of text messages, view web history, block content, track location, and log phone history. Visit www.spectorsoft.com for product information.

- ✔ **SpyBubble** gives parents the ability to track calls, read text messages, track location of the mobile device, see phone contact information, log e-mail, view web browser history, and view all photos being taken with a mobile device. This software is available at www.spybubble.com.

Mobile Phone Safety Concerns

Many parents think about mobile phones and safety together because chances are that they purchased a mobile phone for their children for safety reasons. Although having the ability to call emergency services and stay in touch with parents while out with friends are some of the positives of mobile phone ownership, several safety concerns arise with mobile phone use.

GPS and your children's privacy

I cover the potential dangers of GPS in Chapter 3. Enabling GPS on your child's phone allows you to locate your child via their mobile phone, but it also allows applications, services, and potential predators to locate them.

If you and your child choose to keep the GPS function activated on mobile phone, consider asking your teen to opt out of allowing applications — such as Facebook and Twitter — to access this function. Applications that allow your teen to check in at specific locations publicly alert strangers to your child's current location. Some programs even allow friends to post your child's location without your child's permission.

Consider the following:

- ✔ Talk to your children often about privacy settings on their phones.

- ✔ Create specific rules about location services on apps that allow strangers to find them.

- ✔ Ask your children not to download applications that provide location access to Friend lists.

- ✔ Ask your children to remove location from online social media posts, such as those on Facebook and Twitter.

Texting and driving

A 2012 study by the University of Michigan found that more than 25 percent of teens admitted to reading or sending a text message while behind the wheel, making them far more likely to be in an accident.

```
www.ns.umich.edu/new/releases/21000-driver-distraction-
         do-as-i-say-not-as-i-do-or-what-you-think-i-do
```

You can place apps on your child's phone to help prevent them from texting and driving, but be sure to talk to your children about the danger of texting and driving. Be sure to include rules about texting and driving within your Digital Family Policy, such as the following:

- ✔ Ask your teens to sign a pledge to never text while at the wheel.

- ✔ Ask your kids to ask their friends not to text while driving while they are in the car.

- ✔ Create and enforce consequences for texting while driving.

Kids watch you to know what behavior is appropriate. If you don't want your kids to text and drive, make sure that you aren't texting while driving, either!

Talk about texting and driving with your children as soon as they receive their first mobile device rather than waiting until they are also old enough to drive. Consider the following talking points when having this discussion:

- Be clear with them about the potential consequences of texting behind the wheel including serious and possibly deadly accidents.

- Point out that texting while driving is illegal in many states.

- Include consequences for texting and driving in your child's mobile phone contract.

- Ask your kids to take a pledge to never text and drive, such as the It Can Wait pledge found at `http://itcanwait.com`. (See Figure 17-7.)

- Discuss ways to avoid texting and driving, such as the use of apps and choosing an out-of-reach phone storage location in the car.

Figure 17-7: AT&T's It Can Wait pledge prompts kids to pledge not to text and drive.

The AT&T DriveMode, T-Mobile DriveSmart, and Sprint Drive First applications that I mention earlier in this chapter will help your teens stick to their pledges to never text and drive. Here are some other ways to use technology to protect your children from some of the dangers technology brings:

- **DriveOFF:** This Android app (found at Google Play) from Esure can detect when the mobile device has reached a speed of more than 10 mph and will disable any potentially distracting apps as well as incoming texts and calls.

- **TextBuster** (`www.textbuster.com`): This system requires parents to install a device on their teen's car and an app on their teen's phone. Text messaging, e-mail, and Internet access then become disabled when the car is moving. Phone calls, however, can still be received, and GPS applications will still work.

- **DriveScribe** (`http://drivescribe.com`): This free app blocks text messages and incoming calls when the owner's car is in motion. It also tells drivers to slow down if they are going too fast, and creates a report for parents to show if the teen exceeded the speed limit while driving.

- **Canary** (`http://thecanaryproject.com`): This free application allows parents to see whether their children used their phone while driving more than 12 mph. This app also sends parents an alert if it has been disabled by the teen.

- **DriveSafe.ly** (`www.drivesafe.ly`): This application reads text messages and e-mails aloud and responds without the need for drivers to touch their mobile phones.

Talking to your children about sexting

According to the Pew Research Center (see link below) *sexting* — sending a sexual text message with or without a photograph — affects at least 15 percent of teens; that is, they've received this type of message via their mobile phone.

```
www.pewinternet.org/Reports/2009/Teens-and-Sexting/
        Overview.aspx
```

Snapchat and sexting

One of the key messages throughout this book is that parents need to explain to their children that after you share an image digitally, *you can never take it back.* The application Snapchat has changed that, and unfortunately, some teens are taking advantage of the app to send inappropriate pictures to people in their contact list. Snapchat is a photo-sharing app that allows the user to take a photo and share it with friends. What makes this app unique is that moments after the picture is shared, it disappears completely. However, some users have found ways to save the photos sent to them through a screenshot and similar methods. The message for kids? Even with Snapchat, assume that anything you send digitally may be captured and shared with others.

In Chapter 3, I talk about the dangers of participating in sexting, including possible legal consequences. Parents need to talk frankly with their children about sexting before providing them with access to a phone that supports text. When talking with your children about sexting, consider covering the following:

✔ Discuss the rules regarding sexting in either your Digital Family Policy or mobile phone contract including consequences if your teen sends an inappropriate text or picture.

✔ Create a plan for what your child should do if he receives a sexting message from someone.

✔ Remind your children not to delete messages sent to them that may be inappropriate, especially those from people they do not know. These messages may be needed should you need to report inappropriate or potentially dangerous behavior.

✔ Discuss the consequences of sexting ranging from hurting another person emotionally to breaking sexting or even child pornography laws.

✔ Remind your kids that after they send an image, they have no control over who sees or shares that image.

✔ Encourage your children to feel comfortable coming to you if they feel pressure to participate in this type of behavior.

Part V
Utilizing Online Family Resources

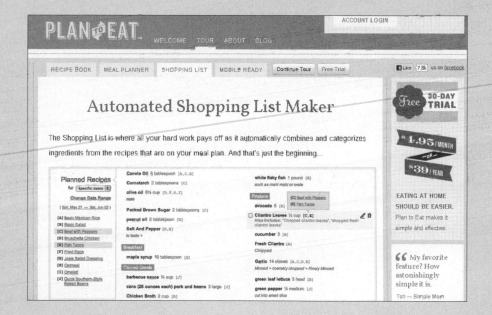

Find more about how educational websites can boost your child's school performance at www.dummies.com/extras/raisingdigitalfamilies.

In this part . . .

- ✔ Explore educational sites that support your children's learning while also entertaining them.

- ✔ Discover a wealth of online tools to help parents organize all aspects of modern parenting.

Chapter 18

Reading, 'Riting, 'Rithmetic — Online?

In This Chapter

▶ Determining the educational value of sites for kids

▶ Encouraging appropriate use of online sources

▶ Using online courses

▶ Understanding the digital role of your traditional school

Raising digital natives means raising kids who have unprecedented access to online resources for everything from education to entertainment. One of the challenges of raising a digital family is evaluating the constantly changing online world for both safety and appropriateness — which, when it comes to online education, can be especially challenging. Sites may claim to provide educational content to your children when really their purpose is to simply entertain or even advertise to your children. This chapter takes a look at ways to valuate online content for educational value as well as understanding the role that the digital world plays in your child's school life.

Determining the Educational Value of Learning Websites

There are scores of educational websites with great content and fun tools for kids. Here are just a few that your children may enjoy:

✔ **Starfall** (www.starfall.com): The focus of this site for children preschool age and older is to learn to read. The site is free of advertising and provides material appropriate for various learning stages.

- **GridClub** (www.gridclub.com): Aimed at elementary school age kids and older, this fee-based site covers a variety of curriculum areas including math, reading, and science.

- **Sesame Street** (www.sesamestreet.org): This site is great for toddlers and preschoolers learning basics, such as numbers, shapes, colors, and letters.

- **BrainPOP Jr.** (www.brainpopjr.com): BrainPOP requires a subscription for kids to use it. The main target of this website is children in lower elementary school.

- **Funbrain** (www.funbrain.com): This educational site is a sister site to the popular online world, Poptropica. Unlike Poptropica, Funbrain provides educational games that build on the skills your child is learning in elementary school.

- **ZiggityZoom** (www.ziggityzoom.com): ZiggityZoom was created for kids preschool age and older and focuses on reading, coloring, drawing, and other printables and crafts.

- **PBS Kids Play!** (www.pbskidsplay.org): This site for preschool kids and older is advertisement-free and covers topics from shapes and colors to reading and math for older children. There is a $9.95 per month subscription fee for the use of this site.

- **Ready to Learn Reading** (www.pbskids.org/read): The goal of this site, which is funded by the U.S. Department of Education, is to help kids develop core reading skills and reading readiness.

- **ABCya** (www.abcya.com): Kids hoping to find practice for math and reading skills they are learning in school will enjoy ABCya.com. The content is organized by grade level making it easy for kids and parents to know that they are spending time in the right area of the site.

- **National Geographic Kids** (www.kids.nationalgeographic.com): This site provides kids with fun factoids and interesting articles about topics ranging from geography to science. There are also games, puzzles, and quizzes for elementary school–age kids.

However, unlike the preceding sites, anyone can create a website with a clever, educational-sounding name and claim to provide a resource to students. So how do you know which websites are both safe for your kids and worthwhile?

Monitoring for difficulty level and content

One of the best places to begin when evaluating the educational websites your children would like to use is to take a close look at the difficulty level and content. Take a look at the sites that your child frequents and ask the following questions:

✔ **Who is the educational authority behind the site?** Many online learning and educational game sites claim to provide worksheets and games by grade or ability level. However, who is determining the level of the content posted? Look for websites from trusted educational authorities, such as state teaching associations, departments of education, and well-known child development experts (such as PBS).

✔ **Is the site monitored and updated?** Avoid sites with outdated content. If the site contains a current topics or news section and none of the items are current, this is a good hint that perhaps the site's content is not up to par.

✔ **Is there a variety of content, or will your children quickly reach the site's maximum potential?** Some sites contain two or three fun games or applications but no other additional content with increasing difficulty level.

✔ **Is the site accurate and well written?** Read through some of the content and check for accuracy. If you find discrepancies in anything from spelling to math problem answers, you know that the educational value of the site is low.

✔ **Is the site's appearance professional and is navigation easy?** Although many educational sites may not appear as "clean," uncluttered, and professional as websites aimed at an adult audience, it is still important that they appear clean and easy to use for your children to get the most out of them.

Ask your child's teacher for a list of recommended websites. Your teacher will know your child's ability level better than anyone and can likely recommend age- and ability-appropriate sites.

Many websites aimed at children contain a section specifically designed for parents. The best sites will use these sections to explain the sources of their online content as well as their credentials. For example, Figure 18-1 shows a popular children's reading site, www.starfall.com. This page of the site explains to parents that the site's research-based methods are modeled after the National Institute of Child Health and Human Development.

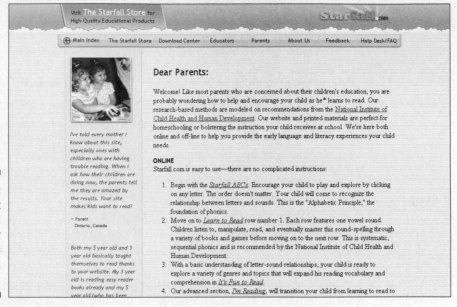

Figure 18-1:
The parent
page on
the popular
children's
website,
Starfall.

Watching for advertising

Advertisers know that online education sites are a great way to access children. When evaluating which websites are appropriate for your children, look at a variety of pages of content to watch for advertising aimed at your children. Ask the following questions:

✔ Does the site include pop-up ads?

✔ Does the site include *advertorial* (an advertisement in the form of an editorial) and sponsored content within the educational content?

✔ Does the site contain advertisements that are not in line with the target age of the content?

Ideally, you want to find sites with as little advertising as possible with clear delineation between educational and advertising content.

One way to avoid advertisements aimed at your children while they are learning online is to select sites with a subscription fee — fees, not ads, cover site expenses.

In Chapter 9, I cover online advertising to children, including how to spot advertisements hidden in special content.

Observing the graphics and sounds

The first aspects of a site that you will notice are the graphics and sounds. Many educational sites and games use animation and other graphics to engage your children in learning. Likewise, sites often use music and other sounds as part of their learning tools. However, the best educational sites will find an appropriate balance between engagement and distraction. Spend some time at the site that your child wants to use to see whether the graphics and sounds used are appropriate or likely to simply overwhelm your young student.

Researching listed source information

As I mention earlier, many quality educational sites for children include lists of sources, regulating bodies and organizations with which they are associated, and information about author credentials. Some sites, such as National Geographic Kids, enjoy a brand recognition that immediately lets parents know the site is associated with a respected educational authority that provides educational and interesting content.

Most sites for kids, however, aren't associated with an educational authority. To help determine whether a site your child enjoys is educationally sound, look for an About page or similar link to content sources and site ownership. Because this content exists for the comfort of parents (rather than the enjoyment of kids), links to resources, sources, and site ownership are often found at the bottom of the site's main page.

Then, you can try to research the organization to find out whether it is a trusted authority. Wonderopolis, for example, shares on its About page that the site is funded by philanthropic partners and created by the National Center for Family Literacy (NCFL; www.famlit.org). At the NCFL website, you can see that NCFL is a well-established literacy authority that uses volunteer hours of certified teachers.

If you can't locate information about educational and research sources — or even site ownership or sponsorship on a site that your children would like to visit — you may want to suggest that your children visit a different site instead.

Parent information on children's websites may seem hidden because the site's audience is the child, not the adult. You may need to scroll to the bottom of the page and click various links before finding parent resources and privacy policies.

Educational Resources: Talking to Kids about Credible and Crediting

Kids as young as preschool age can benefit from visiting learning websites and downloading apps for entertainment and, through drills and games, gain educational substance and skills (such as identifying colors). Although you may think of educational sites and skill-building apps first when you consider the "Internet and learning," many elementary and high school students rely on the Internet as a resource tool, turning to search engines for help when writing papers and creating presentations.

Helping children differentiate between resource sites

The Internet is an amazing resource for students, providing access to information that previously could be found only during a visit to a library, if that. Of course, because there are just as many inaccurate sources available online as accurate, helping your kids locate the most reliable sources and distinguish between useful and untrustworthy sites is important.

Ask your children to answer the following questions when searching for information online:

- **Does the site contain user-generated content?** Sites such as Wikipedia are populated with content created and submitted by users, who are (in many cases) not authorities on the topic.

- **Does the site reference primary sources?** Even websites that contain opinion pieces or secondary sources should reference and share primary sources that act as the basis for the other information on the site.

- **Is the site up to date and current?** Check whether the site includes dates for when the content was created as well as revision dates. If it's difficult to decipher whether the information is updated or outdated, it's time to walk away.

✔ **Is the site professional in its presentation?** Show your kids how to recognize and avoid sites containing glaring spelling and grammar errors, links that don't work, clutter, and lack of organization.

✔ **What is the purpose of the site, and who funds or created the site?** See whether its purpose is to provide information or to persuade. Sites meant to change opinions will likely present only one side of a story, and sometimes separating fact from opinion may be difficult.

✔ **Who are the site authors?** Just as you should check for credentials and affiliations when evaluating an educational website, always check author credentials and affiliated groups when evaluating online sources.

✔ **What is the URL?** Look for online addresses ending in `.edu` (affiliated with educational institutes) and `.org` (typically affiliated with organizations) and `.gov` (the government). Online businesses typically use `.com` and `.net`. Be sure to research the organization associated with the site.

Teaching kids proper crediting of online sources

A survey from *Education Week* (`www.edweek.org`) found that more than one-half of high school students surveyed admitted to copying and pasting directly from the Internet when completing assignments. Surely the Internet is a fantastic resource for students, but kids need to know how to cite all sources correctly, including Internet sources. Your kids will hopefully learn these guidelines in school, but take the time to reinforce these rules when helping your kids with their homework.

Some resource sites — such as World Book (`www.worldbook.com`) — provide students with a proper citation for their web page that can be copied and pasted into a student bibliography.

Your child might be asked to format references according to MLA (Modern Language Association) style (`www.mla.org`) or even possibly APA (the American Psychological Association; `www.apastyle.org`).

Remind your kids that they need to cite online sources, and properly.

Ask your child's teacher for a list of recommended and school-approved resource sites.

The following sites are a great start when looking for online research options for students.

- **KidsClick!:** `www.kidsclick.org`
- **World Almanac for Kids Online:** `www.worldalmanacforkids.com`
- **World Book Encyclopedia:** `www.worldbookonline.com`
- **Internet Public Library – Kidspace (ipl2 For Kids):** `www.ipl.org/div/kidspace`
- **Library of Congress American Memory Project:** `www.memory.loc.gov/ammem/index.html`
- **National Geographic Kids:** `www.kids.nationalgeographic.com/kids`
- **BrainPOP:** `www.brainpop.com`
- **Fact Monster:** `www.factmonster.com`

Discovering Online Learning

Just as the world of education has merged with the online world in the form of educational websites for kids and online sources for students, the Internet has also entered the classroom. Traditional schools have integrated technology into their classrooms, and some institutions have even taken their courses online.

Evaluating online courses

The increase in availability of online courses makes it possible for teens to gain high school and college credit from home, often replacing basic requirements, such as summer school and general education classes. The problem for the digital family, however, is determining which courses are the most appropriate in a sea of options.

The best place to begin in selecting an online course is your child's school. Most guidance departments and college advisors can point you in the right direction in the selection of the online educational institution as well as the selection of the most appropriate course.

Also consider the following when choosing online coursework:

- ✔ **What company or educational institution is offering the course?** Many accredited colleges and universities also offer fully accredited online coursework. Selecting classes from respected and recognizable educational institutes provides you the assurance that the online course is legitimate. Likewise, many online universities have established themselves over time as respected and accredited sources for online coursework. Be sure to research how long the organization has existed, what affiliations they can boast, and what accreditations they hold.

- ✔ **Will the course fulfill a class requirement?** Many students take online courses to fulfill a requirement necessary for graduation or to achieve a degree. Be certain to confirm with your child's school that the chosen online course actually fulfills that requirement before registering and paying for the course.

- ✔ **Does the institution hold a regional or a national accreditation?** Accreditation simply means that the school has been evaluated by regulating bodies and education authorities stating that the school is offering quality coursework. Some schools choose to seek accreditation from one of six regional accreditation agencies, all of which are recognized by the U.S. Department of Education as well as the Council for Higher Education Accreditation. National accreditation is generally based on the type of school (such as distance or technology learning) rather than on the geographical location of the school. Some programs also seek specialized accreditation, such as medical and law programs. Accreditation may be a concern if your child wishes to transfer credits in the future or apply online coursework to a degree program.

- ✔ **Will your child have access to a teacher or professor?** Some students thrive when given the opportunity to complete coursework online, but many students need the supervision and structure of a traditional classroom setting. Before enrolling your child in an online course, find out what access your child will have to their teacher including how your child's questions will be answered and what progress checks are standard during the course of the classwork.

Check with your child's school before selecting an online course. Ensure that the course will count toward a diploma or degree.

Recognizing the digital role of your traditional school

Many schools have integrated technology and the Internet into their daily routines. Elementary teachers often use educational websites to provide extra practice of skills they're teaching in class and sometimes even require use of these sites as part of homework assignments. Many classrooms are also now equipped with SMART Boards (`http://smarttech.com/smartboard`), which are interactive white boards that help teachers create dynamic lessons that integrate technology.

Chances are that your child's school may expect a certain level of technological understanding from you as the parent of one of their students. Some examples of this may include

- Communication with teachers via e-mail
- Placement of the class syllabus online
- Announcement of school-wide messages on a listserve, website, or password-protected school forum
- Communication in the case of emergencies via text or online message
- Access to class-wide projects online
- Use of the Internet for homework assignments
- Reading of parent newsletters online or in PDF rather than paper
- Use of school-provided devices

Device usage in schools

In Chapter 5, I talk about school technology use policies, encouraging you to locate the policy for your child's school. Similarly, in Chapter 17, I discuss finding out whether your child's school allows mobile devices on property before sending your child to school with a cellphone. Some schools are now implementing a BYOD (bring your own device) policy because as they implement technology in daily instruction more and more, school are often also facing budget concerns. So, some schools now ask kids to bring their Internet-enabled devices (from smartphones to laptops) to school with them.

If your child's school has implemented a BYOD or similar program, be sure to find out what the school's policy is regarding the device throughout the day. Is your child allowed to keep that device with them all day or only in certain classrooms? Is your child allowed to use that device all the time or only during certain lessons?

Some schools do have the budget to provide students with tablets and laptops to use in class or to check out from the school library or computer lab. If your child's school allows students to borrow devices, find out answers to the following questions:

- ✔ How long is your child allowed to borrow that device?
- ✔ What is the charge for returning the device late?
- ✔ Who is responsible for the replacement of the device if something happens to it on school property?
- ✔ Who is responsible for the replacement of the device if something happens to it while the child is using the device at home?

Connecting with your child's classroom online

Many teachers use technology not only in lesson planning but also when giving those lessons as well as communicating with parents and students outside the classroom. Just as parents are expected to keep track of school calendars and school requirements for everything from paperwork to immunizations, many schools now expect parents to facilitate their child's access to online materials and information.

Most school systems now allow parents to check their children's grades online. Be sure to inquire with your child's school.

And school websites are one common place where traditional schools have moved into the digital age. Many schools now use a website to communicate with the parent community, including posting policy changes and school calendars (see Figure 18-2), and many teachers also maintain websites for the following:

- ✔ Posting curriculum or the class syllabus
- ✔ Maintaining a classroom calendar with assignment deadlines
- ✔ Taking and responding to student questions
- ✔ Hosting interactive class-wide projects
- ✔ Posting password-protected access to grades and progress reports
- ✔ Highlighting student work
- ✔ Sharing supplementary content or extra credit activities

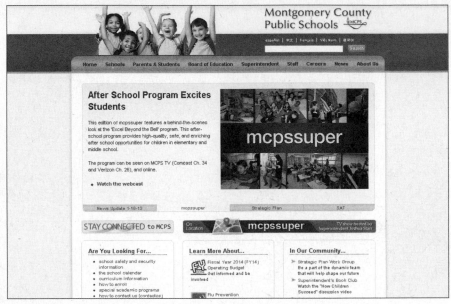

Figure 18-2:
One example of a school system website with parent resources.

Another online location where teachers can connect with students and parents is Edmodo (www.edmodo.com). This platform allows teachers to manage their classroom online — everything from assignments to grades — via a password-protected website. And students can interact with their classmates and their teacher within their teacher's Edmodo community.

Your traditional school may be more tech-savvy than you realize! Connect with your children's teachers to find out how they are using technology to teach the "digital natives" in their classrooms.

Chapter 19

Managing Your Family with Digital Resources

In This Chapter

▶ Using digital resources to manage your family's daily life

▶ Planning meals with the help of online tools

▶ Stocking the family pantry via technology

▶ Following an online family budget

Raising a family in the digital age brings with it challenges that are constantly changing, forcing parents to stay up to date with the current technology and potential dangers. However, as a parent or caregiver, you can find an amazing wealth of resources to not only help you raise your children but also manage nearly every aspect of your daily life.

Orchestrating Life

Online tools and downloadable apps are available for everything from potty training to chore chart creation. Some resources specialize in one particular area of family management, and many others help with a variety of needs within one site or application.

The following are a snapshot of the types of online tools available for parents, highlighting some of the ways how this digital age has made parenting easier than ever:

✔ **Springpad** (www.springpad.com) enables families to create online notebooks where they can collect everything from favorite recipes to family photos. Rather than simply collect your information, this digital tool's enhanced capabilities include other features, such as a map to a favorite restaurant or show times for a movie the family wants to see. What makes Springpad and similar services great for families is your ability to share your notebooks with friends and family. Parents can collaborate on family vacations or projects and access them anywhere via the Internet.

✔ **Remember the Milk** (www.rememberthemilk.com) helps the digital family organize lists and projects, which enables families to create and organize tasks. You can use this app to create task lists from bill paying to child pick-up as well as add tools you need to make those tasks easier (such as maps to task locations). You can share the task with other family members and share duties as well as prioritize jobs and add tasks to shared family calendars.

✔ **Intuition, Mom's Assistant** bills itself as a "personal assistant for moms," helping moms to organize everything from to-do lists to wish lists. This family management app doesn't focus on simply one area (say, grocery lists or tasks) but allows you to integrate as many aspects of your life as you choose by offering an Everything Else category. Users can sync with existing iCal or Google calendars. You can read more about this app at www.iconapps.com.

✔ **Cozi** (www.cozi.com) is another app that chooses to tackle every aspect of family management rather than focusing on simply one area. With the Cozi app, you can manage your family's calendar, which your entire family can access, sending appointment reminders and even getting week long agendas delivered to family inboxes. Cozi also allows you to sync your Cozi calendar to other calendars, such as Microsoft Outlook or Google Calendars. This online organizer offers

- Family calendar

- Shopping lists

- To-do lists

- Family journal

- Meal planner

✔ **AboutOne** is a family management system that not only helps you organize your online task lists and calendars, but also provides you with a way to organize offline information, such as pet records, receipts, and car maintenance. Unlike some other family management products, AboutOne uniquely focuses on its incredibly high level of security assurance, helping digital families reduce paper clutter by storing paperwork and receipts in a safe and secure online location. AboutOne offers a complete system for families looking to move beyond a shared family calendar and task lists to actually digitize every aspect of their lives. You can find more about AboutOne at www.aboutone.com.

✔ **Famundo** (www.famundo.com) is a free service to help simplify family schedules. This online calendar service provides a social network of sorts for families, allowing you to send messages to family, friends, and anyone connected to your family hub. You can use Famundo to upload and share photos, lists, and blogs with family and friends while also creating and sharing a schedule. Famundo also offers services to organizations (such as schools and churches), but the tools included in the service are very useful to busy families trying to stay connected online.

✔ **Famjama** is very similar to other online family management tools that enable you to create and share shopping lists, schedules, and to-do lists. Famjama, found at `www.famjama.com`, enables you to connect existing online calendars as well as e-mail accounts, making it easy to share calendar events and message your entire family via the service. A unique feature of Famjama is its connection to a coupon service, allowing you to add items to your shopping list and locate related coupons all from one app.

✔ **Google Calendars** (`www.google.com/calendar`) is a free service with which you can create calendars linked to your Google account. You can share individual calendars with family members as well as receive calendar notifications on your mobile device. You can also provide editing access to calendars, allowing multiple members of the family to edit the same family calendar.

Here are some tools that help you manage a specific aspect of family life:

✔ **Babysitters:** Care.com (`www.care.com`) and Sittercity (`www.sittercity.com`)

✔ **Family party planning and invitations:** Evite (`http://new.evite.com`) and Paperless Post (`www.paperlesspost.com`)

✔ **Playdates:** RedRover (`www.redroverapp.com`)

✔ **Family packing tool:** Baby Pack & Go (`www.babypackandgo.com`)

Planning Family Meals

One popular area where many parents have turned to their computers for help is planning family meals. The following services are some popular sites for families hoping to save time and money while finding inspiration for their meal planning:

✔ **Plan to Eat** (`www.plantoeat.com`) enables users to collect favorite recipes in one location, organize and share the recipes, and even download and print them. After you load and organize recipes on your account, just drag and drop them into a weekly meal planner. Then, you can create a shopping list based on the recipes in your weekly meal plan. Just open your shopping list via your mobile phone to follow while at the grocery store.

✔ **ZipList** (`www.ziplist.com`) is a tool for digital families to create shopping lists, collect recipes, and locate grocery savings. Families can use ZipList to save favorite shopping lists, such as those created for a special meal or holiday gathering. The free mobile app that accompanies ZipList allows users to access their recipe box and shopping lists while in the store. Like Plan to Eat, ZipList also allows users to create meal plans that use your saved recipes and grocery lists. And similar to the family management tool Famjama (earlier in this chapter), ZipList also provides access to sales on grocery items, acting as a shopping circular, integrated into your family's meal planning.

✔ **Allrecipes.com** users can create a recipe box containing their favorite recipes from around the site, create a menu planner, or use existing site-created plans, and create shopping lists based on saved recipes. One fun aspect of this site is the feedback on uploaded recipes. Users try recipes and then return to provide a rating as well as suggestions to make the recipe better. The site also allows families to change serving sizes — automatically adjusting the recipe to accommodate the change — which is great for large families with more mouths to feed as well as families on their way to an empty nest looking to have fewer leftovers after meals. You can learn more about this free service at www.allrecipes.com.

✔ **KeepRecipes** (www.keeprecipes.com) combines some of the recipe collection capabilities of the other tools I mention here with the feel of a social network. Users can locate recipes and collect them in an online cookbook, but they can also take photos of their completed meals and share them with friends. KeepRecipes calls this function their Social Recipe Box. KeepRecipes users may also choose to follow other users according to their interest or because of another social media connection.

✔ **Epicurious** is far more than a meal planning site for families, with articles, online communities, and even a shopping function. It also includes a recipe box where users can create a profile and collect favorite recipes. Like many other recipe and meal planning sites, Epicurious users can download their recipe box and create shopping lists based on favorite recipes. Learn more at www.epicurious.com.

Purchasing Essentials

So, you used online family management tools to organize your family's calendar for the week and visited your favorite meal planning site to create the week's meal plan. You clipped your coupons, and your grocery list is ready to go on your mobile device. Grab the keys and. . . . Wait a moment. Do you really even need to leave your home to stock your pantry?

The emergence of online grocery and home essentials shopping services is another wonderful benefit of raising a digital family. Check out these services, which allow you to purchase groceries and other necessities from home, some even delivering them to your door for a small fee.

✔ **Alice** (www.alice.com) vows to keep your busy digital family from ever running out of essentials. Users can create a shopping list of everyday items and indicate how often they would like these items replaced. Items are then automatically ordered in the allotted time interval and delivered to your home. Other helpful features include the ability to search by deals, browse green and organic products, and even shop by room.

✔ **Peapod** is an online grocery delivery service although it's available only in specific service areas. This service allows users to create and save shopping lists and have their groceries delivered to their homes. Users can even order their groceries from their mobile device (yup, there's an app for that) and have them delivered. Learn more at www.peapod.com.

✔ **Amazon Grocer** (www.amazongrocer.com) provides online shoppers with access to thousands of nonperishable household essentials, from cereal to coffee to diapers. Amazon Grocer allows users to shop based on the following categories:

- Top sellers
- Breakfast foods
- Canned and packaged goods
- Snacks, cookies, and candy
- Household supplies

✔ **NetGrocer** (www.netgrocer.com) delivers groceries nationwide via FedEx. Users can create and save shopping lists as well as recurring orders. Like the other online grocery sites, NetGrocer also provides users easy access to weekly specials via their site as well as specific shopping categories, such as health and beauty and organic.

Budgeting Online

Some families may find that the most useful aspect of living in a world with nearly endless online tools means being able to budget for the family with these tools. The following three online services offer families a way to organize family expenses online, sharing access to secure accounts and eliminating some of the paper clutter that overwhelms many families:

✔ **Mint** (www.mint.com) is a service that lets you organize all your financial accounts in one location, create a budget, and track goals. The free mobile app connected to Mint.com allows account holders to access their financial information in one place via their mobile devices. Families can use Mint.com to set family goals, such as vacations or purchases for the home, and then track the progress toward this goal.

- ✔ **Manilla** allows families to securely upload all financial information in one location for free. From your home computer or mobile device, you can use Manilla (www.manilla.com) to create bill pay reminders, manage online accounts, and organize paperless statements.

- ✔ **PearBudget** focuses on budget creation and after a 30-day free trial is available for $5 a month. This online tool is great for families who perhaps haven't ever created a budget in the past and are looking for an online tool to help them get started. This service is located at https:// pearbudget.com.

Before entering any sensitive financial information, verify that the site is secure by looking for an https URL, a lock icon in the URL or lower-right hand corner of your browser, or by checking the properties of the site to verify encryption.

Part VI

The Part of Tens

Discover ten great blogs for parents of digital natives at www.dummies.com/
extras/raisingdigitalfamilies.

In this part . . .

✔ Discover a few basic tips to empower you as you learn more about the digital world that comes naturally to your children.

✔ Get to know some of the popular websites where your children may be spending time.

✔ Learn about other top sites that your teenagers may be frequenting.

Chapter 20

Ten Quick Tips for Parents

· ·

After you create your Digital Family Policy (see Chapter 2) and set clear rules for every aspect of your family's fast-paced, plugged-in life, it's time to take a step back and look at how to continue to promote digital safety within your family without having to revisit each step of your family's in-depth policy. In this over-connected world, you want to find ways to enjoy the company of your loved ones without power cords, screens, and Wi-Fi.

These ten tips are designed to be used independently of the other tips throughout this book as well as independently of each other. Some are helpful reminders for parents, while others are action items to keep your digital family on track.

Always Pay Attention

Being aware of the dangers of the digital life and creating a Digital Family Policy are just the first steps. Paying close attention to when and where your kids are plugged in, what they're doing online, and what media they are being exposed to is critical not only to enforce your policies, but also to be aware of changes. Continue to pay attention to changes in the technology used in your home, such as updates to privacy policies and automatic download updates to gaming systems.

Also, watch for cues from your children that might indicate areas of concern such as potential exposure to an online predator or harassment from a cyberbully. By being aware of changes in your child's behavior and digital habits, you may realize that an issue needs to be discussed.

Be a Good Digital Role Model

The reason why this book refers to digital *families* — and not just digital *children* — is adults also live in this incredibly plugged-in world. Kids are keen observers of the world around them and are often the first to notice when parents appear to be connected to a smartphone, tablet, or laptop.

Kids who are Friends with their parents on Facebook also have the opportunity to observe how their parents interact with friends, share information, and discuss personal topics.

Set a good example for your children by being a good digital role model yourself. Would you like to clean up your social media language? Are you trying to cut down on complaining about work in status updates? You may even want to include notes in your Digital Family Policy addressing digital best practices that you will also aim to follow!

Focus on Safety

Although many digital etiquette issues concern parents, safety concerns certainly take precedent over such issues as gaming time, posting silly pictures on social media, or purchasing a download without permission. When creating guidelines for your digital family, including crafting or revising your Digital Family Policy, always keep safety at the forefront of your decision making. Some examples include sharing of identifying information or agreeing to meet an online friend in real life. Allowing safety concerns to inform all decisions will help you set guidelines that protect your children in many other areas. Check out Chapter 3 for extensive coverage of safety concerns in the digital world.

Spotlight Public versus Private

Focus on public versus private when discussing best practices to guide your children when sharing info (and anything else) online. Children should constantly consider what's appropriate to share publicly when using social media (including YouTube), playing online games, interacting with requests for information, and even chatting with friends. Remind your children — often — what information is okay to share publicly and what to always keep private (such as a Social Security number).

Take the Time to Establish Limits

Yes, creating a detailed Digital Family Policy is a time-consuming task. Setting vague guidelines for your children about how much screen time is too much or what information is too personal to share publicly is taking the easy road. Without clear limits, children have no way to know when a (digital) behavior is crossing a line. And you can't enforce consequences without clear guidelines. Rather than writing a nonspecific policy that says "Don't watch too much television," for example, specify exactly how many hours of television viewing can occur in a week. When time is up, time is up — without question — making enforcement much easier for parents.

Enforce Accountability

When clear limits are established, parents can ask children to hold themselves accountable. For example, creating a rule that game consoles can be used only on the weekends is easy to remember, simple to follow, and easy to enforce. Sure, you can use programs to monitor device use and change Parental Controls and settings, but let your children know that they're in charge of monitoring their behavior as well. This teaches your children responsibility, shows that you trust them to follow the guidelines set for your family, and makes any necessary punishment a consequence of their own actions.

Be consistent about enforcing consequences if rules are broken so your kids understand that the Digital Family Policy is meant to be followed.

Use Available Resources

Don't feel like you have to navigate the digital world alone! A huge variety of products and resources are available to help you create your Digital Family Policy and establish safe boundaries for your kids on the devices and applications they use. Each day, new resources appear online and in stores. Be sure to check often for new monitoring and protection tools and plans as well as informational resources to guide you through emerging technology and changes to devices your kids already use.

Communicate with Your Kids Offline

Many parents use texting, instant messaging, and even social media platforms (such as Twitter and Facebook) to communicate with their children. Make sure to also set aside time to communicate often with your children offline. Certain aspects of communication — facial expressions and body language — don't exist or translate well in digital communication. To more easily protect your children online, be sure to spend time communicating with them offline — nothing beats face-time.

Encourage "Unplugged" Time

Setting limits for screen time is a great start, but don't forget to encourage unplugged time as well. Encourage your children to go on a family outing without a smartphone, MP3 player, or tablet for in the car. Try a TV-free day or even take an entire weekend to unplug and just enjoy the nondigital life. Make this unplugged time a special treat rather than a punishment to be endured. Be sure to follow your own advice and unplug as well. Point out to your children that it's okay to experience life without documenting every second of it online.

Join Them!

If you can't beat 'em, join 'em! One way to understand the digital world in which your children live is to join them there. Make time to learn to play their favorite video games, Friend them on Facebook, and visit their favorite social gaming platforms. Not only will this give you time together as a family, but you'll be better able to understand both the pitfalls and the highlights of each aspect of their digital lives.

Chapter 21

Ten Social Networks for Kids

With social media infiltrating nearly every aspect of the Internet (and our daily lives), it's no surprise that you can easily find social networks created specifically for children. These sites typically mimic adult platforms (with account profiles, gaming options, and even chat functions), but they do tend to offer more privacy options and kid-friendly themes.

Even though the platforms I mention in this chapter are designed for children, you should still visit each site and get to know its features before allowing your children to play on their own. Also pay close attention to how each site protects privacy before you allow your child to create an account. Look for sites that adhere to the Children's Online Privacy Protection Act (COPPA; www.coppa.org/comply.htm), which regulates the types of information online sites can collect from children. Finally, find out how other users may interact with your child before allowing them to have unsupervised time on these networks.

Club Penguin

www.clubpenguin.com

Perhaps the most well-known of the social networks for kids, Disney's Club Penguin is a massively multiplayer online game (MMOG) site for children. The game play is moderated at all times, and parental consent is required before children can join the site. Children may play at Club Penguin for free or upgrade to (and pay for) membership, which begins at $5 per month and offers a few more features:

- ✔ Unlimited access to member-only areas
- ✔ Exclusive gifts at special events
- ✔ Style your penguin character with new outfits
- ✔ Upgrade and decorate your igloo, your home on Club Penguin
- ✔ Adopt up to 20 puffles (Club Penguin pets) in any color

Children need their parents' e-mail address to create an account at Club Penguin.

To activate a new account, parents click an activation code that arrives by e-mail. Clicking the link takes you to the site, where you can set a chat option for your child:

✔ **Standard Safe Chat:** Players type their own messages. The Club Penguin word filter and moderators stop the use of inappropriate language and personal information sharing.

✔ **Ultimate Safe Chat:** Players can choose only from a set menu of phrases and see other Ultimate Safe Chat messages.

In the Parents section of Club Penguin, parents can create their own password-protected access to their child's Club Penguin account. There, you can see your child's account activity, edit chat settings, and set a play timer.

ScuttlePad

www.scuttlepad.com

ScuttlePad is a free social networking site designed for kids ages 6 to 11. Much like Facebook, users can upload photos and update their status, but status updates and comments can include words only from an approved list. Images uploaded are all manually reviewed before they may appear on the user's account. There is currently no advertising on this site. ScuttlePad teaches kids the basics of social networking but doesn't have any extra games, activities, or applications like many adult social networking sites.

ScuttlePad provides kids with the chance to learn the basics of social media, but it doesn't contain much else to entertain kids or hold their attention. Still, it's a great resource for parents looking to teach their children about social media without exposing them to too much content or allowing them unsupervised interaction.

Webkinz

www.webkinz.com

Webkinz is one of the first online worlds created primarily for children. The site connects the offline and online worlds by providing an online code with every stuffed animal that Webkinz has sold. Kids can type these codes into the online site to play with the virtual version of their stuffed animal.

This site includes a Parents Area where parents can manage their children's use of chat, limit time spent on the site, and even turn off third-party advertisements. In addition to the many games and activities available for free on

Webkinz.com, there are also opportunities to purchase virtual goods — so you may want to include a rule in your Digital Family Policy about whether your child is permitted to spend real money on virtual products. ***Note:*** This incredibly popular site is used by adults as well as children.

YourCause

www.yourcause.com

This platform is more than just a social networking tool for teens. YourCause allows kids to raise money for a favorite charity while Friending other account holders, sending e-mail, and posting testimonials. This site is free for a basic account. Account holders must be 13 years or older to create an account and may choose from a list of pre-approved nonprofits. The user then creates a page and asks people to visit and make charitable donations. Account holders can choose from more than 1.5 million available charities.

Sweety High

www.sweetyhigh.com

Sweety High is a social network for girls age 10 and older. All members younger than 13 must have parent-verified accounts, though, and parents of those users are given parent access to those accounts. This site is carefully moderated with strong privacy settings. Member profiles are visible to member friends only. User-generated content is moderated, as are comments from other "Sweeties." The themes of this site rely heavily on style, fashion, and celebrity.

Parent tools on Sweety High encourage parents to help their daughters become "Savvy Sweeties." This includes talking to your daughter about such issues as keeping private information private and bullying. Because Sweety High is a closed community, nonmembers cannot access or view profiles, photos, or user-generated content.

Yoursphere

https://yoursphere.com

This social networking site (for children age 17 and younger) includes a virtual world where kids can play games, participate in shared interest "spheres," write their own blog, and earn credits for positive interactions. Yoursphere members that positively contribute to the community can redeem the credits in the Gift Gallery for music, electronics, magazines, and more. Users can also play hundreds of games and interact within a virtual world.

Yoursphere strictly adheres to its membership rules and even compares account requests against a database of registered sex offenders. The staff at Yoursphere has teens who help ensure that the content is relevant to its teen users, but also includes a Law Enforcement Task Force to advise the site on how to best protect its users.

Additionally, Yoursphere includes a resource site for parents at `www.internet-safety.yoursphere.com`. This site includes information about topics (such as cyberbullying), offers tutorials, and recommends products. Content is updated regularly and walks parents through a variety of technology related parenting concerns.

Both parents and kids can create an account on Yoursphere. That way, parents can monitor what their child is doing.

Fanlala

`http://www.fanlala.com`

Formerly called Imbee, Fanlala is a social media platform for kids ages 8 to 14 with a focus on entertainment and popular culture. Content and activities are geared toward tweens, though. Fanlala creates its own web-based shows and specials, but account holders may also upload their own photos and videos, chat with other account-holding friends, and join groups.

Only parents can create a Fanlala account for a child. You also are in charge of the security settings, so be sure to set age-appropriate parameters. Fanlala provides a base account for free but requires a $1 parental credit card verification.

Fanlala also includes a chat feature allowing Fanlala users to chat with other users in real time. To chat with an account holder, you must be "Friends" with that account holder. These chats are not moderated, and users can create their own content during these interactions.

Unlike some children's social media platforms that focus on learning the ins and outs of social networking, Fanlala is very content driven and does include quite a bit of advertising with a heavy focus on celebrities and pop culture. Parents may want to supervise their children to be sure that the content they are viewing is appropriate.

giantHello

www.gianthello.com

giantHello (formerly, FaceChipz) is a social network for tweens and teens (ages 7 to 17) patterned off Facebook with a heavy focus on gaming. Friending another member allows account holders to send private messages to that user and see the content that they've created, including comments on other accounts, group activity, status updates, and uploaded photos.

To "Friend" another account holder on giantHello, users must e-mail their friends or print an invitation code to give them in real life. Accounts must be verified by parents via a small credit card charge or by providing the last four digits of their Social Security number.

The games section of the site is available to the public without a required registration. This section of the site includes advertisements but also questionable content, such as games with violent and sexual themes. Even though this platform is open to the public, registered tween users cannot be contacted by strangers, nor can they contact strangers through their account.

When creating the social networking section of your Digital Family Policy, be sure to discuss the varying functions of giantHello and set specific rules regarding which features may be accessed.

Everloop

www.everloop.com

Everloop was designed specifically for kids ages 8 to 13 although kids younger than 8 and as old as 15 may join. Account holders can create a custom profile, including changeable background images, color schemes, and stickers. In the Everloop chat function, users can interact in real time through instant messaging and chats within their approved loops. The site also contains the Everloop Arcade that contains more than 1,500 games. Account holders can also earn credits that allow them to purchase virtual items, such as premium stickers for their profile page.

Everloop is different than other social networking sites in that it contains "looping" technology, which allows kids to locate what interests them, such as sports or fan groups, and then share those interests by joining loops. Within loops, they can share photos and information. Before kids are allowed to participate in loops, parents must give their approval. Everloop contains user-created loops but also partners with a variety of educational and entertainment partners to create branded loops: National Geographic, Mattel, and Monster High are some partners.

Other features can be accessed only after parents have approved the account. For parents concerned with bullying and bad language, Everloop promises to filter both chats and posts as well as screen uploaded videos and photos. Not only does the Everloop staff monitor these messages, but kids can flag upsetting or bothersome site content.

For even greater monitoring, parents can create their own account and receive notifications about their children's actions on the site. Parents can also control the permission settings for their children's account including whether or not their children may participate in chats and whether their children can send messages through Everloop to their friends.

Jabbersmack

`www.jabbersmack.com`

Jabbersmack (formerly Kidsocial), calls itself a "social entertainment network" and provides branded content and entertainment pages as well as access to streaming content. The site also allows kids to interact with friends and play social games. This site is open to kids of all ages, but kids younger than 13 must have parent approval to have an account. Parents may also monitor their child's account via a parent account.

Many of the branded pages on Jabbersmack will be familiar to parents. Content from Grooveshark, Zynga, YouTube, Playmobil, and more is presented through Jabbersmack after being filtered for inappropriate content.

Jabbersmack allows kids under 13 to connect with real-world friends only through friendship codes. When children are invited to connect, parents are notified. Pages created by account holders under 13 are never visible to strangers. Users over 13 can join and connect with new Friends, much like Facebook users.

Unlike some social networking sites for kids, Jabbersmack doesn't have a maximum age requirement and adults can create accounts and interact with teens. You may want to discuss this public interaction with your children before allowing them to create an account.

Chapter 22

Ten Other Places Your Kids Might Be Online

• •

Twitter and Facebook continue to reign as the top social media sites, Google holds its place as the number one search engine, and YouTube is all-powerful in the land of video sharing, but many other online locations are incredibly popular with teens. If your kids aren't already familiar with these platforms, chances are that they will be soon. They are definitely worth getting to know and discussing in your family when creating or updating your Digital Family Policy, and many of these platforms offer a great opportunity to discuss appropriate versus inappropriate content and private versus public.

Pinterest

`http://pinterest.com`

Pinterest is the third-largest social media platform (only behind Facebook and Twitter). The Pinterest mission is "to connect everyone in the world through the 'things' they find interesting."

A virtual pinboard, account holders use Pinterest to organize and share items found on the Internet by "pinning" an image or graphic from the web location. Pinterest account holders use pinboards to plan projects, share favorite recipes, collect beautiful pictures, organize vacation ideas, and more. Pins from other users are searchable, and many account holders browse public pinboards to re-pin images of interest. Users add pins to pinboards via a Pin It button on their web browser toolbar, a phone app, or a plug-in from the site they're pinning.

Pinterest accounts are free, and new users can use current social media accounts to sign up. Users need to be 13 or older and agree to this when accepting the terms of service.

After you create your Pinterest account (by Facebook, Twitter, or e-mail account), you can customize your username, bio, profile picture, how you share pins via Facebook, e-mail notification preferences, and privacy settings. To hide your privacy settings, open the drop-down menu next to your account name (upper right of the screen), and choose Settings⇨Hide Your Pinterest Profile from Search Engines⇨On.

You can't, however, make a pinboard private.

Pinterest asks that account holders follow Pin Etiquette, which includes being respectful and crediting sources. If your teen is interested in joining Pinterest, use this opportunity to discuss items in your Digital Family Policy, such as copyright and appropriate images to share publicly. Also discuss with your teens that although you can hide pinboards from search engines, you can't hide pins from users browsing Pinterest pinboards. Pinterest users should assume that everything they pin is public and may be shared.

Google+

```
https:/plus.google.com
```

Created in the summer of 2011, Google+ is a social network created and owned by Google. Google+ is open to anyone age 13 or older and is accessed via a free Google account. Google+ users may post in their "stream," much like a Facebook or Twitter status update. They can also use "circles" to organize their contacts into groups, such as friends, family, and acquaintances. Users may add a contact to more than one circle — say, a circle called "High School Friends" and another called "Friends."

Google+ also includes the Hangout social feature, where group chats, including chats with video, may be held. To join a Hangout, users must know the unique URL assigned to that event. You can also communicate instantly with people in your circles via a Messenger function, and share photos.

Because of the variety of ways to use Google+, the possibilities are nearly endless. Some teachers use Google+ Hangouts as a way to share homework information and a place for teens to collaborate on assignments. Sports and extra-curricular activities can use Google+ circles as a way to share information, calendars, and messages.

If your teen is using Google+, discuss those online privacy settings. Unless you change your Google+ account settings, your profile is visible to the public. The default settings for teen Google+ account holders are different than the default settings for account holders over age 18, and teens can override these settings.

To change your Google+ privacy settings, sign in to your Google+ account, click your account image in the upper right, and then click the Privacy link. On the Profile and Privacy page that appears, click the Edit Visibility on Profile button next to Public Profile Information. Next to each item in your Google+ profile, select the globe icon to edit the visibility for that aspect of your profile. Click Done Editing to save your changes.

You can't hide the following information from being public: Full Name, Brief Description, Gender, and Profile photo.

Ning

www.ning.com

Unlike other social media platforms where users create profiles, Ning allows users to also create what Ning calls "social websites." Ning site creators can make site design changes, add members to their social website's community, generate content, connect to other social media platforms, and even use their Ning to earn money. Pricing begins at $25 per month for Ning users who want to create their own site. However, you can have a free Ning account in which you can be a member of Ning social websites created by other users.

After you join a Ning site, you can change aspects of your profile (such as profile picture, gender, location, and website). Ning users need to be at least 13 years old.

Schools, clubs, and other groups use Ning as a way to share information and chat with other members, but Facebook groups and school-owned forums are the most popular vehicles.

Foursquare

https://foursquare.com

Foursquare is a social media tool that allows users to share the places they've visited. Foursquare easily connects to other social media platforms, such as Facebook and Twitter, allowing users to share their locations and thoughts about those locations across platforms.

After you create a Foursquare profile online (you do need an e-mail or a Facebook account), download the free app to your smartphone to check in to locations. When checking in, you can add information about the location, including tips and reviews for others. You can also use Foursquare check-ins to earn social media badges as well as tangible rewards such as coupon codes and free offers.

For many parents, Foursquare creates a variety of privacy concerns because users allow the public to see their current location. This is also a concern to parents, out and about with small children, checking in publicly to places like stores, restaurants, and parks.

You can still use Foursquare while protecting your privacy:

- **Friend Requests:** Users who want to find your check-in history must request to be your Friend on Foursquare — and you must approve this request.

- **Private Check-Ins:** You can opt for a Private Check-In, which allows you to add a place to your check-in history while keeping that check-in completely private, even from Friends. You can still earn points and badges without sharing your location.

- **Disabling Sharing:** Foursquare accounts can be connected to Twitter and Facebook, or you can disable these settings to keep check-ins from being shared with those audiences as well as their Foursquare Friends. To choose sharing settings, log in to your profile and then

    a. *From the drop-down menu in the upper right, choose Settings.*

    b. *On the Settings page that opens, select Sharing with Other Networks (from list on the right) and set whether to connect your Foursquare account to Facebook and Twitter.*

- **Customize Privacy Settings:** Follow the steps for setting sharing, but go in to the Privacy Settings (list on the right) and make changes.

Vimeo

`http://vimeo.com`

Vimeo is a video-sharing platform where users can upload and search video content for free. Account holders may also upgrade to Vimeo Plus or Vimeo PRO for a monthly fee. Like other social media–based platforms, Vimeo includes a community feature beyond its video-hosting capabilities, but participation in that community is not required to upload or search the video content on Vimeo. Social engagement on Vimeo includes liking video content, leaving comments on videos, following Vimeo users, and participating in Community Forums.

Vimeo content restrictions prohibit sexually explicit material but do allow nonsexual nudity. Vimeo content filters *do not restrict videos that contain nudity*. Because of the type of content available on Vimeo and the lack of site-run filters to make the site child-friendly, you may want to restrict access to Vimeo in your home or include other Vimeo-related guidelines in your Digital Family Policy.

Ustream

http://www.ustream.tv

Ustream is a free platform that allows users to create live broadcasts of events. The largest live streaming platform, Ustream broadcasts commercially produced content as well as user-generated content. Ustream users can search the site by subject and keyword for content or use a provided link to go directly to a live broadcast or event. Ustream events also allow you to participate in a chat via a chat window while watching the live video content. The chat platform allows users to connect their chat to their existing social media accounts to share their Ustream participation across those platforms.

Teens may be asked to view specific content on Ustream related to learning goals or broadcasts created by educational experts. Although this content is likely safe, you may want to screen the content with your teen. Because there are no safety search filters on Ustream like on some other video-sharing sites, you should discuss Ustream search rules with your teens when creating your Digital Family Policy.

Flickr

www.flickr.com

Flickr, owned by Yahoo!, is a photo- and video-sharing website where you can share and host your photos and videos for free. You can also use Flickr to explore content uploaded by other Flickr users. Users can upgrade their free account to a Pro account for a small monthly fee. This service allows them to upload unlimited pictures. You must be at least 13 to have a Flickr Pro account.

Flickr users may include a variety of descriptions with their content (titles, tags, location, and people), and content can be organized by sets, collections, and as part of Flickr groups.

Account holders can upload content from mobile devices, e-mail, browser, third-party apps, and the Flickr desktop app. Uploaded content can be shared through e-mail, Facebook, Twitter, Pinterest, Tumblr, Blogger, LiveJournal, WordPress, or RSS feed. Users may also grab a link to their photo or HTML code that can be embedded.

Flickr also offers a social media component, where users can add contacts to their account and send messages. Users may also join Flickr groups where they can view and upload shared content.

You do need an AT&T/Yahoo! account, or sign in with your Facebook or Google account.

You may select a default privacy setting that applies to all your content. If you add a photo or video to a group, group members can view and comment on that content regardless of your default settings, though.

From the Privacy & Permissions section (under Your Account), you can select everything from who can tag you in a photo to who can find your content in searches. You can also elect to activate Safe Search from this page, which allows you to see only those photos and videos that Flickr believes are safe for a global, public audience.

Instagram

http://instagram.com

Instagram is a popular photo-sharing social media tool. Using a free, downloaded application, this service allows users to take a photograph with their phone or tablet, apply a filter, and then upload the photo to the social sharing platform. Users can share these uploaded images with other Instagram users and also on other social networks, such as Twitter, Flickr, Facebook, and Tumblr. Instagram may also be connected to Foursquare; Instagram users can be checked in on Foursquare by specifying a location when they upload a photo. This application, acquired by Facebook in 2012, is available for use on both iOS and Android platforms.

You need to download the Instagram application before opening an Instagram account. Find the app at Instagram online, at the Apple Store, or on Google Play (on an Android device). You need to provide an e-mail address.

Users can follow the accounts of other Instagram users and also use hashtags to search for photos as well as other users. *Note:* All photos uploaded via Instagram are public by default, so they are visible to anyone using Instagram as well as on the Instagram website. You can change Instagram account settings to private, though, so that only people who follow you on Instagram can see your photos (from the Photo Privacy section).

After setting your account to private, new followers have to be authorized by you before they can see your images, and only authorized followers will be able to view your photos. Changing this setting doesn't affect existing followers, though.

Here's a great reason to keep your photos private, especially if you're worried about copyright infringement: When you upload images to Instagram, you grant Instagram the right — royalty-free — to modify, reproduce, and distribute your content unless that content is listed as private.

To use Instagram, you have to be 13 or older, agree to not post sexually suggestive or nude photos, or use the account to threaten or intimidate other users. You may also not use URL's in your Instagram account name without permission.

MeetMe

www.meetme.com

MeetMe (originally MyYearbook) is a social media site originally created to connect with friends from the past. It now is a platform where users can make new friends. MeetMe calls using social media to meet new people "social discovery." MeetMe users can use games and applications to meet other MeetMe users and can access the platform online or via apps for iOS and Android operating systems.

Anyone 13 or older can create a MeetMe account. You don't need a credit card, but you do have to provide an e-mail address.

Changing user settings to make an account private kind of defeats the goal of the site for user profiles to be public, allowing users to find and connect with each other. Much of the content shared on accounts is inappropriate for children, though, and may involve sexual references and inappropriate language. Parents should supervise teens very carefully if allowed to create a MeetMe profile.

Tumblr

www.tumblr.com

Tumblr is one of the most popular social media platforms with teens today. A virtual scrapbook, Tumblr allows teens to share their favorite content from around the web on their pages called Tumblrs. Users can post text, photos, quotes, links, music, and videos from platforms ranging from their phone to their web browser. Teens can customize the look of their Tumblr pages. Tumblr users can blog original content, but the site is most often used to "reblog" (share) other content they've discovered.

Many parents allow their kids to have a Tumblr as a way to express themselves online. Tumblr allows anyone 13 or older to create an account. You do need an e-mail address.

After you create an account, you can connect to people you know via Facebook and Gmail.

Tumblr is a great way for teens to express themselves, but it can also put teens at risk for oversharing very personal information. Even though Tumblr allows users and commenters to remain anonymous, many teens share their Tumblrs with friends and follow their friends' Tumblrs as well. There is also no way to control who follows your Tumblr, and users of any age may choose to follow the content uploaded by your teen. *It is not possible to make a Tumblr private.* If your teen uses Tumblr, discuss the public nature of this platform and the ramifications of oversharing. Be sure to include Tumblr content guidelines in your Digital Family Policy.

Index

• *Q* •

• *R* •

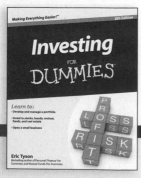 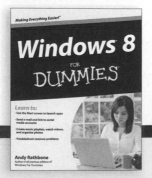  

Math & Science

Algebra I For Dummies,
2nd Edition
978-0-470-55964-2

Anatomy and Physiology
For Dummies,
2nd Edition
978-0-470-92326-9

Astronomy For Dummies,
3rd Edition
978-1-118-37697-3

Biology For Dummies,
2nd Edition
978-0-470-59875-7

Chemistry For Dummies,
2nd Edition
978-1-1180-0730-3

Pre-Algebra Essentials
For Dummies
978-0-470-61838-7

Microsoft Office

Excel 2013 For Dummies
978-1-118-51012-4

Office 2013 All-in-One
For Dummies
978-1-118-51636-2

PowerPoint 2013
For Dummies
978-1-118-50253-2

Word 2013 For Dummies
978-1-118-49123-2

Music

Blues Harmonica
For Dummies
978-1-118-25269-7

Guitar For Dummies,
3rd Edition
978-1-118-11554-1

iPod & iTunes
For Dummies,
10th Edition
978-1-118-50864-0

Programming

Android Application
Development For
Dummies, 2nd Edition
978-1-118-38710-8

iOS 6 Application
Development For Dummies
978-1-118-50880-0

Java For Dummies,
5th Edition
978-0-470-37173-2

Religion & Inspiration

The Bible For Dummies
978-0-7645-5296-0

Buddhism For Dummies,
2nd Edition
978-1-118-02379-2

Catholicism For Dummies,
2nd Edition
978-1-118-07778-8

Self-Help & Relationships

Bipolar Disorder
For Dummies,
2nd Edition
978-1-118-33882-7

Meditation For Dummies,
3rd Edition
978-1-118-29144-3

Seniors

Computers For Seniors
For Dummies,
3rd Edition
978-1-118-11553-4

iPad For Seniors
For Dummies,
5th Edition
978-1-118-49708-1

Social Security
For Dummies
978-1-118-20573-0

Smartphones & Tablets

Android Phones
For Dummies
978-1-118-16952-0

Kindle Fire HD
For Dummies
978-1-118-42223-6

NOOK HD For Dummies,
Portable Edition
978-1-118-39498-4

Surface For Dummies
978-1-118-49634-3

Test Prep

ACT For Dummies,
5th Edition
978-1-118-01259-8

ASVAB For Dummies,
3rd Edition
978-0-470-63760-9

GRE For Dummies,
7th Edition
978-0-470-88921-3

Officer Candidate Tests,
For Dummies
978-0-470-59876-4

Physician's Assistant Exa
For Dummies
978-1-118-11556-5

Series 7 Exam
For Dummies
978-0-470-09932-2

Windows 8

Windows 8 For Dummies
978-1-118-13461-0

Windows 8 For Dummies
Book + DVD Bundle
978-1-118-27167-4

Windows 8 All-in-One
For Dummies
978-1-118-11920-4

ℯ Available in print and e-book formats.